Justice Denied

Justice Denied

Friends, Foes & the Miners' Strike

Edited by
DAVID ALLSOP
CAROL STEPHENSON
& DAVID WRAY

MERLIN PRESS

First published in 2017
by The Merlin Press Ltd
Central Books Building
Freshwater Road
London
RM8 1RX

www.merlinpress.co.uk

ISBN 978-0-85036-730-0

British Library Cataloguing in Publication Data
is available from the British Library

Printed in the UK by Imprint Digital, Exeter

Contents

Contributors

Dr David Allsop is a Principal Visiting Lecturer at the University of Hertfordshire.

Debbie Ballin is a Senior Lecturer in Film and Media Production at Sheffield Hallam University.

Eric Eaton is Chairman of the Nottinghamshire Miners' Association.

Barbara Jackson is secretary of the Orgreave Truth and Justice Campaign.

Siân James was Member of Parliament for Swansea East from 2005 to 2015.

Esther Johnson is a Professor in Media Arts at Sheffield Hallam University.

Ian Lavery is the Member of Parliament for Wansbeck, Northumberland.

Peter Smith was a member of the Cokemen's Area Association, of the National Union of Mineworkers.

Keith Stanley is the former Vice-President of the National Union of Mineworkers.

Carol Stephenson is a Principal Lecturer in Sociology at Northumbria University.

John Stirling is the former Head of the Social Sciences Department at Northumbria University.

David Waddington is Head of Communications and Computer Research at Sheffield Hallam University.

Granville Williams is a founder member of the Orgreave Truth and Justice Campaign and a National Council member of the Campaign for Press and Broadcasting Freedom (www.cpbf.org.uk).

David Wray is a Senior Visiting Research Fellow at the University of Hertfordshire.

List of Abbreviations

ACPO	Association of Chief Police Officers.
AIS	Area Incentive Schemes.
CCU	Civil Contingencies Unit.
COSA	Colliery Officials and Staff Association.
DMA	Durham Miners' Association.
ISTC	Iron and Steel Trades Confederation.
ITN	Independent Television News.
LGSM	Lesbians and Gays Support the Miners.
MFGB	Miners' Federation of Great Britain.
NACODS	National Association of Colliery Overmen, Deputies and Shotfirers.
NALGO	National Association of Local Government Officers.
NCB	National Coal Board.
NEC	National Executive Committee.
NFYFC	National Federation of Young Farmers Clubs.
NRC	National Reporting Centre.
NUM	National Union of Mineworkers.
NWMA	Nottinghamshire Working Miners' Association.
SWAPC	Sheffield Women Against Pit Closures
UDM	Union of Democratic Mineworkers.
WAPC	Women Against Pit Closures.
WWA	Welsh Women's Aid.
YMCA	Young Men's Christian Association.

Timeline of Events

May 1966–April 1968. The National Power loading agreement introduced.

9 January 1972. The first national miners' strike since 1926.

10 February 1972. 10,000 Flying pickets used to close the Saltley coke depot at Birmingham.

October 1973–April 1974. The oil price shock.

12 November 1973. NUM begin an overtime ban.

6 December 1973. The NCB confidential Wilfred Miron Report.

31 December 1973. The Conservative government introduces a three-day week.

4 February 1974. The miners' strike.

28 February 1974. Ted Heath calls a general election on 'who governs Britain'.

June 1974. The implementation of the NCB Plan for Coal.

11 November 1974. First national ballot on a national incentive scheme.

October 1977. Second national ballot on a national incentive scheme.

1 December 1977. District Incentive Schemes introduced.

27 May 1978. The Ridley Report published.

September 1978–March 1979. The 'winter of discontent'.

23 February 1979. Nottinghamshire decides to ballot its own members to oppose the closure of Teversal colliery.

3 May 1979. The Conservative Party, headed by Margaret Thatcher, returned to government.

July 1980. Closure of Teversal Colliery in Nottinghamshire.

1 January 1981. The 1980 Employment Act comes into operation.

13 February 1981. NCB announces proposals for the 'accelerated closure' of 23 collieries. In response NUM threaten to ballot its members on strike action. Meanwhile, a proliferation of strikes occurs throughout the UK coalfields.

18 February 1981. Mrs Thatcher's Conservative government withdraws plans to close 23 pits.

December 1981. Arthur Scargill elected president of the NUM.

28 March 1983. Ian MacGregor appointed Chairman of the NCB.

1 March 1984. Cortonwood Colliery closure announced

5 March 1984. Yorkshire Area Council votes to implement the 1981 ballot decision and instructs Yorkshire NUM branches to stop work from the last shift on Friday 9 March.

4 March 1984. 170 collieries are in operation.

6 March 1984. NCB announces a reduction of 4 million tonnes capacity entailing the loss of 20,000 jobs. The Scottish Area Executive call a strike from 12 March in response to the cut-backs.

14 March 1984. High Court grants NCB injunction to prevent Yorkshire miners from picketing other areas.

15 March 1984. David Jones killed while picketing at Ollerton Colliery. Nottinghamshire. NUM leaders call a strike pending the outcome of an area ballot. Yorkshire Area Executive of the NUM agree to defy the court injunction on picketing.

16 March 1984. Nottinghamshire miners vote 73 per cent against supporting the strike.

19 March 1984. NUM national delegate conference reaffirms the strike as official and in accordance with the national rule book, which superseded all decisions taken at Area level.

6 April 1984. Operation Police Watch launched in Sheffield.

25 April 1984. NCB launches a back to work campaign advertisements.

26 April 1984. Arthur Scargill calls for a national demonstration in Nottinghamshire.

1 May 1984. NCB grants Nottinghamshire miners a day off with pay to demonstrate against the strike and 7,000 demonstrate at Berry Hill Mansfield.

8 May 1984. Chris Butcher forms the 'Nottinghamshire Working Miners' Committee'.

14 May 1984. NUM hold a mass rally in Mansfield in favour of the strike.

16 May 1984. Anne Scargill arrested on a picket line for 'wilful obstruction'.

23 May 1984. Mass picketing began at Orgreave Coke works lasting for some three and a half weeks.

25 May 1984. High Court grants injunctions upholding the Nottinghamshire miners' 'right to work' in defiance of union instructions.

30 May 1984. Scargill charged with obstruction at Orgreave.

11 June 1984. Pro-strike branch officials heavily defeated in Nottinghamshire branch elections.

18 June 1984. The most controversial encounter at Orgreave Coke works, 5,000 pickets, ninety arrested and over one hundred injured.

21 June 1984. MacGregor writes to all NUM members, predicting they will lose the strike.

28 June 1984. NEC proposes rule changes for disciplining members for actions 'detrimental to the interests of the union'.

2 July 1984. Working miners take control in Nottinghamshire Area Council elections.

8 July 1984. Nottinghamshire strikers occupy committee rooms to prevent Area Council meeting to mandate representatives to oppose the new disciplinary rule.

12 July 1984. MacGregor announces scabs will not lose their jobs if expelled from the NUM, thus, terminating the closed shop agreement.

18 July 1984. Sir Robert Megarry rules the new disciplinary rule unlawful.

19 July 1984. Thatcher describes striking miners as Britain's 'enemy within'.

22 July 1984. First national conference of Women Against Pit Closures held at Northern College.

10 August 1984. Special Delegates Conference (SDC) boycotted by delegates from Nottinghamshire, Leicestershire and South Derbyshire. Reiterates the disciplinary rule 51 change.

11 August 1984. Women Against Pit Closures demonstrate in London.

15 August 1984. Twelve collieries have closed since the strike began. First scab in Yorkshire (Gascoigne Wood Colliery).

20 August 1984. 1,000 police escort a solitary miner back to work at Gascoigne Wood Colliery.

16 October 1984. NACODS calls a national strike from 25 October after failing to agree a settlement over colliery closures.

24 October 1984. NACODS call off the strike in return for a modification of the colliery review procedure.

25 October 1984. High Court orders the sequestration of NUM assets.

2 November 1984. NCB offers a Christmas bonus and holiday pay to miners who return to work by 19 November.

9 November 1984. Mass picket at Cortonwood in response to a solitary strike breaker.

24 November 1984. NCB claim 5,952 miners returned to work this week.

30 November 1984. High Court appoints Receiver to administer NUM funds, a taxi driver was killed driving a working miner to the colliery, three strikers charged with murder.

11 December 1984. Nottinghamshire miners vote heavily in favour of a new constitution giving greater autonomy from National Union.

20 December 1984. Nottinghamshire Area Council endorses rule change.

30 December 1984. NCB claims that miners who return to work would receive £1,000.

12 January 1985. Henry Richardson, General Secretary of the Nottinghamshire Area, is suspended.

26 January 1985. Amnesty for sacked miners becomes an issue.

30 January 1985. Sequestrators recover 5 m NUM funds.

7 February 1985. NCB refuses to negotiate.

22 February 1985. NCB plans a final push to encourage more miners to return to work to reach over 50 per cent.

28 February 1985. NEC calls SDC.

1 March 1985. Durham, Lancashire, South Wales and COSA Areas vote for an organised return to work. Yorkshire votes to continue the strike.

3 March 1985. SDC votes to return to work on 5 March.

4 March 1985. Yorkshire Area Council votes to return to work unconditionally. Scotland and South Wales vote to stay on strike as amnesty for 718 sacked miners unresolved.

5 March 1985. Miners return to work. Half the miners in Yorkshire and Scotland still out with Kent.

10 March 1985. Kent and Scotland vote to return to work; Richardson dismissed by Nottinghamshire Area Executive.

22 April 1985. NEC meet and find Roy Lynk guilty of gross misconduct and terminate his contract of employment as a Nottinghamshire Area official.

16 May 1985. Nottinghamshire ballots members opposing the rule changes made at the SDC August 1984, specifically Rule 51 that allows the removal from office of any official who actively worked against the union. They gain 73 per cent support.

6 July 1985. Nottinghamshire votes in favour of breaking away from the NUM.

1 September 1985. Nottinghamshire changes its name to the Union of Democratic Mineworkers.

1 May 1986. NCB unilaterally abandoned the conciliation agreements that had been in place since 1946. New conciliation procedures were agreed with the UDM and based on the majority-minority principle.

1 January 1987. NCB renamed British Coal Corporation.

19 March 1987. Newstead Colliery closes.

3 March 1988. Linby Colliery closes.

31 January 1992. Sherwood Colliery closes.

1 January 1995. 31 remaining collieries were privatised, the largest owner being RJB Mining.

15 May 2001. RJB mining was renamed UK Coal.

1 March 2005. Ellington Colliery closes.

10 July 2015. Thorseby Colliery, the last deep mine in Nottinghamshire, closes.

18 December 2015. The last remaining deep mine in Britain, Kellingley Colliery, North Yorkshire, closes.

Introduction

Carol Stephenson

There have been many fine books written about the miners' strike of 1984-1985. Collectively, they explore the events that took place during the dispute and the political and social legacy for Britain, the industry and the mining communities themselves. This book, however, is written by or is focused on those who were personally and directly involved in the strike and its aftermath, as strikers, trade unionists and activists, filmmakers, witnesses and researchers. It explores the events, legacies and controversies of the strike from an eyewitness standpoint.

The book is organised into three parts. The early chapters provide a biographical insight into the personal day-to-day experience of individuals directly involved in the dispute, and its legacy for the lives that followed. This is followed by a series of chapters that critically explore the political controversies that surrounded the strike and the wider support for it. The final section of the book examines issues that endure thirty years on from the end of the dispute.

It would not be unreasonable to question why so much has been written about *this* particular industrial dispute, above all others. The answer is relatively simple: those on both sides of the political divide agree that the outcome of the dispute was fundamental to determining the political and social nature of Britain in the decades that followed. Indeed, when Margaret Thatcher died in April 2013, commentators from both the political left and right assessed her legacy, and in doing so, few failed to mention the 1984-1985 miners' strike. For Thatcher's supporters, the defeat of the National Union of Mineworkers in 1985 'saved the country' from radical trade unionism and a moribund economy based on nationalised industries.

From this foundation of victory, she moved the Labour Party, and indeed the country as a whole, to the political right; her self-professed 'finest hour'. The working class was 'transformed', freed from the shackles of the past. The children of shipbuilders, miners and steel workers were liberated, it was claimed, from the tyranny of bullying trade unions and limiting class-based ambitions. They could stop being what their parents were, and there was no longer a need to depend on failed sunset industries as their parents were forced to do. Margaret Thatcher, her acolytes concluded, was good for the working class.

The question of Thatcher's legacy will be explored later, and her detractors will then have their turn. Before that, it will be useful to continue to explore Thatcher's interest in social class. Owen Jones[1] writes that Thatcher hated the very idea of class. At a number of levels class was problematic for Thatcher, not just the working class and their annoying tendency to stick together, but the very idea of social class itself was anathema to her.

The organised working class, particularly as it existed in the late 1970s and early 1980s, was highly problematic for those who, like Thatcher, put their faith in market economics. For supporters of a free market, trade unions, collective bargaining and industrial action block the free functioning of the market, pushing up wages and undermining job security by making industries unprofitable. If allowed, collective industrial action disrupts and reduces the production of profit.

This miners' strike had its roots in mining communities that fostered a high level of class-consciousness. Evidence of this, if more is needed, is present in the biographical chapters offered in this book by Siân James, Ian Lavery and Peter Smith. Each of these writers point to family heritage, and union and community pride, as the foundation of their political consciousness. Despite the hardships of the year long dispute, there was no faltering of commitment to the cause. Each writes about the good humour, kindness and inventiveness that characterised the strike and the support networks that worked tirelessly, enabling thousands of mining families to survive for a year without wages. These accounts are a reminder that many of those who went on strike did so primarily for the benefit of others, to protect their way of life and their communities: they chose strike action over individual gain in the shape of redundancy payments.

Ian Lavery, a teenage apprentice at the outset of the dispute, remembers marvelling at the knowledge that a Welsh miner nearing retirement (who he had never met and would never meet) chose to strike in defence of his job, instead of settling for early retirement and a hefty redundancy pay-out. This is the nature of solidarity and collectivism, to make a sacrifice as an individual for a collective cause in the understanding that others will make that sacrifice for you in turn. Mining communities were especially strong in their class-based identities, but they were not alone. In chapter two Barbara Jackson describes the 1970s and early 1980s as 'a rebellious time'. Jackson's chapter explores her burgeoning interest in politics and trade unionism and the education that was available to her through trade union activism. These biographical chapters demonstrate the degree to which reflective and intelligent working-class people understood that their strength and security was not embedded in free market economics, but in collective solidarity and working-class identity. Such solidarity was a problem for Thatcher and for the free market.

Class-based identities are typically underpinned by an understanding of class injustice which can be the foundation for a direct challenge to the politics of Thatcher. She sought to eradicate not just effective opposition to free market economics, but the root cause of it – identity based on class. Jones recalls Thatcher's 1994 meeting with the Chilean dictator Augusto Pinochet, and argues that Pinochet had achieved through a bloody coup what Thatcher sought to achieve through the mobilisation of the state against the miners: the wholesale selling-off of nationalised industries; and a legislative assault on workers' and trade union rights. Her ultimate aim was to shift the collective consciousness of these people from 'workers' to 'entrepreneurs' and 'individuals' in order to prepare an ideological and political climate sympathetic to unfettered global capitalism.[2]

As free market economics rests on the belief that the economy is best served if individuals act in their own individual economic best interests, this shift to individualistic and competitive thinking was vital. The new gods of neoliberal politics must become the new gods of Britain: individualism, aspiration, and competition. If Thatcher's far-reaching ambition to re-shape Britain was to be realised, working-class identity and solidarity had to be decisively defeated, and the battleground for this was to be the defeat of the National Union of Mineworkers.

In chapter eleven John Stirling examines the implications of the miners' strike, and suggests that it must be understood in the wider context of an assault on the trade union movement generally that was, at that time, witnessing a decline in membership numbers and in activism. Part of that assault introduced by the Thatcher government was the legal insistence on secret ballots for strike action. The absence of such a ballot was used by the state to undermine the legitimacy of the miners' strike and by some as an excuse when refusing to support this dispute. In chapter six, David Allsop and David Wray, both striking miners at the time, examine the legitimacy of the call for a national ballot. They conclude that the ballot was an attempt at interference in trade union democracy through the imposition of a strategy of divide and rule: the needs of vulnerable mining areas were set against the needs of those who believed themselves to be secure.

Nottinghamshire was one such 'secure' area and a majority of miners there continued to work, citing the absence of a national ballot as defence for their actions. In chapter nine David Allsop, Eric Eaton and Keith Stanley give a first-hand account of striking in Nottinghamshire while a majority of their colleagues continued to work. This chapter examines the consequences of this failure of solidarity for them personally and for coal mining in Nottinghamshire where, despite the confidence of working miners following the defeat of the NUM, their coalfields too were put to the sword. The right-wing Union of Democratic Mineworkers failed to prevent the loss of jobs in the area but paid back the government for their support by providing a prototype for company style unionism and the sweet-heart deals which were to follow in the late 1980s and 1990s.

Whether the miners' strike came about as a result of careful and meticulous planning (on the part of the Thatcher government, and/or the NUM) or as a result of 'cock up' is still a point of controversy. David Waddington takes this question up in chapter seven. Whatever the impetus for the dispute, it was a political showdown for both sides, and once begun, victory became an imperative for the Conservative government. It is little wonder then that the full force of the state was set against striking miners. Granville Williams's account, in chapter ten, of police attacks on striking miners at Orgreave on the 18 June 1984, and the subsequent vilification of injured and arrested pickets, is indicative of that force. Peter Smith describes in chapter four how he was targeted by the police because of his picketing activities, found his liberty of movement curtailed, and was ultimately sacked for his activism.

The miners' strike uncovers a great deal about political power and where it is held in Britain. Waddington's account, in chapter eight, of media misrepresentation of the actions of both police and pickets at Orgreave reveals how the BBC and ITV misused their position of trust and impartiality to misrepresent the actions of the police and to incriminate miners who were depicted as being 'out of control'. The strike was both a physical and ideological battle against the miners, in which the police, the courts and the media played their part.

In the years that followed the dispute, the implications of Thatcher's dislike of the concept of class have become apparent. For supporters of the free market, acceptance of the idea of socially created class inequalities opens the door to the possibility that these can and should be overcome. Thatcher wanted to see a wholesale cultural and political rejection of the notion that inequality is *socially* created, to be replaced by the view that each individual holds their destinies in their own hands. For the notion of class injustice to be refuted, individualism and competition had to be seen as the only legitimate and effective route to security. Here, we see the real goal of the Thatcher government in defeating the miners in 1985: denial of class as a socially constructed phenomenon depended upon the defeat of organised labour and class consciousness in its most potent form, and with it confidence in the power of collective resistance. Defeat of the miners, it was hoped, would deliver a platform upon which to undermine the very idea of the power of the British working class, and of class itself.

In the years since the miners' strike, much has been done to demean the working class and the idea of socially created class inequalities. The notion that the poor are poor because of their own failings, their lack of judgment, and their poor taste is embedded now in newspaper commentaries and television comedies alike. These views are not merely offensive, but have a direct and material impact on the lives of working-class people. The assault on the moral worth of the low waged, the unemployed and the disabled is used to legitimate cuts to benefits. In reality, there is little evidence of a culture of dependency among the long term unemployed, even in post-industrial areas experiencing high levels of deprivation.[3] Peter Smith's account of his attempts to find employment after the dispute is testament to this. Ian Lavery's anguish at the decline of Ashington, his home town, the closure of shops and pubs and the problems young people face in finding secure employment, is repeated across the post-industrial landscape of Britain.[4]

Owen Jones has led the criticism of the assault on the British working class which followed the strike. His work on what he calls the demonisation of the working class is well-known and influential, but he is not alone in his views.[5] A growing number of researchers and academics point to sustained attempts on the part of right-wing politicians, newspapers, and cultural commentators to deny the very existence of social class in favour of a supposedly meritocratic society where reward follows ability and endeavour.[6] If the poor and vulnerable can be blamed for their own failings then class, as a socially created phenomenon, simply disappears. It is not the system to blame; it is those who lack competitiveness and tenacity. It's a neat trick: the denial of class achieves a great deal for those on the political right. It presents the position of the poor and vulnerable as legitimate, beyond salvation and sympathy, while simultaneously confirming the superiority of the powerful. Eradicating the idea of socially and systematically created social inequalities from the minds of the British people, and most importantly from the working class, simultaneously removes the likelihood of opposition, and legitimates and reinforces the position of both rich and poor. The corrosion of the idea of class was essential if a free market was to thrive; individualism, aspiration, competition – all these were to be the unassailable gods of the new era, a new hegemony.

Those who condemn the working class as idle and feckless would do well to read the early chapters of this book, which convey the dedication and endeavour that epitomised the struggle to see out the dispute. From Peter Smith's honesty and determination not to become, as he put it, a 'professional sacked miner', to Siân James's excitement and pride at her community's defence of a valued way of life, the tenacity and abilities of working-class people are evident. These biographies, far from revealing a lack of ambition and aspiration, reveal a commitment to an aspiration for collective advancement and security.

To turn attention again to the question of Thatcher's legacy in the wake of the miners' strike, most credible commentators would struggle to suggest that the defeat of the miners was a victory for the working class, or indeed for working people in Britain as a whole. In the years following the strike, much of what underpinned the security of working-class people and, increasingly, middle-class people, have been undermined. The miners' strike provided a platform for Thatcher and her Party to further undermine workers and trade union rights and to push ahead with the process of privatising national assets in housing, education, transport and health.

Those who provide biographies here have been, relatively speaking, fortunate in their lives following the dispute. Barbara Jackson, David Allsop, David Wray and Siân James went on to study at university. Ian Lavery is now MP for his beloved Ashington. Peter Smith struggled initially, but went on to find employment, and has just recently retired. While their stories are not unusual, they are not necessarily representative of the outcomes for those who depended on the coal industry in the early 1980s. Many miners did not find employment following redundancy, nor did those working in dependent industries. Former coal communities are now characterised by depravation and decline as a result of high concentrations of unemployment and ill health associated with the industry, poor infrastructure and the absence of investment in alternative forms of employment. Three academics based in Sheffield Hallam University have argued that twenty years after the initial mine closures of the late 1980s, recovery of lost male jobs stood at around 60 per cent.[7] However the picture is bleaker that this figure suggests. Low levels of claimant unemployment presented a misleading impression of the extent of recovery as large numbers of working age men had diverted into other forms of economic inactivity, in particular onto incapacity benefit.[8]

For those involved in the dispute, the strike was about future generations and a way of life that offered some dignity. Counter claims were made by the Thatcher Government for greater freedom and prosperity for young people, if the tyranny of collectivism and nationalisation could be overcome.

What of the condition of Britain's young people today?

Far from being 'freed' by free market economics, those from low and middle income backgrounds are more likely to remain in the economic bracket into which they were born than at any time since the Second World War. Then prime minister, David Cameron, conceded at the Conservative Party National Conference in 2015 that Britain has the lowest level of social mobility in the developed world. So much for the meritocracy. This is just one of many problems facing Britain's young people. The inflated cost of private housing, and the sell-off of social housing, has left huge numbers of young people struggling to live independent lives and to plan their futures with dignity. The collapse of employment opportunities and meaningful apprenticeships, offering recognised and transferable qualifications, combined with the removal of economic state support for those entering higher education, has trapped many thousands of young people in debt, low wages and zero-hour employment.

At the same time the economic and political position of the wealthy has increased dramatically in the past thirty years. In the aftermath of the strike the Conservative Government cut the top rate of income tax from 80 per cent to 40 per cent, reduced capital gains and inheritance tax, and loosened stock market controls under the Financial Services Act of 1986. [9] This provided a basis upon which a minority of the super-rich could build their wealth further, while laying the foundations of the banking crisis of 2008 and, consequently, the savage cuts to benefits under the guise of austerity. It is little wonder that Andrew O'Hagan, writing in the *New York Review of Books*, claimed that Thatcher's moral legacy for Britain was to leave it greedier and seedier.[10] Thatcher was not 'good' for the working class and nor was she good for Britain.

Given this overview some might argue that Thatcher's mission to move the country irrecoverably to the right was achieved. Not so: there are clear indications of the failure Thatcherism to impose the ideology of individualism and competition on the collective British consciousness. On her death, the sociologist Huw Beynon, himself a chronicler of the events and implications of the miners' strike, wrote that despite her best efforts, by her own admission there was still too much Socialism in Britain for Margret Thatcher, 'she never won over the whole of the population, or even half of it'.[11]

Beynon points to the resurgence of the Durham Miners' Gala as evidence of a commitment to unionism and collectivism, in a region where such efforts were made to stamp those sentiments out.[12] In chapter twelve, Carol Stephenson and David Wray suggest the Gala is evidence of a full-blooded pride in the coal industry, its institutions and to and identity based on class. Thatcher wanted the children of the working class to stop being what their parents were, and yet the very act of the Gala is an act of resistance, an act of memory, and a rejection of the attempts to denigrate the working class. In chapter five Esther Johnson and Debbie Ballin explore the memories and contemporary views of the children of striking miners. Far from rejecting who their parents were, their lives had been positively touched by the strike and their ideas and attitudes very much aligned with those of their parents.

Beyond mining, Beynon points to high levels of public approval for the re-nationalisation of key industries, particularly, the rail network. Collectivism and public service, the desire to provide for the common good, is locked into everyday life and institutions, and continue to have deep roots. Two of the most popular institutions of British life, the NHS and the BBC, remain publicly-funded and controlled, which is anathema to the politics of the free market. Thatcherism may have weakened the ideas of public service and collectivism, but she could not destroy them. Consecutive right-wing governments have found it impossible to expunge these sentiments; individualism and competition have not provided Britain with a new hegemony.[13]

Had Beynon written that critical commentary on the legacy of Thatcher just three years later he could have pointed to more evidence to support his claims. He bemoaned the rise of Tony Blair and the Thatcher-light politics of New Labour, but in 2015 the Labour Party elected a socialist, Jeremy Corbyn, as its leader. Membership of the party increased to 338,103 by the end of 2015, an increase of 194,349 on 2011 membership. In the five days following Corbyn's election 40,000 people joined the party.

Activism and campaigning did not die in 1985 and recently there has been a noticeable growth in confidence in the left. The Orgreave Truth and Justice Campaign and the events of that day are explored in this book by Granville Williams and Barbara Jackson. The landmark ruling, in April 2016, that 96 people were unlawfully killed at Hillsborough has increased pressure for a public enquiry into the actions of South Yorkshire Police and other forces active at Orgreave. If, such an inquiry is eventually held, it is inevitable that more evidence will emerge of the state's misuse of power at that time, providing fuel for a growing public appetite for a critical assessment of the legacy of Thatcherism for Britain.

NOTES

1 Owen Jones. *Chavs: The Demonization of the Working Class,* 2011, London: Verso.
2 Ibid. p. 45.
3 Rob MacDonald, Tracy Shildrick & Andy Furlong, 'In search of "intergenerational cultures of worklessness": Hunting the Yeti and Shooting Zombies.' *Critical Social Policy*, September 2013, Vol. 34, Issue 2, pp. 199-220.
4 See: David Waddington, Chas Critcher, Bella Dicks, & David Parry, *Out of the Ashes? The Social Impact of Industrial Contraction and Regeneration on Britain's Mining Communities,* Jessica Kingsley: London, 2001; Carol Stephenson & David Wray, 'Emotional regeneration through community action in post-industrial Communities: The New Herrington Miners' Banner Partnership', *Capital and Class,* Vol. 87, pp. 175-199.
5 Jones, op. cit.
6 See: Stephanie Lawler, 'Disgusted subjects: the making of middle-class identities', *The Sociological Review,* Vol. 53, No. 3, 2005, pp. 429-446; Imogen Tyler, 'Chav Mum, Chav Scum: Class Disgust in Contemporary Britain.' *Feminist Media Studies* 2008, Vol. 8, No. 2., pp.17-34; Lisa McKenzie, *Getting By: Estates, Class and Culture in Austerity Britain,* Bristol: Policy Press, 2015.
7 C. Beatty, S, Fothergill, R, Powell, 'Twenty years on: Has the economy of the Coalfields Recovered?' *Environment and Planning*, Vol. 39, 2007, pp. 1654 –1675.
8 Ibid. p. 1671.
9 Huw Beynon, 'Still too much socialism in Britain: The legacy of Margaret Thatcher', *The Industrial Relations Journal.* 2014. Vol. 45, No. 3, 2014, pp. 214-233.
10 A. O'Hagan. 'Maggie', *New York Review of Books*, 23 May 2015.
11 Beynon, op. cit., p. 229.
12 Ibid.
13 Ibid. p. 230.

Part 1

The People

Chapter 1

A young miner's view of the strike: 30 years on

Ian Lavery

The 1984–1985 miners' strike was a conflict born out of a desire by a Tory government to confront, and fatally wound, political trade unionism through any and every means available. It was also a strike that fundamentally changed my life. Looking back with the benefit of hindsight, new information and my own maturity give a wonderful sense of perspective and the clarity to see that we were right all along. It is easy to forget that at the time I was a boy, barely politically conscious and just entering the world of work, who along with all other miners was lured into a strike by the state itself. I come from a family of miners: my father was a miner all his life, as was my grandfather. My great-grandfather came from Ireland to work in the mines in the north-east coalfield, and that's where it started on the Lavery side of the family. On my mother's side, mining runs back generation after generation. So basically, I come from a family that is of 100 per cent mining stock.

Despite this family heritage in mining, my first employment was not in mines but on a government Youth Opportunity Scheme working in the construction industry. When they started taking men and boys on at the Northumberland mines, in January 1980, I successfully applied for a job, and started my mining career at Lynemouth Colliery. It was working in the coal industry that I really learned the value of work, of solidarity, and of camaraderie. Prior to the strike, I had been fortunate enough to be accepted onto an apprenticeship in mining craft. This was a huge opportunity for me, as mining craft apprentices were expected to go on to become colliery officials, with some even set on the long path to becoming a colliery manager.

After a few months at Lynemouth Colliery, I was offered the opportunity to go to nearby Ellington Colliery, or the 'Big E' as it was known locally, to take up this mining craft apprenticeship. Unlike many of their modern namesakes, which are short term and really equate to little more that slave labour, these were real apprenticeships, with study involved as well as work and leading to globally recognised qualifications and with a secure job at the end. This involved working in the different specialities underground, and gave me an early opportunity to understand the inner workings of mining coal. This was, of course, a huge opportunity for a young man. Under the apprenticeship system you were trained very early to work on the coalface, which was a big thing because working on the face brought good wages.

With my training barely underway, worrying signs began to emerge of industrial unrest across the national coalfield. The newspapers, radio and television outlets were all full of stories about the threats of closure hanging over some collieries, those same collieries that had made Britain great. Fresh from dismantling the British steel industry, Ian MacGregor had been brought in to do the same thing in the coalfields, regardless of the cost to those that lived and worked in those mining communities. Following the announcement of the closure of Cortonwood Colliery, near Barnsley in Yorkshire, what started as a local walkout soon spread across the national coalfield, with miners coming out on strike in defence of their jobs, their industry, and the very future of their communities. The media vividly portrayed, through words and images, picket lines that were inevitably set to hit the Great Northern Coalfield. Eventually those images became reality for us, as picket lines formed at the gates of Ellington Colliery. From that day forward, although I did not know it at the time, my life was to change forever.

When the strike started in Northumberland, mass meetings were called at all the mines, and I thought it was tremendous the way that people were sticking together to fight the closures, even when their mine was not in danger. While this was something that I had never experienced before, the majority of miners had experienced this togetherness in the strikes over wages in 1972 and 1974. While there had been local industrial relations problems at Ellington Colliery, I had not experienced any kind of industrial action on this scale before. That people were willing to stand by each other in this way was new to me, and would remain with me throughout my life. At the outset of the strike, while I was a member of the National Union of Mineworkers (NUM), I was not particularly active and was politically naïve. For the next year, my family – my father, myself, and two of my brothers – would go without wages, would be demonised by the state, and would experience the working-class solidarity that shaped my life and my political beliefs.

My own involvement in the strike was not without complication. The NUM had sanctioned a continuation to work for mining apprentices, and as one of those apprentices, I was expected to continue to go into work. My father was a loyal union man, believing the old adage that 'together we are stronger' and had always supported instructions and policies of the NUM wholeheartedly, but on this occasion, he rebelled against the Union. He told me that despite what the union was saying, if I crossed the picket line I would always be viewed as a 'scab'. This is the best piece of advice I have ever been given, and as far as I am aware, I was the only apprentice in the North East of England that refused to go to work. I am proud to say that I never did cross a picket line, and from that day I became an active participant in the dispute.

My first experience as a striking miner came in the very early days of the dispute when Blyth Power Station, a site in my constituency now reduced to rubble, was the focus of a mass picket intended to choke off the supply of coal and restrict the generation of electricity. Busloads of miners had come to the area, many of them from the Scottish coalfields, to join what was to be a mass picket. I travelled to the picket line from Ashington, making the short journey with my father, who had been through the bitter disputes over wages in the 1970s. But this was an altogether different dispute, with jobs and communities now being defended rather than demands made for decent wages and conditions. I can still vividly remember that first visit to the picket line: the noise and the almost audible crackle of tension in the air.

However, my first stint on a picket line ended hastily with my arrest only minutes after arriving. This was my first experience of being arrested, and I was perplexed by the actions of the police. This was not the way I believed a picket line would be policed, nor how law and order was upheld. The illusion I had held about the police being there to protect the population was shattered. In the next twelve months I was to learn a lot about the state and its willingness to use all of its machinery against its own citizens. In the aftermath of my arrest I was sent to appear at the court at the rear of the old Ashington police station. This was my first arrest and first encounter with the judicial system, a system that I did not understand. I believe that justice was served that day; standing in the dock in that cavernous courtroom, I was cleared of all charges. Even now, it is difficult to put into words just how confusing this experience was for me, a young man being dragged into a fight with the state for my job and my community, that I had neither picked nor wanted. I had always thought that the state was there to protect ordinary people like myself, my family and my neighbours, to be there to maintain law and order, not wage pitched battles with its citizens, and use the courts to rule fairly on disputes. My world was turned upside down.

Our community always believed that the dispute would be settled and the strike would end the following week. In the early months we thought this every week, and this was a belief that was replicated up and down the national coalfield. We believed that our reasons for going on strike were right; we had won in 1972 and in 1974, so why should it not end soon? In the communities themselves, there was an unshakable belief that our case was just. This was a dispute in which a miner from Wales in his sixties, and near retirement, had downed tools to protect the jobs and the communities of apprentices like myself, who lived hundreds of miles away. In the long history of industrial relations, has there ever been a more noble or justified dispute?

My own involvement in the strike gave me a political education that even the best universities in the world could not have delivered. The dispute gave me an experience in, and education of, the trade union movement, as well as insights into industrial policy and politics in general. It also allowed me to listen to some of the finest orators I have had the pleasure to listen to, not only the Scargills, the Benns, the Skinners and the Bickerstaffs, but also people from my own community, men and women from ordinary mining families who were empowered by their involvement in the strike. It was simply fascinating, not to say uplifting, to hear the wide and varied opinions of men who had worked all of their lives underground, men who were often portrayed by those in power as being ignorant, uneducated and unpleasant. There was a veritable encyclopaedic knowledge of the world stored in those people: the men who earned their living deep underground and their wives and families who populated their communities. Articulate and intelligent people who had been denied the opportunities afforded to young people now, but who had found work in the colliery. The dispute also brought mining women to the fore in defending their communities. From those that steadfastly supported their families in the communities, to those who became part of the Women Against Pit Closures network, and played a huge role in assisting the NUM in that long dispute. The burden of the consequences of the strike, particularly the poverty that broke many families and individuals, politicised and energised many others.

During the strike, though I was courting my future wife, I was unmarried and lived with my mother, father and three of my brothers. It became evident from the very outset of the strike that our family, and our simple way of life, was under threat, primarily through the deprivation of our basic finances. Like all other ordinary mining families, we relied on a weekly wage and could not exist on our meagre savings. It was the same for all the mining families throughout our town, and in other mining towns and villages up and down the UK. From the early days of the strike, many families struggled with the financial practicalities of being on strike. This lack of money was an issue for every family of a striking miner, particularly for those people with mortgages, car payments, and young children. It was an extremely difficult time, but as the struggle continued the communities did their best to support each other. Throughout the strike, communities were able to maintain themselves through weekly food parcels and what became known as 'soup kitchens', even though they supplied much more than soup.

The NUM was eventually subjected to the sequestration of its assets by the extremist Thatcher government, in an attempt to mortally wound the embattled union. In the nations coalfields, miners and their families were forced to become creative in order to survive. Predominantly, these efforts took the form of trying to secure financial support from different sources locally, nationally and internationally. This was not a choice but a necessity forced upon us in order that we were not to be compelled to go back to work through starvation. The realities of this meant that while some were on picket duty, others were sent out collecting funds. In communities up and down the country, miners and others sympathetic to the cause knocked doors and rattled tins to collect money and groceries to keep their impoverished communities fed. In villages, towns and cities, despite the barrage of propaganda from the Tory media, the generosity of ordinary people was heart-warming. The financial solidarity from the wider trade union movement was also generous and much needed. It would be easy to fill this chapter, and many other chapters, with stories of the solidarity and support for mining communities; stories that have become in many communities the stuff of legend, but perhaps these should be left for another time and another publication.

As an individual, I have to admit that I was more at home on the picket line, at rallies or demonstrations than being sent out collecting. However, due to the increasing militancy of the police, the judiciary and government I found myself in a position that, in order to help the cause, I had little choice but to do so. Having been prevented from exercising freedom of movement by the courts, and being effectively barred from joining the picket lines, the only way I could contribute was through collecting funds, which was always interesting. There was a wide and varied set of views across the country about the strike, and the media were predominantly against the miners. However, the vast majority of people that I met when collecting were positive and supportive. Some though were negative, and a few offered downright rude opinions of miners and their leaders. Whatever the reception those collecting received, it all had to be endured so that the miners and their families were not starved back to the coal face.

Few if any of us in the coalfields believed that the strike would go on until Christmas. As the months passed, and the days grew shorter, the possibility that the strike could be won increased, at least in our minds. However, some miners were becoming disillusioned by the worsening situation, particularly as their financial position worsened. Even for people steadfast in their belief in the strike, hardships were beginning to tell. The imminent arrival of Christmas in the coalfields was cause for more than a little concern in the communities, and a slow trickle of men began to abandon the strike and return to work. As a result, the picket lines became increasingly hostile and volatile places, especially with friends and family members now on both sides of the line. The Tory tactics of divide and rule, implemented remorselessly, appeared to be having an effect. Despite this slow but increasing return to work, the message from the NUM rang out loud and clear: 'victory is imminent'.

Along with my family, I fully believed that this was the case, and I still to this day believe that the strike, which we were provoked into, was justified. It was an attempt to protect the very lifeblood of our community from an increasingly extreme government, determined to consign the communities they saw as hotbeds of socialism to the dustbin of history. This was a fight we simply could not have backed down from. Christmas came without the hoped settlement between the NUM and the National Coal Board (NCB). Far from being bleak, the Christmas of 1984 was one of the best I have ever experienced. The solidarity afforded to the miners and their families from their supporters was a joy to behold. International comrades, from far and wide, expressed solidarity with the mining communities under attack across the coalfields in a way that has rarely, if ever, been seen before.

The Confédération Générale du Travail, (CGT)* in France gave a cast iron commitment that no child from a striking miners' family would see Christmas Day without a gift. They lived up to this commitment by sending juggernaut after juggernaut full of gifts across the English Channel to ensure that the presents were received in time. This, without doubt was one of the most magnificent demonstrations of international working-class solidarity that I have ever experienced. Food parcels, including chickens and turkeys, were also sent and then distributed throughout the communities to ensure that every miner's family could have a traditional Christmas dinner. The toys and food that allowed those families to forget their hardships for even

* The Confédération Générale du Travail, or 'General Confederation of Labour' in English, is one of five trade union confederations in France.

a short period of time were perhaps the greatest gift of all. At my family home on Christmas Day, the small chicken we received did not go far in such a large family, but the message of solidarity it brought with it was more important that any morsel eaten. This was a chicken that had found its way to Ashington, paid for by people little better off than ourselves, who we had never met, and from a country that we had never visited.

Christmas came and went, but the bitter struggle for our communities we had found ourselves in showed no sign of abating. As the trickle of miners continued back to the coalface, the picketing continued and the volatility of the situation grew. My family and I stayed resolute until the end, never even considering joining those miners who had abandoned the strike and returned to work. I am proud to say that I and my family were there at the beginning and were also there at the end. We were also very clear that the strike had been the correct thing to do, and that the struggle to preserve jobs and communities had to be continued.

Even toward the end of the strike, when many miners had returned to work, we maintained the hope that there would be a negotiated settlement that would somehow save our towns and villages from the ravages of what we knew would follow. However, false dawn followed false dawn, meeting followed meeting, and we eventually came to understand that any hope of a return with an agreement would not be realised. In the weeks leading up to the end of the strike, in my heart of hearts I think I knew that no agreement would come. The state had used every weapon in its arsenal, and had spent millions of pounds to win the strike, and with people returning to work in a steady stream, all they had to do was wait. When I embarked on the strike I was politically naïve, but by its end I was hardened and knew this attack on hardworking communities had been a political, not an industrial, issue.

As we moved on toward the NUM conference in March, people had become desperate. After almost a year of severe hardship for the mining families and the communities we lived in, opinion was split as to what should happen next. We could not bear the thought that, after a year on the picket lines, and after an epic struggle, we had lost. The March conference voted to return to work, and this was one of the lowest points of my life. I had entered the strike a young man and had experienced the full force and brutality of the state. As I said earlier, this was a year that changed my life, and it changed many other lives as well. The defeat and subsequent demise of what had been, without doubt, the most powerful trade union in the world, has had a devastating impact on working people the length and breadth of the country. The government's victory opened the floodgates for an all-out attack on the trade union movement and workers' rights that continues to this day.

The end of the dispute was only the beginning for the mining communities that had put their very survival on the line against the might of an ideologically driven state. The impact of what the government's victory actually meant for the country, and for the mining communities themselves, can still be seen today. Since the late 1970s successive governments had introduced legislation that weakened the rights of people in the workplace. Through confrontation, rather than negotiation, taking on and smashing the spirit of trade unions, the Thatcher government was able to fundamentally alter the relationship between the state and its citizens, breaking with the decades old post war consensus championing individualism, and all for the benefit of the already rich and powerful.

From the end of the Second World War, and right up until the 1980s, collective bargaining was the main way of regulating employment relations and pay and conditions across the British workforce. Since the end of the strike, the NUM and the wider trade union movement have been weakened and are in serious decline. The number of workers represented by trade unions has dropped dramatically, from 80 per cent in the 1970s to under 20 per cent today.

With the decrease in membership, along with the erosion of collective bargaining, it is no surprise that the UK has one of the highest levels of wage inequality in the developed world. Workers across the UK have seen their real terms pay reduced, the casualisation of their labour increased, and their health and safety protections in the workplace diluted. Power has been stripped away from working people and put in the hands of those for whom profit is the ultimate goal.

Britain's industrial landscape has changed almost unrecognisably in the last four decades. The primary industries, such as coal and steel, which employed millions in the 1970s, are all but gone, as are many of our manufacturing industries. Despite the fact that the last deep mine in the UK closed in December 2015, the UK still produces up to 30 per cent of its electricity from coal imported from abroad, while rich seams of coal still extend below our feet. The journey from the end of the strike to the situation we now find ourselves in, can be best described as nothing less than wanton industrial vandalism. The ideological desire to curtail trade unionism has left destruction in its wake and has changed British society for the worse.

Towns like mine have never really recovered from the loss of the mines that they were built up around. Those mines not only provided employment, directly and indirectly, they also provided a rich social fabric that bound the communities together. The industrial revolution that made Britain great was built on the backs of the miners who toiled underground to provide the fuel for growth and expansion. Through their union, and their political party, they helped to make the areas they called home safe, relatively prosperous, and somewhere to be proud of. They rose from their supposed lowly station in life, with coal dust and socialism running through their veins, and began to challenge the long-established order. Those in power have always sought to curtail the power of the NUM, and to put those coalfield communities back in what they saw as their rightful place. The coming to power of Margaret Thatcher, with her extreme policies, provided the establishment with the power and opportunity to do so with vigour.

This was a conflict born out of a desire by the Conservative government to confront, and fatally wound, political trade unionism, using any and every means available. Margaret Thatcher and her government of political extremists, if not vandals, set about their task by targeting the trade union that they feared most, the NUM. The NUM, in order to achieve higher standards of health and safety and pay and conditions in their industry, had brought down a Conservative government only a decade earlier. This strike can only be seen as retaliatory attack on the members of the NUM and the coalfield communities they and their families called home.

Looking back, after thirty years, it still strikes me as sad that trade unionism, and all it stands for – the working together for the better of all, not just the few – was seen as such a threat to the British establishment. Post-war, that establishment had been bloodied by working people seeking to better their lives and the lives of their families. Those defeats at the hand of the trade unions were still fresh in their memories, and revenge was on their minds. Margaret Thatcher always claimed that she was but an innocent bystander in this strike but the cabinet papers relating to the strike, released during the last parliament, paint a very different picture, confirming what the inhabitants of the mining communities have always known. Not only was she involved in the detailed command of the government's response to the strike, but she sent out senior politicians and civil servants to mislead the country, demonstrating that she was prepared to stop at nothing to defeat the miners. This was a prime minister who was intricately involved in micro managing the strike. While she lied to the country about the scale of the proposed closure programme, she simultaneously schemed to use the armed forces to ensure her victory over the miners. In 1984, Thatcher's state apparatus unleashed a politicised police force and judiciary on men who were simply defending jobs and their communities. The National Union of Mineworkers spoke often of the secret plans to destroy 75 collieries and

65,000 jobs. But the government of the day and senior civil servants in its pay lined up to dismiss the claims as the fanciful dreams of militants and revolutionaries. Not only did this list exist but it was well known to those right at the very top of government.

It seems absurd, when considering the energy needs of our nation, that vast reserves of coal still lie under our feet. It is equally absurd to think that a whole primary industry would be sacrificed in an ideologically based crusade to crush trade unionism. The failure of the strike did indeed deal a blow to trade unionism, but it was certainly not fatal, and perhaps the current governments' anti-union rhetoric can still be linked back to those distant memories of ordinary people organising to force change. Again, in looking back on the strike, I see two contrasting but concurrent disputes. Firstly, there was the desperately sad side, where a government, hell bent on the mass destruction of the coalfields, was prepared to use any and every means possible to win. Second, there was another more positive side, where communities banded together fighting for what they knew was right, existing on the breadline for a full year in defence of their jobs and communities.

The strike and its hardships brought out things in people that were unknown, even to themselves, from the men who had worked their whole lives underground to the women involved in the Women Against Pit Closures. From masterful and articulate oratory that would put the grandest public speakers to shame, to the ability to comprehensively get over the point in a debate, that legal representatives train their whole lives to achieve. It was a situation of all hands to the pumps, and people found the talents required to meet those emergencies, from organising and speaking at meetings and rallies, to the collection and distribution food. It was amazing to witness, and amazing to be involved with.

In 1984 it was desperately depressing to think that an industry that had provided my town with work for over a century was being targeted in such a vicious way. Thirty years on, looking at the same town, it is even more depressing. The unprecedented destruction caused by the closure of our mine has taken its toll. The social and economic fabric of Ashington was ripped apart, and little has been done to repair it. The same can be said of any of the now post-industrial communities in the UK. At the beginning of the strike in 1984, 170 mines remained, employing almost 200,000 men. These mines were the life blood of their communities that had grown up around them. Today none remain.

Those communities still bear the consequences of those closures, and it is no surprise that in almost all of the economic indicators, the former coalfield areas fare far worse than the rest of the country. From job density to rates of employment and levels of business formation, those areas lag behind. It is no surprise that ill health is prevalent in those communities, and that deprivation exists in many areas. In communities where once there was a vibrant social scene and thriving high streets there is now blight: empty shops and boarded up bars and clubs. Ripping the economic heart from towns and villages with absolutely no plan to provide alternative work has allowed this terminal economic decline to occur. Years of struggle to build a better life for generations of miners, their families and their communities were washed away in the tsunami of closures that hit in the wake of the miners' strike. As is so often the case, the meticulous weaving of social fabric and the building of traditions and institutions can take many decades. Destroying what others have fought and died for can take a matter of minutes.

Writing this chapter has given me the opportunity to look back and reflect on the strike, and many things come back to me. While I saw how the power of the state could be wielded against a section of the population, I also witnessed at first hand, how communities can come together to fight for their very existence. I first stood on a picket line as a young man unsure of what the future held. Now, thirty years on and more weather beaten by the same fight, in the same circumstances I would do exactly the same in a heartbeat.

Chapter 2

I am Woman, I am Strong!

Barbara Jackson

I would describe myself as a socialist, and a feminist and a republican as well! I came to all of these in my mid-30s. My family had always voted Labour, but none of them were actively involved in politics, as far as I knew. My parents were just part of that Second World War generation, grateful for the post-war settlement and the welfare state. They always said, 'You vote Labour because they look after the working man'. It didn't matter that my mother was working as well, and this view just sort of bubbled away in the background. I had an awareness of some questions: why am I not getting a decent job? Why have my parents never got any money? Why does she look worn out? So, it was a gradual but growing political awareness.

In terms of qualifications, I have two O Levels that I got after I left school. My school was a secondary modern, and like most I left without any qualifications; it wasn't expected of you, and you just left with your school report. I left school at fifteen and my first job was in a big department store in Sheffield, on the hosiery counter. It was a huge cultural shock for me because I was brought up in Pitsmoor, which is a really poor part of Sheffield. I had no idea that Sheffield had a big department store because it wasn't for the likes of us; our world consisted of going to Woolworths and the market. My family was so poor, by which I mean poor physically, emotionally, psychologically.

Becoming an activist, socialist, trade unionist

Ours was a world of deprivation at every level, but as a person I've always been pretty good when somebody faces me up. In my middle twenties someone said to me, 'why don't you join the Labour Party?', and I thought, 'why not'? The jobs that I'd had in admin were not unionised, so it was from quite a low level of political understanding that I got involved. I wouldn't have called myself a socialist at that point because I had no understanding of what a socialist was.

When I went to Labour Party meetings in the early 1980s, it was not that different to the party it is today, but with less women and ethnic minorities. I started to read *The Observer* and thinking 'I want to know more about things'. I was meeting people who were really interesting, both men and women that I had never met in any other area of my life. There was this completely hidden world going on all the time, which was not obvious unless you were part of it. In an accidental way, I had become part of something that just fitted with me, how I thought.

In 1981, I started working at the National Coal Board (NCB), working in administration at the regional office in the Pensions and Insurance House in Sheffield.[1] I was really pleased and excited to have that job, and I can remember that in the interview I was told that I had to join a union to work there, because union membership was mandatory. I readily agreed to join as I had always wanted to join a union. You might not say that openly today, but it was totally accepted at that time. I joined the Colliery Officials and Staff Association (COSA), which was part of the National Union of Mineworkers (NUM). I could have joined another union rather than the NUM, but I thought it a better union.

I had some understanding of mining and mining culture, through newspapers, radio and TV. Regularly on the news you would hear about the mining industry, and I could remember in the 1970s when there were the three-day working weeks due to miners being on strike. I worked in a private company at that time, and in our particular office we were all really excited about what the miners were doing. We were in this ludicrous situation, working by candlelight part of the time, and the women that I worked with were all saying quite openly they were going to vote Labour. Once I had joined, I started to attend the COSA meetings. I had no experience of going to meetings other than the Labour Party, and I had never attended a trade union meeting before. With all the strikes that were going on, it was a rebellious time.

I was aware of Thatcherism and what it represented, and this was one of my reasons for joining the Labour Party. I was naïve then but I had enough sense to realise I wasn't bothered or impressed that she was a woman. It was her politics that I hated, and Sheffield was really big in fighting back against her policies. What particular upset us was what happened to our transport policy, which was 10p for any bus journey. We were so proud in South Yorkshire of that transport policy, and the whole country knew about us, and then the Tories deregulated transport and the people of Sheffield knew what Thatcherism stood for.

Once I had settled in at Pensions & Insurance House, I started attending the lunch time union meetings. The union was led at the time by a marvellous older woman called Audrey, and there was a saying that if you had a problem 'leave it to Audrey, she'll sort it out'. When Audrey went on long-term sick leave, there was a small group of activists and younger people left to pick up the pieces. There were a number of us who got stuck in, taking up positions in the union and making it more political, and more radical than it had been. A lot of the workers regarded what management said as gospel, thought that the trade union's role was to just pass that on as an instruction. Management's attitude was the same: 'this is what management wants to do, you tell your members that.'

There was a small group of us, I think about six or seven, that did not like this attitude, and we became more challenging toward management. We had people working on short time contracts that were coming to an end, and there was anxiety over whether they would be renewed. We tried to get stuck in over these and other issues and became a younger, sharper, more radical branch. Our main focus was to say to our members 'we're fighting to get these contracts made permanent and to end this uncertainty' and stuff like that.

We were also involved in the Doncaster Area Panel,[2] representing South Yorkshire, where COSA branch officials would go. A couple of us started attending these meetings, and of course we were then exposed to men who were representing COSA in the various collieries of South Yorkshire. They were streets ahead of where we were in our thinking, and in the way they dealt with things. It was useful to me, to link up COSA representatives from Coal House in Doncaster,[3] which also had a large number of white-collar workers who were members of COSA. We were aware of all the issues around pit closures, and we were involved in an overtime ban in November 1983. Our office regularly worked overtime on Saturday mornings and in order to support the miners our branch decided that we would also implement the overtime ban. This was our first big involvement in industrial action, taking on the management in our office by implementing the national overtime ban.

The overtime ban was fully supported by the activists in the branch, and was largely supported by the membership, as they were fed up with being put under pressure to work overtime. They also supported our aim to make temporary contracts permanent, allowing people to settle down, and getting rid of the uncertainty in their lives. We went big for this, and got a picket line organised. I have to say we did this in great fear and trepidation. We had no history of striking, or organising a picket line, but we were able to get a few activists to staff it.

It is difficult being on a picket line; you are asking people that you work with to join in with the ban. Some were conflicted because they wanted the money but were sympathetic with the ban. Others were not conflicted at all, and just wanted the money. Also, you may be working with people who have crossed the picket line. Overall, we saw it as a success as we managed to turn some people away, but others were determined to go in to work. In order to deter those who had crossed the picket line, we announced that we were going to name those who continued to defy the ban and went into work. We were supported in this action by the NUM. Some of the people employed in the NUM offices came down on Saturday mornings and joined us on the picket line, and some Derbyshire miners also came and stood with us. On some occasions we were thirty strong and by that time hardly anybody crossed the line, it just grew and grew. Somehow we managed to stay strong and stay together, and it did not disturb people too much as they still received their weekly salary. In the end, our management decided they would not ask for overtime, so we had won. It was a time of confidence and a steep learning curve.

The strike

When we were asked to attend the Area Panel, we knew something big was coming unless something was sorted out between the NUM and the NCB over the proposed pit closures. We were very nervous, because it is one thing having an overtime ban with a picket line on a Saturday morning, but an all-out strike is another thing altogether. As we were trade union branch officials and activists, it was like putting your money where your mouth is. It is all very well when times are good, saying what you will do, and how you will get this, and how you will talk to management about an issue but now, all of a sudden you have really got to follow through.

There was no doubt in my mind that I would do it, I mean I was scared and worried about the implications of it and how it would go. I had become a bit of a leader, you know, a front person, and I realised that I would end up talking to people on the picket line and explaining it to them. It was just really, really difficult, the lead-up to the strike. The night before we actually went on strike I don't think I slept at all from worrying about it, were we going to hold together, this little group of young, untried branch officials? Of course we had no idea we were going to be out for a year. At the time you're thinking, miners usually win strikes fairly quickly in recent times. I start getting a bit emotional about all of this because these were difficult times.

We decided what we were going to do, that we were going turn up at our workplace, and because we were on flexitime we could come in any time between eight and ten. We decided that we would get there at half past seven because we were quite sure the office would be open and that people would try and come in early to avoid us. That first morning we got there early and people had started to arrive for work. We tried talking to them, telling them that this is for real, the decision has been taken and we are now on strike. In no time at all we had this huge crowd milling around on the pavement outside, unsure about what to do. They knew that they had until 10 a.m. to go in, so they had time to think about it. There was quite a big foyer to the office, and there were all sorts of managers milling around. There was a small number of people that had gone in and people were outside, waiting for some kind of collective decision to be made. There were about 700 to 1,000 people there, from a mix of unions. There were steps up to our office and I can clearly remember being at the top of the steps saying 'you can't go in, this is it, this is us on strike', and stuff like that. Then at about five minutes to ten, the deadline for flexitime, there was a big surge to go in. I think we were left with about forty people at that stage who said that they were not going in as they believed in the strike.

I cannot remember what we did after that, but we knew we would have to do it all again the next day, and the day after that, and the day after that. We were insignificant in terms of the strike, because there was no attention paid to our picket line. We were literally one hundred yards away from Westbar Police Station, the main police station in Sheffield, and they only came to see us once, because the thing about being on strike is if you are not successful in stopping people going into work, you can be there forever. The police are only interested in you when you're successful.

Over the following days, we lost most of those forty people, and it was really tough, turning up to that picket line every day. We only did it for a couple of hours, until ten o'clock because it was more than we could bear. It was tough because some of the forty people who started out with you would not tell you that they had gone into work, and you only found out when other people came and told you. That was really distressing because by then things were appearing on the news about miners, such as the violence on picket lines, which was hugely influential, especially to white collar workers and to people who were looking for a justification to go back into work. That was really, really tough, and we were eventually left with nine people who stayed solid until the end of the strike. Interestingly, the gender make up of those that were left was fifty-fifty.

We lost some of our branch officials who had been strong in the beginning, but who could not cope as it went on. They had been fine with the overtime ban, and were initially fine about the strike, but I think they believed that we should take a decision whether we were going to stick it out or not, and out of that collective decision, decide what we all should do. If that had gone to a vote, it would have been to go back into work. However, we never took that collective decision so we kept on saying to ourselves, the ones who had remained strong, 'we are not going back, we're going to carry on, and we're going to stay out on strike'.

We tried to seek advice from the Area Panel but nobody was interested in us because everything was in chaos, and we were on the margins of the strike. There was nobody to come and help us out of this big hole that we were in. Our own branch officials who went back into work were angry with those of us who remained out, because they argued that we had always done everything together. They argued that they could be more useful to us by going into work and raising money for miners on the inside, but we correctly saw that as little more than an excuse to go back to work. This split resulted in the ludicrous situation of our own branch officials crossing their own official picket line.

But the picket line did survive until the end of the strike. Two of those who did not go back left us to take up work elsewhere, and one drifted off to university. One of our group always wanted to get out of the NCB and concentrated on music, while his girlfriend carried on working. Our branch chair found part-time work on an ice cream van, and occasionally came to the picket line. So there were five of us who stayed out until the end, with four running the picket line.

My husband at that time ran his own garage as a one-man operation. He fully supported what I was doing, but he had no political comprehension or comprehension of trade unionism. For him, the strike was just something that affected me and something that I was really involved in, so he would support me, both financially and emotionally. Like others on strike, we got some food parcels, and other support occasionally. Here is a letter from one of our members who worked at Coal House and was on strike – 'Dear Barbara ... yeah, more food vouchers, and you know, related to all the tins we received … a lot of tinned meat, and me a vegetarian'!! Sheffield City Council were marvellous with us, and did what they could in terms of offering free school meals to the kids. Sheffield had no pits, but they were hugely supportive and they organised vouchers for us occasionally. Unlike in the mining communities, there was nothing regular for us.

Most of the speaking that I did during the strike, the audiences were more interested in Women Against Pit Closures, rather than the personal story of our particular picket line. To be frank, when we went out on many of the marches, a lot of the miners were amazed that we were out on strike with them. They used to say to us quite openly, 'Get back to work, why are you doing this?', or, 'You can go back to work and there'd be no recriminations'. There may not have been any recriminations from other strikers, but there would have been our own internal emotional, moral and psychological recriminations. Those of us who were out at the end just could not have done it.

In the early days of the strike, the miners were really strong and they felt that they did not really need anyone else; it was their strike and they could win it on their own. It was only after the summer, when things started to go wrong, that there was this realisation that they could not win it on their own and there was more appreciation of what we were doing. To all intents and purposes, our little group was insignificant. In lots of ways, we were simply following a personal path of trade unionism and political commitment. We had a lot of support from NALGO, the local government trade union. A couple of those people adopted us part way through the strike, and they would come down and join us on the picket line, with tea and toast and hot sausage rolls. Even their kids came and joined us. It was really heartening to know that we had this little group who we knew would come every day with some hot drinks and stuff.

Any money that was being raised was largely going to Sheffield Women Against Pit Closures, rather than towards us as a group. We got two guys that joined us every day on the picket line, one was in COSA and the other one in the NUM at Brodsworth Colliery. The Area Panel had announced in the early days of the strike that we were really struggling and would people go and support us on the picket line. They took this request literally and every day for a year they travelled in by train and stood with us on the picket line. Eventually we took in three young lads who were working at a Fence workshop at Woodhouse. They were members of the NUM/COSA who were on strike. It appeared that no one in the NUM knew about them, they did not know where to go, and nobody appeared to be interested in them. Eventually they heard about us, and came and joined us. We also had a couple of people who lived in Sheffield but worked at Coal House in Doncaster. It was easier for them to come and stand with us than travel to Doncaster, so we always had a little group of twelve to fifteen, on any day. Not many, but we were a presence.

Sometimes when days of action were called, you'd get a bigger group coming down to join us, and they'd be really into it, shouting as people crossed our picket line. These people were also amazed that we were not shouting. That was difficult because they didn't understand how draining and emotional the daily picket line had become for us, constantly confronting our colleagues. The emotion involved in that is just so draining. They were saying: 'why aren't you shouting?', and we were thinking, 'you're being a bit too enthusiastic'. I do not think they realised that we had gone inwards to survive, as a group and individuals.

Despite all of our troubles we remained buoyant, and we still thought we were going to win the strike, right up until the end. Of course, Mel and Alan, coming in from pit villages every day, brought news of what was happening in their pit villages. So, for a two-hour daily session of picketing, it was quite buoyant. I had a little van at the time, and every day I would turn up with our placards and park for free on this parking meter outside our office for a year. We were never challenged, and the parking meter people just ignored us. The police only came once, very early on in the strike. This police contingent came along, marching. I do not remember what exactly I said, but words to the effect that we worked in this building and we were on strike, and we were polite, respectable people and that there would be no trouble. They left and we never saw them again.

The couple I was closest to at work were not political, or anything like that, but they were nice women and good fun. Occasionally before the strike we would go out together and they still wanted to talk to me on the picket line. This was really bizarre, we were on strike, and they wanted want to chat as though nothing had happened, and then they went in to work. In the big foyer, there was a drinks machine and they'd say, 'Can we go and get you a hot drink from the drinks machine?' and we would reply, 'No, we don't want anything, thank you'. I believe that they were uncomfortable and possibly guilty about still going into work.

Yes, people were still going in, and it was really difficult for all of us to deal with. We found the only way we could deal with it was to turn inwards, into the group, and ignore people if they tried to talk to you. We pretended to be having a conversation with one of our fellow pickets. The picket line was great in so many ways because every day there had been a new event that had happened nationally somewhere, and there was something to talk about every day, you'd seen a television programme where Arthur held his own in an interview, when the interviewer insisted that he gave yes or no answers.

It was hard, but for me the saving grace was that I found out about Sheffield Women Against Pit Closures (SWAPC). Meeting people like that got me thinking, and especially after I had joined. This was about a group of fifty women, who met weekly, and a lot of them were middle class but a lot of them were working class. The thing was that many of them were political, and had some further education beyond mine, and it was seeing how they handled themselves in the meetings that attracted me. As you can imagine, it was quite difficult to hold fifty women together with different points of view. It could have easily split into groups between miner's wives and middle-class intellectual professional women. That it did not was down to the chairwoman, a communist called Cath Mackie, and she was just marvellous. She held it all together by building bridges between the two groups. It was just so vibrant and so exciting and they were just a group of women who thought, 'we can do anything', and you know, they could do anything. They were full of confidence and ideas and possibilities. It was a complete contrast to what the picket line had become. They say you cannot carry on banging your head against a brick wall without some support, but those women helped me get through, emotionally. I had friends in the Labour Party who also supported me, so I also had huge psychological and emotional support elsewhere.

The thing is, an event like the strike turns out to be the most exciting experience in your life. For me, it represented freedom. My personal commitment to the strike was to go to the picket line for a couple of hours, five days a week, for a year. That left me with an awful lot of free time, and being involved in Sheffield Women Against Pit Closures filled that space. Once you joined an organisation like that you were immediately accepted, and there were no questions asked. It is the same when you meet somebody who was involved in the strike, there is an affinity straightaway. You know nothing about them, and you may never see them again, but all of a sudden you put your arms around one another and you start telling your stories. Being involved in the strike pulled all of us into this alternative world that introduced us to new ideas, and new people.

I realised as soon as the strike finished, that a lot of women did not want the strike to end, because they had been given freedom, attention and enormous power during that year, all of it dependent on the strike. I knew that a lot of that would dissipate when the strike ended, and that Women Against Pit Closures needed to find a role in its own right. I personally didn't want us to be affiliated to the NUM, and when the NUM vote went against us, I was pleased because I didn't think that that was right for us. I think we needed to stay outside of the NUM, and joining would have been seen as us clinging to their coat tails. There was a lot of misogyny within the ranks of the NUM, with attitude of the 'women will be told what to do', and some of the women were underpinning these attitudes by seeking reassurances from the men about what they were doing. I just thought, fuck it, this is not what I'm about. I did not need their reassurances, or their affirmation, and I was glad when we failed to get a role within the NUM.

Defeat and after

We cried when the strike was called off, and when I returned to work it was just dreadful. The thought of going back into that office, and working alongside those people that had crossed our picket line day after day. The five of us that stayed on strike decided to meet at eight o'clock as usual, and return to work together. I had another sleepless night thinking 'how am I going to get through this'? So the four of us went back together, and immediately we got into the foyer, four managers appeared, and we were all taken to different offices and given a talking to. A couple of us were put on probation for three months, and told to go home and think about whether we wanted to continue working for the NCB, and by half past nine I found myself back out on the street again.

So I went home, and I can remember being in the kitchen and starting to cry. My husband, Ken came into the kitchen and said 'I thought you were going back to work today'? I told him what had happened, and I told him that I did not want work there anymore. He said that this was fine by him and that he had no problem with this at all. Fortunately, a reasonably well-paid a job came up at Sheffield Centre Against Unemployment shortly after my decision to leave the NCB, and I applied for it and got it. While all this was going on, I had made enquiries into going to Sheffield Polytechnic, never expecting anything to come from it. However, I was called for an interview and to my amazement I was offered a place, and in September 1985 I became student. I thought, 'right, another big step forward, Barbara'!

I think, looking back, that I had been given this opportunity because of my experiences in the strike, but I felt like an imposter. It was as if people were thinking 'who do you think you are, coming here with no qualifications'. Then I had to do my first essay, and I had no idea how to write an essay. When I was at school, they called these 'compositions'. I was given advice from the tutor and managed to get a B-, and the next hurdle was an exam that I managed to get through. After that I was on my way. I am quite competitive and I loved learning and developing myself. I approached all of it very seriously as I wanted to succeed, and I ended up with a 2:1 which made me immensely proud of myself.

Returning to activism

After the strike the big issue was to settle down again, and I think I was in a process of mourning. The NUM needed to hold itself together as well, to try and work with the modified colliery review programme that had been introduced to 'manage' pit closures. There were also 900 miners who were sacked during the strike, so the big campaign was to get these men reinstated. The suggestion of a 50 pence levy to support the sacked miners was lost in a ballot, which was an absolute disgrace. There were all sorts of internal things going on across the coalfields, as the workforce and the union were trying to pick themselves up, and Sheffield Women Against Pit Closures ceased to exist in 1987.

I was coming up to my final year at the Polytechnic and I wanted to make sure of getting a reasonable degree. Then there was the issue of what I was going to do next, what type of work am I going to find? I also started a new relationship at this time as well, so I was gradually being diverted away from what had gone before. There was a sort of feeling, almost of embarrassment, that started to creep in about the strike, and also a bit of shame as well. We had gone through all of the troubles and stress involved in the strike, and we had lost. I would meet people after the strike, women who had been involved, and you'd automatically assume that they still had the same mindset as you. I would get talking to them and many of them would say 'Oh, we've left all that behind'. I could not think like that, and just discard what I had experienced as if it was of no consequence.

There was a period where I did not know what to do with my anger and my despair. The Tories had been re-elected and the country had, in effect, said 'we're quite comfortable with what's happened to the miners. We can live with the pit closure programme.' When in 1992 the pit closure programme was intensified, some friends of mine who had supported the miners told me that they were going down to London on a march against the closures. When they asked me to go with them I said no, because I did not think it would do any good, it would not change anything. There was huge public support for the miners, and a dawning realisation that the coal industry was in freefall, but that support had nothing to ground itself in. The NUM were going through a period of internal conflict, particularly about the use of strike action, and I thought that the whole situation was hopeless.

Activism didn't really start for me again until in 2004, when I went to the Chesterfield May Day rally. I found Ann and Betty, two of my friends there, running a stall for Barnsley Women Against Pit Closures, and I felt ashamed because they had kept the faith, and I had drifted away. In the end it did not take that much to pull me back in, so I went to Wortley Hall in October 2004 where women who were active during the strike were brought together for a residential weekend school. It was great, but there was again nowhere to channel your energies or your organisational skills, and women were asking what they could do, or get involved in. New Labour was in office, but they were doing nothing on trade union issues.

It was not until 2012, following an 'Inside-Out' programme in our locality where the BBC spent thirty minutes looking at Orgreave and the police statements that they had obtained, that I had something to focus on. They had interviewed police officers who admitted openly on camera that they had been told what to write in their statements, and I thought, wow, someone is interested at last. Nobody had ever talked about Orgreave since June 1984 – it was a no-go area for discussion. This was a serious professional programme made by a journalist called Dan Johnson, who had been born in Barnsley during the strike. Then the Hillsborough campaigners had their independent panel hearing and they were completely vindicated in their version of what had happened. People were saying, 'Wow, it's great that they've kept at it all these years and they've finally achieved success', and then people began to say that something like that should happen about Orgreave.

I had been on a miners' email list for a number of years and I can only describe the majority of contributors as a load of 'gobshites'. They were mainly men, and quite a few were always sounding off about what should be done on every subject. I expected one of them to take the initiative. After two weeks, I realised that nobody was going to do anything, and it was like one of those moments during the strike when you think, 'I'm being pushed out to the front'. I thought if it was not going to be me, then no one is going to do anything. I thought I should call a meeting, and I contacted my friend Lesley Bolton from the famous photograph of her nearly being truncheoned by a mounted police officer. She was also part of SWAPC, so I trusted her. I told her that I was going to call a meeting to try and do something about Orgreave, and that I wanted her to come as I was too scared to do it on my own. She said that she was up for it, and that if no one turned up, we could just have a drink and go home. I sent out an email to all my contacts notifying them about the meeting, and eight others turned up beside Lesley and myself. Granville Williams, editor of the book *Shafted: The Media, the Miners and the Aftermath*,[4] came to the first meeting, and he suggested the name of our little group: the Orgreave Truth and Justice Campaign. Joe Rollin, a UNISON community organiser, turned up to the first meeting as well.

The campaign just took off, and it has taken over my life. It is massive, it is independent, it is a political campaign, but it is not party-political though we are fully aware that we are dealing with a political issue. We decided we were going be bold because from the outset we had 28 years to make up for, so that's why we've always had the objective of a full public enquiry to get to the truth of what happened at Orgreave. That is not to say that other issues were not important, such as the general policing of the strike. As a small grass-roots campaign that had few resources, we needed to concentrate all our efforts on what happened at Orgreave. When we had stalls at different events, men who had been at Orgreave would come and tell us their stories. These men had been telling their stories for thirty years, and I used to think, 'what do you want to do with your story? You can't just keep telling your story, yes it happened to you, you were arrested, but what have you done about it?' Then I realised that it was down to a lack of confidence, caused by thirty years of being crushed, and they were now daring to believe that something might happen that could be good and positive for them.

The legacy of the strike

I always say to people who want to talk to me about the strike that I am not representative of the vast majority women in the strike. I am not representative because I am not a miner's wife, as most people assume. No, I am actually a woman who was on strike in her own right, and I am very proud of that. But neither am I representative of a typical woman who would have been involved in the strike, mainly because I come from Sheffield, a large city, and a city provides you with lots of opportunities. It is different for the women who lived in the pit villages, where when the mine closed everything around also closed, so please don't take me as any way representative because I'm not. This is now true of many people in the working class, not just miners and their families. As a result of the general deindustrialisation that has taken place since the strike, there are people who have very little political consciousness at all. It is not just the working class who are on the back foot now; you have to be pretty wealthy to feel comfortable and safe. It is the denial of class that I find most problematic, but people like Owen Jones and others are continually identifying how the working class is being stigmatised, and how class itself is being eradicated from our thinking.

The period of the strike was an extraordinary time, and I feel privileged to have played a small part in it. We had no idea that we were making history at the time, but we were making our own history. Now we can take ownership of that history and we can talk about it with a full sense of ownership, and a full sense of pride. Some people who were involved will say 'don't ever mention the strike', but not me.

NOTES

1 Pensions and Insurance House was the national administrative centre for the National Coal Board's pension scheme.

2 Because of the large area of the Yorkshire Coalfield the NUM organisation in Yorkshire was divided into four Area Panels, of which Doncaster was one.

3 Coal House in Doncaster was the Headquarters of all mining operations in the Yorkshire Area of the National Coal Board.

4 Granville Williams, *Shafted: The Media, the Miners and the Aftermath*, London: Campaign for Press and Broadcasting Freedom, 2009.

Chapter 3

From the Picket Line to the Palace of Westminster

Siân James

At the beginning of 1984 I was a young mother and contented housewife, married to a husband who was employed as a fitter underground for the National Coal Board (NCB). As a family, all we were concerned about was enjoying the raising of our children in the community we both grew up in – the Upper Swansea Valley. My life overall was a very traditional one, revolving around family, local community, and chapel, and also including a burgeoning interest in politics, though with a small 'p'. However, within a few months, my life had been turned upside down and changed forever, due to the most exciting year of my life. That year saw our community, our lives, and in my case my whole future, change out of all recognition from what I had thought it would be. The events of that year set me on a journey that would lead me from a picket line to the Palace of Westminster.

The decision by the National Union of Mineworkers (NUM) to strike in March that year is well documented, and I will not comment here on the reasons for the decision which led to a year-long series of experiences that are still causing reverberations in my life thirty years later. Little did any of us realise at the time that the bitter conflict between Arthur Scargill's mineworkers and Margaret Thatcher's government would become a struggle of epic proportions resulting in one of the longest strikes in British trade union history. It was a strike that would become the stuff of legends, and one the likes of which this country will probably never see again.

To fully understand the course of the strike, you have to appreciate the symbiotic relationship between the mining communities and the NUM. It is my firm belief that no other trade union could have sustained a strike of that length. We, as the wives, partners, mothers and children of the nation's miners, fully understood the nature of that relationship and, given what was at stake, we also understood that there was no option other than fighting to defend our communities. Win, draw or lose, the families in the South Wales coalfield were on strike together, as were the majority of mining communities across the UK coalfields. We all had a common enemy (Thatcher) and a common purpose: to fight the pit closures that would destroy our communities and, in doing so, destroy a culture and way of life that we all valued and cherished.

Traditionally, the NUM provided advice, support and guidance, not only to its members, but also to the communities those members lived in. It was there to help to solve any problems, not just those associated with work. Its officials were well known to all members of the community it served, and in our community older miners were always there to help out anyone experiencing hardships, with the local Lodge officials providing a direct link to the NUM at area and national levels. Very quickly, after the strike began, our communities established a support network specifically designed to provide food and practical support for all striking miners and their families. We lived a good distance from my husband's colliery at Abernant, so we chose to become involved with the Neath, Dulais and Swansea Valley Miner's Support Group, which covered the area where we lived. It was a decision we never regretted and a truly amazing group of people became involved, many of whom are still our friends today. Our Support Group was organised around nine support centres, three located in each of the three valleys we were responsible for, offering complete support and welfare for just under one thousand individuals. We covered the major towns of Neath and Ystradgynlais and more rural locations such as Penycae and Abercraf.

The rules were simple – every penny raised and any items donated were to be pooled and each miner would receive an equal share. In addition, every person who turned up to the weekly meeting would be entitled to a vote, regardless of status in the union or gender; a truly liberating idea for the women involved with the strike. In the past, our roles had been very much ones of passive supporters, not active doers, working behind the scenes in a support role, but here we were encouraged to express our opinions and to 'get stuck in'.

At first, my role was a very traditional one, selling raffle tickets and garden plants from door to door, raising money and collecting donations of food, clothes and toys for redistribution or sale in Abercraf Miner's Welfare Hall. I talked to our neighbours and friends about why we were on strike and how they could help us, which proved an important link into the local community as most of my neighbours had relatives who worked, or had worked, in the mining industry, and their support and goodwill was crucial.

From these conversations we learned about their concerns, and the bitterness they felt towards the government. Youth unemployment was high in the Valleys, despair about the lack of opportunities and concerns about future employment were all around us. Many understood from the outset that the strike was an attempt to preserve jobs and provide opportunities for future work for their sons and brothers. I relished these discussions, exchanging views on politics and learning at first-hand about their worries, but as time went on it became apparent that this strike, unlike previous strikes, could very well go on for many months. I was becoming more and more immersed in the work, and my involvement in the Support Group was growing ever deeper, as was the involvement of my husband. We were both totally committed to the aims of the strike and we were fearful of the future if the strike was to fail.

While I was involved with local community based activities, Martin, my husband was picketing, helping to shift food and supplies at the local food centre, and cutting and distributing wood for pensioners whose concessionary coal supplies had been stopped. These activities took him to picket lines across South Wales and his stories of the aggression of the police on the picket lines worried me. I knew he had to support the NUM in this way but it was frightening to realise that the police were being used by the government to repress miners who were simply exercising their rights to picket. We discussed how committed we were to the strike and what limits we would set on our activities, and very quickly we realised that we were in for the long haul and that we would have to become more active with the support group and on the picket lines. I can't say our families were thrilled by this increase in our commitment, but we both felt it was necessary. Staying at home doing nothing was not an option for us and we knew that we had the determination and commitment to support our community and union.

One crystallising moment, for me personally, was when Thatcher described the striking miners and their families as 'the enemy within'. This incensed me, and created a resolve within me to become even more involved, and I remember thinking that I had now been given some sort of moral permission to be more active and to fight back. If it had not been obvious before, it was now becoming clear that the women of the British coalfields were the 'backbone' of the strike. Their commitment and resolution were the key reasons why our communities were holding out so steadfastly against Thatcher and her disreputable government. Through my links with the other women in our valley, I began to attend the weekly meetings in Onllwyn Miners' Welfare Hall, more commonly known as 'the palace of culture'. Here, at the heart of all activity related to our support group, we were encouraged to express our views and participate in decisions on food purchases, picketing schedules and the wider political situation. I drank it all in, wide eyed and excited by everything that was going on around me.

For the first time, my opinion mattered outside my family circle. The thoughts and ideas of the women were not shouted down, but listened too and discussed rationally. We might not win the arguments, but at least our suggestions were considered and cogent reasons given as to why they could or could not be implemented. This was truly liberating experience for me, and I went home every Sunday afternoon to report back to Martin what had been discussed, and what decisions had been made. In this way, we both felt part of the bigger picture, and our political education continued within our own home.

As part of the support group structure, we had a policy of inviting any group who raised monies on our behalf to come and stay with our families and see for themselves where their money was being spent. In mid-September, we received a letter from a group of gay and lesbian activists based in London, who had collected monies on behalf of striking miners and their families. Calling themselves Lesbians and Gays Support the Miners, (LGSM) they identified closely with us and our communities, united by a common hatred of Thatcher and her pernicious brand of politics.

I remember the meeting where their initial letter was discussed. It was clear that they desperately wanted us to accept their donation, but had experienced a great deal of negativity from other coalfields and support groups they had approached. A full and frank discussion then followed debating whether we should, or should not, accept their donation. The comments from around the table ranged from typical working-class jokes about gay men, through to comments that the sight of men, dancing together at our social events, would be too shocking for the local community! As usual, the women in the group cut to the chase. Our opinion was that if this money had been raised, we didn't care who the fundraisers were and it was just good manners to accept their donation. The next stage of the fledgling relationship was to send representatives of the support group to meet with LGSM. The rest, as they say, is history. Within a short space of time we had twinned with LGSM and invited their representatives to visit our communities, to stay with us in our homes, and to witness for themselves how their donations were being used.

Martin and I volunteered to welcome two gay people to our home and very quickly accommodation was found for all the members of LGSM who had expressed an interest in visiting. They would be spread across the three valleys, and would experience, at first hand, the hardship being endured by our hard-pressed families.

Our main concern in Cae'rbont was not that our visitors would be gay or lesbian, but that they might require a vegetarian menu! After much discussion, Martin suggested that simple meals of baked beans, pizza and mushroom omelettes would be both suitable and cheap enough for our much-reduced budget. We need not have worried, the gay man who stayed with us proved to be a meat eating Northerner, who fully understood the class struggle and was a delight to host. I can honestly say the weekend that followed proved to be one of the best experiences of our lives. Yes, we did see men dancing together, but we women had danced together for years, as our macho husbands propped up the bar. What was so different? Truthfully, nothing.

The relationship between the Neath, Dulais and Swansea Valley Miners Support Group and the LGSM went from strength to strength, with new friendships being forged and family links maintained to the present day. Along the way, we lost many good comrades and friends to HIV and two deaths in particular caused much grief in our home. The tragically early deaths of Mark Ashton and Derek Hughes were bitter losses to me personally, and to Martin and the children. We have such happy memories of them and the specialness of their support. Both were true comrades, willing to go the extra mile to help others and the world is a much poorer place without their shining presences.

It was those links, forged between our mining community and LGSM that gave us the determination to support the recently premiered 'Pride' film, and allow our names to be used for two of the characters. 'Pride' is a story that has touched the hearts of millions of cinema audiences across the world. The fact was that in two such disparate communities, we had discovered that we were not that different. We had more in common than we had ever imagined, the bonds we forged and the links made between our two communities would go on to help break down the prejudices of generations and help gay men and lesbian women gain the rights denied to them for generations. Our actions in the strike and the decision to accept donations from this brave group of people helped achieve full equality for gay men and lesbian women in the UK. Without a doubt, we helped change public opinion and our partnership was ground breaking. Of course, not all barriers have been removed and there remains a great deal to do but, oh, how different life is for a young gay person in today's Britain, than that experienced by them in the early 1980s.

LGSM became one of our largest donors, and the most consistent. They never missed a week after we accepted their support, a wonderful record when you realise how vicious the anti-gay feeling was, fuelled by hysteria around the burgeoning AIDS crisis. Newspapers carried stories of the 'gay plague', and encouraged heterosexuals to fear anyone who was different to them. Thankfully, in our small way, our support group played its part in breaking down the prejudices of the time.

Running parallel with my activities within our Support Group was my increasing involvement with women active in the struggle, not only across Wales, but also across the UK. Inspirational women such as Hefina Headon, secretary of the Neath Dulais and Swansea Valley Support Group, Edwina Roberts of Seven Sisters and Ann Jones of Hirwaun led by example within their communities and motivated me to do more on a personal level. These women became true comrades and friends who continue to inspire me to this day. As the strike progressed, I become more and more involved with the South Wales Women's Support Group and the wider Women Against Pit Closures movement, attending meetings and speaking out against the government and British Coal wherever and whenever I could. Eventually, I would become the Chairperson of South Wales Women's Support Group, an honour and a privilege I cherish to this day. What greater recognition could any woman involved with the struggle achieve?

As the strike progressed, the attacks on the NUM and our mining communities continued to grow. The majority of the media provided the British public with highly skewed images of violent miners, hell bent on destroying democracy in the UK. Our communities were portrayed as disloyal, greedy, and led like sheep by a politically motivated leader. The Police were cynically used by Thatcher to suppress our freedoms and the state adopted draconian anti-trade union legislation in an attempt to control our rights to picket and to protest. Was it any wonder that some sections of the public believed the lies and carefully manicured stories they saw on their televisions and heard on their radios? I and many others were left feeling frustrated and angry at these orchestrated attacks on our union, our men, and our communities. We were being systematically marginalised and the whole weight of the British establishment was being brought to bear on the NUM. Truly, on their terms, we were the enemy within, but not because we were extremists or unreasonable but because we, as communities, refused to accept that the government was right to shut our mines and make the UK reliant on imported coal.

For the first time in our lives, we were meeting women from other mining communities and coalfields. We were also meeting representatives of the wider women's movement, such as the women from Greenham Common, as well as activists from Black and Ethnic communities, and other campaigning minority communities from across the UK. Women like myself who had been content never to stray beyond the boundaries of our own valleys, were now travelling from coalfield to coalfield, picketing at some of the most well known, or should I say notorious, mines in the UK. We were, both mentally and physically, putting ourselves on the front-line of the struggle to save jobs and communities. Place names like Annersley, Orgreave, Seaham, Point of Ayr, Wylfa and Didcot peppered our conversation. Speaking engagements on behalf of the NUM, and the Support Groups I was involved with, began to take up more and more of my time.

Supporters of the NUM were realising that it was the women of the mining communities who were coping with the daily juggling act of keeping hearth and home together, while becoming increasingly involved with more direct action such as picketing and protesting. Now, everyone wanted to listen to these amazing women from the mining communities, women like me who had previously been silent and unseen. Suddenly, we were in great demand on platforms at meetings up and down the country, telling the stories of ordinary women who were doing extraordinary things. I, and others like me, were taking these changes to our lives in our stride, eager to talk to whoever would listen, to tell them that our beloved communities were under attack, and why we were compelled to take the actions we were to protect them.

Every evening, in their own living rooms via their televisions, the public were presented with images of violent miners, confrontational women, and communities in turmoil. Caused, so our critics claimed, by our determination to hold off progress through violent anti-social behaviour. It was essential that we challenged these attacks and miners' wives were speaking out about what life was really like in Thatcher's Britain, where communities and lives were being destroyed by unemployment and poverty, and where greed was good and collective action was an aberration.

Once the fight back started, the demand for speakers from the NUM was so great that I began to undertake speaking events on behalf of overstretched union officials. These speaking engagements took me to other mining areas such as Staffordshire, Yorkshire, Durham and Nottinghamshire. Speakers such as myself and Ali Thomas from Onllwyn, were playing an important role in keeping morale up in these areas. I stood on platforms with Arthur Scargill, Derek Robinson, Dennis Skinner, Derek Hatton and other great orators, who I studied and watched in fascination. They could hold a room in the palm of their hands, and with practice, I improved my public speaking skills at rallies and meetings across the UK coalfields and in London, gaining more and more confidence as I went.

It was the first time I had visited many of these communities and they were so different to ours in Wales. Miners had transferred to work at the new modern mines in those regions from other, declining, coalfields such as Scotland, West Wales and Durham. They were not born and bred in those coalfields, did not live in close knit communities such as the ones they had left, and as a consequence had very little sense of belonging. It was clear that there was some isolation and disconnect from the NUM. When we visited, we tried to take practical and emotional support, alongside messages of solidarity to them and their families. As always, I made friends on these visits that have remained so to this day.

During these visits and speaking events, I began to realise that even though the majority of miners in their localities had returned to work, their own personal solidarity and dedication to the strike was the equal of ours in South Wales. Most were paying a heavy price for remaining loyal to the NUM, feeling demoralised and pressurised by their situation. Indeed, these were brave people, loyal to their union despite facing enormous pressure from scab workers and the NCB managers in their regions. It is never easy for the few to stand up against the many, and I was full of admiration for their actions.

Invitations to speak were flooding in, and London beckoned, with huge opportunities to fundraise within the various boroughs and communities that made up the city. Many of those who supported us were active trade unionists, people from mining communities who had left to work in wealthier parts of the UK, or like those we met in LGSM, sections of the community under direct attack from Thatcher and the state. There were many common bonds but most of us had one basic thing in common, we hated Thatcher and all she stood for. Thank goodness for these comrades, all decent people who wanted to help us on a financial and practical level. From colleges, universities, factories, trade unions, workplaces and local communities they reached out to us to offer help and support. They stood shoulder to shoulder with us, providing us with the resources and encouragement to fight on when it got even tougher in our communities. Some of them had never even seen a mine, or met a miner, but that didn't matter, they supported us regardless, and wanted to hear about our struggle and how we were coping. My memories of these meetings are fond ones, particularly addressing clothing workers in a small factory in Brick Lane, a bar full of black people in a Brixton pub, a classroom of teachers in Wood Green, community activists at Broadwater Farm, and many more. The people who turned up to hear us speak were prepared to stand alongside us and wanted to expose the depths that the Thatcher government was prepared to stoop to in their attempt to keep working-class people in their place.

In Wales, we were in a unique position. In 1982, a Welsh language television station had been established, specifically designed to meet the needs of the 25 per cent of the population of Wales who spoke Welsh, and wanted to watch television in that language. S4C offered us a rare opportunity within the British media to access coverage that was not openly hostile to us or skewed towards a Thatcherite agenda. Many of their journalists, researchers, technicians and actors came from the same valleys and communities as us, and most had relatives who were working, or had worked, in the mining industry. They were keen to tell our stories and despite some suspicion of all journalists, based entirely on the behaviour of the national UK press, some of us were happy to give interviews to Welsh radio, television and print journalists. As these interviews were exclusively through the medium of Welsh, they sought fluent Welsh speakers, who had the confidence to speak on the television or radio. I came from a Welsh language home, my children were attending Welsh medium schools, and the daily life of the upper Swansea Valley was conducted in our language of choice – Welsh. In fact, you stood out like a sore thumb if you were greeted in Welsh and did not reply in the same language. You were immediately identified as a stranger and a good deal of questioning would follow, as to why you were visiting and what had brought you to the area. I quickly became recognised as someone able to conduct interviews bilingually, and who was happy to do so whenever the opportunity was offered. This is how my interest in learning more about my own language developed. It eventually led me to study the written language and embark on a full-time degree course at Swansea University when the strike ended.

Before this we had a strike to win, and with Christmas fast approaching, our minds were focused on providing many of the goodies the children and elderly of our communities would otherwise be missing. Our links with organic farmers in Pembrokeshire, the print unions and our stalwart donors would help provide the basics and the rest we would create ourselves. We had a different Christmas that year but we made sure the children would enjoy it as well as they could. Christmas parties, with Santa Claus in attendance, were organised in our nine food centres. LGSM organised the 'Pits and Perverts Ball', featuring Jimmy Somerville; an event that raised over £5,000. This money helped not only our own Support Group, but we were able reach out financially to other, less well supported mining communities across South Wales.

Volunteers for the role of Santa were numerous and in Abercraf a local councillor volunteered to distribute the modest gifts of basic toys and chocolates. My son and his best friend were very puzzled as to why Sion Corn (Santa Claus in Welsh) was wearing the councillor's shoes. In his excitement at playing Santa, he had forgotten to don the wellington boots that matched his hastily borrowed costume. The eagle-eyed eight year olds had spotted the anomaly and went to bed extremely puzzled by this conundrum.

1985 dawned and the strike was still solid across South Wales, though there were one or two who decided to go back to work. They were such a small minority that we were able to stem the tide, with our efforts focused on picketing the local pits. The sight of a single man being escorted by dozens of policemen, with police vehicles and motorbike outriders was astonishing, and it was obvious that this overkill was purely for the media. There was no way any coal was being produced, but it did create a lot of overtime payments for the police on duty.

Initially, we appealed to those who had returned to work directly through the local NUM officials, asking them to stick with the strike and share our burden. When this failed, more direct action was undertaken outside their homes, where a series of community gatherings were organised, including sessions of community singing. In Wales, we have a great tradition of eisteddfodau or song festivals, so we decided to meet outside their homes to sing hymns and local people responded well, offering us the chance to stand in their gardens and providing us with bathroom facilities. There was a fantastic community atmosphere, with everyone joining in with great gusto or as we say in Welsh, 'hwyl'. One hymn in particular proved to be the most popular. 'What A Friend We Have in Jesus' and when we got to a particular line in the hymn 'do thy friend despise forsake thee', can you blame us that we gave it an awful lot of 'hwyl' and shouted out the words at the top of our voices.

We always tried to be respectful of the neighbours and kept the gatherings peaceful, but often the police became over-excited. There was always a large police presence and it was clear their priority was protecting the scab's houses, and their behaviour towards the singers left a lot to be desired. In particular, the reactions and behaviour of those policemen who were imported from regions other than South Wales were over the top. If we were not in a neighbour's garden, or on the pavement, anyone at the gatherings could be arrested so it was important to keep off the public highway. In all the pushing and shoving it was easy to step off the pavement onto the highway and be snatched up by the over-zealous policemen. On several occasions, police officers from other regions behaved very badly, snatching people off the public pavement, dragging them away, and threatening arrest. One favourite tactic of the police in these situations was to walk along the edge of the pavement facing up to those gathered on it and rely on a local policemen to point out potential trouble makers. On one particular occasion, I was horrified to realise that the policeman walking along with the officers from the Midlands was well known to me. Indeed, his daughters attended the same school as my children and we had socialised with the family as our children grew up. He made a great show of pointing out the 'troublemakers' facing them, using his finger to point and just pronouncing the word – troublemaker. When he came abreast with me, he stuck his finger out and waggled it in my face, while saying to the officer in charge, 'big troublemaker' and carried on along the line. As soon as the police began to snatch people, I was carted off, along with several others.

With Christmas over, we began to think about the strike reaching its first anniversary. It was not easy but we felt that we had 'hit the wall' and survived, and now we were battle hardened campaigners. With little to lose, the struggle was still integral to our lives and early in the New Year the NUM called a regional meeting of the men to update them on the negotiations and the strike in general. The women went along but were denied access to the meeting, which was a bitter pill to swallow considering how integral to the strike the women had become. Without us, the strike could not have lasted so long, or remained so solid in South Wales, but the union did not seem to appreciate our dedication at that point. We decided to go anyway and lobby outside the meeting and remind those attending of the plight of the sacked and jailed miners. When Martin came outside to tell me what had been discussed, it was clear that he was concerned. He felt that the local union was going to encourage the men to return to work, an action we women found incomprehensible. We had suffered for so long, remained so loyal to the union, and with 98 per cent still solid here they were discussing the possibility of a return to work. Not only without a victory, but without the reinstatement of the sacked miners.

We returned home despondent realising, as the anniversary of the strike approached, our regional union leaders were beginning to think the unthinkable. The rock solid South Wales NUM was being guided by its own executive committee towards a decision which could very well see our region lead the way to a national return to work. This was definitely *not* how the women wanted the strike to end, after all that we had done to save jobs, the mines and our communities. Many tears had been shed but we knew instinctively that there was a lot more damage that Thatcher and her government could inflict on our communities. We were now staring at a future without any hope of preserving our way of life.

Over the next few weeks we watched news reports of miners returning to work across the UK and we became more and more despondent. The trickle of men returning to work was becoming a steady flow, and when we talked to friends in other regions we heard the despair in their voices. South Wales was still pretty solid but, more and more, we heard talk of the strike bring a lost cause and the possibility of an orderly return to work. Another regional meeting was held in Porthcawl and again, the women from across the South Wales mining communities lobbied those attending. The eyes of the world were on the South Wales miners; if they crumbled what hope was there for those striking in regions where coal was being produced. I was interviewed for the World at One radio programme and I reminded the interviewer about those men who had given everything for the strike and how we could not forget them.

Before we knew it, we had reached the beginning of March 1985, the anniversary of the beginning of the strike. Quite fittingly, one of the groups visiting us that weekend was the LGSM. Along with us, they watched in despair the news report on the executive's committee meeting in Pontypridd, where scenes of NUM officials standing outside their headquarters at Sardis Road, endlessly played on our TV screens. This was the end of our hopes and aspirations for our communities; the unthinkable was happening before our very eyes, the South Wales NUM had voted to recommend a return to work.

Much has been written of this period by historians and so called trade union experts, who have consistently claimed that common sense prevailed and that an orderly return to work was the only sensible option open to NUM. We heard this with shock and horror, because they actually believed the government would honour their pledge to save the mining industry. We knew their argument that it was better to sacrifice some collieries to save others, but we believed that this would prove to be more lies. While some wanted to believe, we knew that you cannot deal with intransigence, and you cannot negotiate with an enemy that does not respect you and has no intention of honouring anything previously promised. We were continually lied to, by British Coal, by Thatcher, and by others.

The organised return to work without a formal agreement left the NUM in a much weakened position, with nothing to offer but a docile acceptance that pits would inevitably close. Even worse was the failure to negotiate a deal for the sacked and jailed miners. Ordinary people like us were dismayed by the decision but as soon as it was made, the return to work was organised for the following Tuesday. On that day I watched with a heavy heart as, for the first time in a year, Martin walked to the top of our road to catch the bus to work. I could see from his face and body language that every step was like a knife thrust to his heart. For a year, we had supported the strike and followed the NUM, done our duty to it and to our community, and now we were left shattered by the decision to return to work. Facing us was the prospect of an even more poverty-stricken community, where jobs and opportunity would be even scarcer, as we had little of value to offer Thatcher's Britain. We knew with a cold dread that the full brunt of her revenge would fall on us and everything that we held dear.

Personally, I was terrified when the strike ended, and wondered what would happen to me. I knew we faced debt and a tough period of re-establishing our personal lives but, selfishly, I was also concerned about myself. I had changed so much from the person that I had been, gaining so many new skills and experiences. Friends from all parts of my life tried to encourage me to look forward and not back, and two in particular stand out, Roy James of the Lesbian and Gays Support the Miners and Helen Prosser of DACE.* On separate occasions both sat me down and talked to me about my skills, and how I should not waste them by returning to my past life as a wife and mother. The 'different' me was ready to take my life in a new direction, but that direction would have to include my husband and children, which meant centralising all that I did in the future around my family and our community. Going away to university or to a trade union college in another part of the country was not for me. I wanted to be here for my children and the community I knew and loved. Through Helen Prosser, I approached the Welsh Department of Swansea University and Dr R.O. Jones offered me a provisional place on their full-time degree course. This offer was dependant on me gaining a Welsh Language Diploma and I continued to study with Helen, gaining the diploma before entering Swansea University in 1986.

I had expected university life to be a hotbed of political activity, with memories of the 1969 student uprising in the Sorbonne clear in my mind, and I looked forward to meeting politically aware students who wanted to make a difference to the lives of others. This was a slight over expectation, as I had underestimated the effect of Thatcher and her 'greed is good' message. Many of the students I met were from working-class backgrounds but most were focused simply on gaining a good degree and getting a well-paid post when they graduated. The influence of Thatcherism was everywhere, salaries and job opportunities were the popular topic of discussion, with very little said about activism or giving anything back to the community. Despite this,

* Department of Adult Continuing Education, University of Swansea

I entered university determined to participate fully in the student life, even if I had to make it happen myself. I joined the Student Union, becoming the Welsh Officer, and I also volunteered in the university crèche. I also attended political meetings of all types and organised support for workers on strike, and visits to Greenham Common.

To ensure we had adequate childcare during the period I was in university, Martin worked the night shift at Abernant colliery. Often, we met at the bus stop in the morning, as he got off the works bus and I waited for the bus to Swansea. His support for me was unwavering and I can honestly say that my gaining a degree was as much a recognition of his work and commitment as it was of mine. During the half term breaks the children often sat beside me in lectures.

Much happened to our family during the three years I attended university. Both of our mothers passed away and Abernant colliery finally closed. The options for a transfer for Martin were limited, so the decision was made for him to accept the redundancy offer and start again. Unemployed for several months, he was eventually offered a job at a small engineering unit in Pontardawe. One of the first things he was handed by his new employer was an application for supplementary benefit, something we had never had to consider before. When he asked why he needed the form, the reply was that they did not pay enough for someone with children so he would need the form!

Graduating in 1989, I immediately began to think about getting a job. Feeling I had a great deal to offer an employer, I was anxious to start contributing to our family finances. I had a good skill set, which included the Welsh language, and I began to apply for roles that would utilise them and allow me to further develop as a person. My first full-time post was as Field Officer for the National Federation of Young Farmers (NFYFC), an organisation that was as different as it possibly could be to anything I had experienced previously. The post was an all-Wales one requiring me to travel across the country providing services for young people living and working in the rural communities and industries of Wales. Almost immediately, I was 'outed' as a political activist when being interviewed by a journalist on Radio Wales about my appointment. Halfway through the interview, the journalist paused and asked, 'Are you the Sian James from the Miner's Strike'? I replied that I was, and there started a discussion on how different working for the NFYFC was from my activism during the strike. There were no huge repercussions from the interview, but it surprised me how many young people asked me about being a member of the Labour Party in Brecon and Radnor, and what was Arthur Scargill like? For many, I was the first person that they had met who was openly talking about politics, whether it was their politics, or my dreadful politics of the left.

Over the next 15 years I worked for some of the best known organisations in Wales, including Save the Children, Securicor and The National Trust. My work was in public affairs on behalf of these organisations, and I developed a particular expertise in dealing with contentious issues, such as unpopular planning applications, prison suicides and escapes, the Sea Empress disaster and serious train accidents. I continued with my Welsh language appearances on radio and TV but now there were a great deal more English language opportunities open to me as well. Running in parallel with these roles were my Labour Party activities and in 1997, when the Welsh Assembly was established, I became a lobbyist for the rail industry in Wales. It was then that I became interested in becoming an elected representative, and dipped my toe in the water as a Town Councillor in Neath, the town we had moved to from the Upper Swansea Valley upon my father's death in 1995.

In 2002 I was selected to stand as the Labour Party candidate for the 2003 Welsh Assembly elections in Monmouth. A seat that was very different to the valley communities I knew so well. While having pockets of rural poverty it was, in the main, very anglicised and very wealthy. It was not to be politically for me in Monmouth, and I was beaten by the Conservative candidate. However, the whole experience was a good one and I learned so much about the process of being a candidate, particularly how to lead a campaign and encourage party activists to work for you. I advise any aspiring politician to fight for a seat, even if it's not a winnable seat. You serve your apprenticeship and emerge from the whole experience as a far better candidate.

As soon as the election was over I started in a new post as Director of Welsh Women's Aid (WWA), an organisation that was very close to my heart. It was an honour to work with women and children from across Wales. Each and every one of them was an example to us all on how to survive terrible experiences in their lives and, with the help and support of the wonderful workers of WWA, to go on and make new lives for themselves, free from abuse. At the time of my appointment, the organisation was going through a period of upheaval, and a key challenge was to transform a collective organisation into an organisation with a traditional management structure. This umbrella organisation provided advice, policies and services to 37 member groups across Wales and again, my role utilised my Welsh language skills and lobbying experience.

In 2004 I was selected to fight for the Swansea East constituency, the first woman candidate in its history. The seat was, and remains, one of the safest Labour seats, not only in Wales but in the UK as a whole. I was selected on a Women Only Short List and I make no apologies for that. If we want a House of Commons that truly reflects society as a whole, then we have to take action, if we leave it to chance then history shows us that despite the high standards of the female candidates, men tend to win. I am proud that the Labour Party has had the determination to correct this imbalance and taken positive action. In the history of the Labour Party in Wales, there have only ever been thirteen women elected and I am fully conscious of that honour and want to encourage even more women to participate at all levels of the democratic process.

I was privileged to be elected in 2005, and to serve as the first female Member of Parliament for Swansea East. I felt that I was the ideal match for the constituency, given my background and the journey I had made to Westminster. I had many links with Swansea East and was one of the only Members of Parliament who could say that they resided in the town of their birth, Morriston. It is a typical inner city, working-class constituency, having all the problems faced by far too many people today. Issues such as fuel poverty, bedroom tax and universal credit have hit the constituency hard and I was saddened by the fact that I had come full circle in my career. I was back handing out food parcels to people who have no other option than seek help from my constituency offices.

I am now at another crossroads in my life, and have decided to stand down from Westminster politics. It has been a marvellous period and I have fully enjoyed representing the wonderful people of Swansea East, but I want to return to Wales. I want to focus on community politics once again, and have learned during my ten years at Westminster that there is a danger of becoming isolated from real politics. Westminster can be a bubble, and I want to get back to my grass roots, working alongside local people, speaking out against injustice and helping communities to achieve the things they really need.

My journey from the picket line to the Palace of Westminster has been an exciting one but I learned during the strike that, as one door closes, another opens. I have always walked through the open doors ahead of me, and I am now ready to walk through the next door that is standing tantalisingly open, just ahead of me.

Chapter 4

I Never Went Back

Peter Smith

One of my first jobs after I left school was in the warehouse of a catalogue firm, and this is where I met my wife, Jan. It was not a job that I wanted to do for the rest of my life, but I worked there until I was 21 and old enough to get work at the National Coal Board (NCB) in the Hawthorne coal preparation plant in Co. Durham. The coke works as it was known, processed all of the bi-products out of the coal, leaving coke, the primary fuel used in the steel industry. I started working there not long after the miners' strike in 1972, which was a strike over wages. While the workers at the coke works were in the NUM, they had continued to work during that dispute, and there had been a lot of bad feeling between them and the miners because of that. About six months after starting at the coke works I was on the local committee of the union.[1] One of the reasons I got involved was because it was a union man who had helped me to get the job. I went to all the meetings because I believed, and still believe, that the union is there to protect the workers, and that all should be actively involved. It was nothing to do with politics, because I have never really been particularly interested in politics. I have always voted for the Labour Party, because I believe that it is the party of the working class, but I have never felt the need to join the party itself.

At the coke works, we were just ordinary working men, some of them were as daft as brushes, and when any of them had to see the foreman, or when the manager wanted to talk to one of them, I would always offer to go with them. This was because I believed that no one should go and see management without someone being with them, to support them. I think that these actions carried a little bit of weight with my workmates, and that was why I was voted on to the Lodge committee at the plant.[2] I always told the members that it was important that they attend the monthly union meetings at the plant, to hear what was going on elsewhere in the industry, and to put forward any grievances or issues that they might have had, so that the union could get them sorted out. I told them this was the only way to improve things at the plant, because it is pointless saying nothing when there was a problem, as that way nothing ever gets done. Despite that encouragement, there were only a few of them who attended the Lodge meetings on a regular basis, but during the strike in 1974 those of us active in the union had managed to get things changed around in the coke works, and all our members came out for the duration of that strike. When I say all, it is important to understand that we maintained a skeleton staff to maintain the coke ovens, otherwise if they had been left to cool down they would have all collapsed.

My interest in the union came from my father, who was a Lodge official for the miners at Murton Colliery, so in a way trade unionism was in the family. My father was the one who taught me right from wrong, and he always said that trade unionism was really just about common sense, a situation was either right or it was wrong. He also told me that I should always go with my feelings, and if you feel you are right, then nothing can stand in your way. That was a very good piece of advice, and I have stuck with it, and it was my philosophy all the way through the strike, and in the rest of my life.

Once the strike started we had a show of hands in the plant and everyone voted to come out on strike, all two hundred of us in support of the miners in Durham, who had come out on strike to support the miners at Cortonwood Colliery in Yorkshire. Every one of them knew that we were fighting to save out jobs and communities, and if they went back to work before the strike was over they would be scabs.

At a meeting in Sheffield called by Arthur Scargill, the President of the NUM, the National Executive Committee (NEC) took the decision to make the strike official, and miners across all the coalfields came out on strike. After all, we were all part of the same union, we all wanted the same thing, and we felt that we should all stand together. I can never understand why there has been such controversy about the lack of a ballot, because none of us were forced to come out, we all did so voluntarily. Over the years I have had many arguments with people who want to talk about the fact that the NUM did not hold a ballot. I have always responded by asking them where they work and, if they have never been a miner, I always tell them that they don't know what they are talking about. You needed to be part of the industry and the union to understand why the union acted the way that it did. The critics of the strike always argue that we were forced out on strike by Scargill, but I always tell them two things to set them straight. First, that this belittles the intelligence of the miners, and second, that it was the membership who called the strike, and not Arthur Scargill.

When the strike started those of us in the coking plants were allocated picketing duties at the coal fired power stations across the UK to stop, or at least monitor, the coal that was going in. We also picketed coking plants that were working, to try and stop the coke coming out. I was away from home a lot of the time in the first six months of the strike. We had a sort of roster with the coke works at Monkton, also in Durham, where we would be away picketing for a week and then back home for a week. When we were at home we picketed our own plant at Monkton, or joined other picket lines in Durham, wherever we were needed. When we were away, we went wherever the union sent us. During our weeks away, we would stay in the houses of people who supported the strike and wanted to try and help.

Initially, we travelled in our own cars, but when our cars started to break down, or needed servicing, the NUM started to hire vans to get us around, and I was the driver of one of those vans. One of our first pickets was at the Agecroft colliery feeding directly into a local power station. We were down there for a week and stayed in a student union building at the nearby Manchester University. To show their support for the strike, the students hired a van for us to go back and forth to the picket line.

The NCB was transporting coal into the power stations in all kinds of wagons, and most of them looked as if they should have been scrapped years ago, the tyres were bald and the wagons looked like they were dropping to bits. It was obvious that they were using anything they could to keep the coal moving into the power stations. All in all though, the picketing was usually a futile exercise, as the wagons kept going in, but we had to keep trying. We would travel anywhere we were needed, and I will always remember picketing at Coalville Colliery in Leicestershire. In Leicestershire there were only thirty miners out of about 2,500 who were on strike and they became known as the 'dirty thirty'. They were an example to everyone who was involved in the strike, and we were glad to be down there to support them.

While we were down in Leicestershire, I was billeted with a member of NACODS,[3] the union for the underground management in the mines. While he was in management, like many of his colleagues across the UK coalfield he was very sympathetic to our cause. While we were fighting for our jobs, we were also fighting for theirs as well, and they were well aware of this. I do not know what would have happened to him if the senior management at the NCB had found out, but he was doing this out of solidarity with our cause.

When we were at home we picketed all around County Durham, and as the strike went on we stopped telling the pickets where we were going, because the police were somehow getting to know and would be ready for us. Also, too many of us were getting arrested. We would only tell the lads where we were going when they were all in the vans. Sometimes we would head off to where there was going to be a big picket and if we found that the police were there in numbers, we would drive off and find somewhere else where there were no police. Once we left one of the big pickets, and went to picket the NCB Headquarters in Gateshead, which caused a major panic among the office workers in the building. It was a bit like playing hide and seek, but it was a tactic to move the police around as well, to try to stretch their resources. Once arrived at a site to picket, the police were never far behind.

On one occasion, the van we had been supplied with happened to be the same type as the police were using to deliver their lunches, and we were waved straight through the police lines. Once the police found out that we were now picketing right at the gates of the power station, well behind the police lines, all hell broke loose, and we were escorted back to where all the other pickets were standing. However, as the strike developed, the police were much more efficient at stopping pickets travelling around the country, and keeping them away from power stations.

I am also veteran of the picketing at the Orgreave coking plant. The first time we went down there to picket we were held back at the top of the road leading to the plant, and we never got anywhere near where the coal wagons were going in. On the day the police rioted, we arrived to find lines and lines of buses that the police had arrived in, and instead of keeping us back where they usually did, we were directed to a particular spot where we were all kept together. The police lined up about fifteen deep, and it was obvious that there were many more of them that there were pickets. Police with big shields were at the front, and as they started to move towards us, they began to hit their shield with their truncheons, like the Zulus in that film. Then they stopped and opened up their lines to let the horses through. When the mounted police charged at us, we ran for our lives.

At that time I was eighteen stone and it was a red-hot day; our only escape route from the cavalry charge was up a steep hill. I ran as far as I could and then hid behind some trees with some of the other lads, because I was exhausted and could run no further. They charged up the hill and as they went past us, I could see them hitting the lads as they went. It was a sickening noise when they hit them with their truncheons, and it always seemed that they were targeting the head. After the cavalry charge, other police with little round shields came out, and they started to hit the pickets, again targeting the heads. I saw one of them, on his own away from the others, who was just running through all the pickets hitting them as he went past, leaving them on the ground.

Everyone started to run again, including me, and we ran towards the streets of houses that were near the plant. As we ran, I saw this young woman with a pram who had a massive bruise on her arm where she had been struck by one of the police. After we got her safely out of the way, we caught up to a little old lady who was also running away from the police. We told her that there was no need for her to run away because she had nothing to do with what was going on, but she told us that she was running because they were hitting everyone, not just the pickets.

We kept on going, because someone shouted that they had let the police dogs loose, but after a while I could run no further and had to stop. I told the lads I was with to go on without me, and that I would take my chances, but I just could run no further. I looked up toward where the lads were running, and off to one side there was a group of about ten or twelve police standing with a couple of pickets with them. A sergeant shouted to me to come and stand with them, and that if I did I would be safe. I did as he said because I was exhausted. When the charge was over, and the police had moved on, he said to us 'right lads, get yourselves away back to your buses, you'll be OK now'. The sergeant then marched his officers away from us and back down to the original police line. They actually got a round of applause from those around us, who had seen what they had done. It was obvious that this little group of police officers wanted nothing to do with what was going on at Orgreave that day. That little group of police officers had saved us – from the police.

Not all of the police were aggressive to us, and there were other times when some of them showed that they were not happy with what they were being asked to do. On one picket line, a sergeant asked us when we had last eaten. When we told him to mind his own business, he told us that he was being serious, so I told him that we had eaten nothing that day. He left and came back with a big load of sandwiches and apples that were left over from their own lunch break. He said, 'you take them lads, if they don't get eaten the Inspector takes them home with him, for his family'. However, despite the actions of these few officers, the majority of the police were against us, even in our own village. Once when we were picketing our own plant, where some of our own workmates had scabbed, they even stopped an ambulance with its siren going and blue light flashing, until they got the scab bus into the plant. They would not even help a sick person, until they had made sure the scabs got to work.

It was in my own home that I was arrested in the November of the strike, the arrest that ended up with my becoming one of the group known as the 'sacked miners'. The police had called round to the house three times that day, looking for me, but I was out picketing. We had picketed at Wearmouth Colliery in Sunderland earlier in the day, and then we had returned to our village to picket our own coke works. When I finally got home from picketing, I was told about the police looking for me, so I rang them up to find out what they wanted. Eventually, a sergeant and two constables came to the house and arrested me. The constables wanted to handcuff me in front of my two young children, as if I were some kind of dangerous criminal, but the sergeant told them that this would not be necessary.

When we got to the police station, I was placed in a cell and two detectives came in to ask questions. It was then that I found out that I was being accused, falsely, of deliberately driving the picket van at the car of a scab who was driving into work, although they did not use that term. I had been arrested under the 1876 Trades Union Amendment Act – for driving a transit van! I did not realise that they had transit vans in 1876, but I found out later that I was to be charged under that Act for 'affray', which I was told, carried a maximum sentence of twenty years. This, I can tell you, scared the life out of me when I realised the serious position I was in.

They had me in the cells for three nights before I was released, and my wife and father came to see me during that time. They were told that they could not bring anything in for me, nor would they be allowed to touch me. While they were waiting outside my cell, there were a couple of police officers standing nearby. Jan, my wife, later told me that one of them said to her that he would have to sit down because his wallet was so heavy due to all the overtime payments they were getting because of the strike. My father then challenged that police officer about what he had said, a sergeant came and asked what was going on. When Jan and my father reported what the officer had said, the sergeant immediately sent him away, and apologised for his behaviour.

While I was in the cell, the little flap opened and a police officer said 'do you remember me'. When I told him I did not he told me that we had faced each other on a picket line, and now he was in charge, which you can imagine worried me. However, despite all the restrictions regarding my visit that had been laid out earlier, that same officer opened an interview room for us. He said it would be OK, as long as we did not shut the door. He also allowed Jan to give me the cigar and the packet of Munchies she had brought for me (I still love Munchies to this day). When this officer saw the cigar he said that smoking was not allowed, then told me to make sure I flushed the cigar down the toilet in my cell when I had finished it. This was another example of a decent police officer.

A couple of weeks after my arrest, I was summoned to our coke works to be interviewed by the manager. Looking back to what happened all those years ago, I think I could possibly have saved my job. During that interview with the manager, there were veiled suggestions from him that if I agreed to come back to work immediately I could save my job. I refused, telling him that I could never go against the union, and would never make myself a scab. Because of my new status as a sacked miner, I was unable to get work for two and a half years after the strike.

It was a little incongruous that I had been sacked before the case against me was heard, as I did not attend court until January. When the case started, the scab that I was supposed to have driven the picket van at changed his story several times during his evidence. Perhaps because of this the charge against me was reduced from 'affray' to one of 'intimidation'. Unsurprisingly, given that I was a picket in a highly contested industrial dispute, I was found guilty and fined £40. Another one of our lads driving a picket van in the village that same day was also arrested and charged with 'affray'. His charge was also reduced to one of 'intimidation', he was also found guilty but fined £60. The extra £20 was due to the fact that he had a ski mask in his pocket when he was arrested.

Having lost our cases we were placed under a permanent curfew and not allowed out of our houses between the hours of 7 p.m. and 9 a.m. We were not even allowed in our gardens during those hours. It was very difficult to go picketing outside of our area, because I had to be back for the curfew, but we both continued picketing. We did, however, manage to have the curfew order lifted just before Christmas. I think that this was primarily due to the fact that the person making the decision was from our village, and knew me and my family well. We both appealed our convictions, and our appeals were heard in June 1985, long after the strike had ended. As expected, we both lost our appeals.

Despite having been sacked, I still carried on helping with the strike. I still went picketing locally, although the union would not let me drive the van, so I had to travel to the picket lines in one of the other vans. As a sacked miner, I was sort of an unofficial picket, and I still went to all of the union meetings, because I was still a member of the union. I also spent a lot of my time helping out in our food kitchen, where my main job was mashing the potatoes; in fact the ladies that were running it bought me my own masher. My other jobs were to peel all the potatoes, and then help with the washing up afterwards, and I came to know a lot of great people who were also involved with the kitchen.

One of the Deputies that worked at Murton Colliery and his wife did a fantastic job for us with the kitchen. As a Deputy, and a member of NACODS, he was still working, but he ran his car into the ground during the strike running round all over the place carrying groceries and other stuff. His wife, who was also a local JP, spent most of her time going around the village trying to raise funds and donations of food to help feed the families. I think that it is probably true that without this husband and wife team, we would not have had a food kitchen in our village.

When the strike was finally over, all those who had stayed loyal to the NUM from across all the coalfields decided that they would go back to work together, marching behind their banners. I was asked if I wanted to march up with those going back to our plant, walking in front of the banner, but I told them I would not march with them unless I could go in to work, and Jan was against this idea as well. In fact, Jan was devastated when the strike was over and everyone went back to work, leaving me outside the gates.

After I was sacked, the union did their best to help us as a family, and they kept in regular touch with me, especially after the strike was over. There was talk about the NUM taking a levy from all members to provide financial aid to all those who had been sacked, but I was strongly against that idea. Not long after the strike finished I was contacted by a group of miners from Wales, offering to get us a house down there, and to pay me a wage until I had sorted out a job. These were people we had never met. They were absolutely wonderful people, but we did not want to move away from where we lived and where our families were.

I was signing on at the unemployment office for two and a half years after the strike, and I felt dirty every time I did it. I managed to get a little car, and went round knocking on doors trying to get work, then I would get a bit sick and stop for a while, then I would be off again, looking for any kind of work. The people at the unemployment office asked if I wanted to talk to somebody about my situation, but I never went; these were my problems and I wanted to sort them out myself. I went all over – the Gas Board, the Electric Board, anywhere I thought I might get a job. I was willing to take any kind of work. During that time we just seemed out of things as a family. The lads I had worked with would ask me to go down to the pub, and I'd tell them that I had no money, but they would say 'come on we'll see you all right'. I suppose I could have had a life as a 'professional sacked miner', but that was not for me, I wanted to work.

I was worried about the possibility of being blacklisted because I had been sacked, but I was determined to get a job. I went for an interview at a local bus company, and had references from some influential people in the community. I did a written test, simple maths and English, and I finished it all before the time was up. Then I went for an interview and I thought that I had done well. That was until he asked me what my last employment was, and I told him that I had been dismissed during the strike. He told me that everything seemed to be fine and that he would let me know. However, I received a letter saying that my application had been unsuccessful, but it did not go into detail.

Following that, I called in at the Electricity Board to see if they were looking to take people on, and by chance they were. This lady gave me an application form, and told me to fill it in and bring it back to her so that she could put it in the internal post. A week or two later I got an invitation to go for an interview. I had been told by the people in the Job Centre not to put the fact that I had been sacked on any application form, so I had not put this on the application form for the Electricity Board. During the interview the person who was interviewing me said that they valued their staff and always tried to maintain an honest relationship between management and the workforce. I said to him 'look you've been honest with me so I'll be honest with you. I lied on the application form. I was told by the Job Centre not to put on the form that I had been sacked during the miners' strike.' He told me that he was not interested in what I had done in the past, but I told him that as he had been honest with me, I wanted to be honest with him. I told him the circumstances that led to me being sacked, and told him that all I wanted was a chance to prove that I was a hard worker. I was given the job, and I found out later that he told people that if there had been no job available at the time, he would have created one for me because I had been so honest with him. So honesty really is the best policy. I have worked ever since, and I retire this year.

Over the years people have occasionally asked me about the strike and the picketing and about getting sacked, but not many of them understand what it was like, or how it affected us. I do not think anyone who was not involved in the strike can ever truly understand. Some have asked me how I feel about not getting the redundancy money that all the others got when they closed the coke plants and the mines. I always tell them that what I wanted was a job, and not a hand out to compensate for not having one. They may think that this is my way of coping with the fact that I did not get a redundancy payment, but it's not, it's how I genuinely feel. People also ask me if I have any regrets about my involvement in the strike, and I probably give the same answer that any miner who was involved would give. It was probably the best year of my life and, looking back over the thirty years since the strike, I would not change a thing.

NOTES

1 Unlike the other Area Associations, the Cokemen's Area Association organised on a national level, representing all the workers who worked at what the National Coal Board called Coal Preparation Plants, which produced coke and other by-products of coal.

2 Lodge in the term used to describe the local NUM organisation at the individual NCB workplaces in Co. Durham.

3 National Association of Colliery Overmen, Deputies, and Shot-firers.

Chapter 5

Voices from the Strike

Esther Johnson and Debbie Ballin

The oral testimonies in this chapter were originally gathered for an exhibition entitled *A share of a pensioner's Christmas 'Bonus'* which premiered at the People's History Museum in Manchester from December 2015 to January 2016.[1] The exhibition is part of a larger academic research project called *Echoes of Protest*[2] and was inspired by material held in the People's History Museum archive.[3]

The stories we have collected are largely from adults remembering what it was like to grow up as a child during the strike. They articulate the experience with a maturity they may have been unable to express at the time and can now reflect on the strike with the benefit of hindsight.

Twelve people were interviewed in July 2015 for the project and approximately eleven hours of recorded interview was gathered from this process. The contributors selected for this chapter are four children of striking miners, four mothers and one father. By interviewing parents, as well as those who were children during the strike, we were able to include insights into how they perceived it affected their children. This elicited a wider discussion of the assimilation of political views within families. Contrary to expectations, everybody we interviewed talked about their memories of the strike with great fondness, warmth and humour.

The contributors whose voices are included here are:

Craig, a striking miner's son from South Yorkshire who was born just as the strike ended.

Dave, a striking miner from County Durham and his daughter **Sam** who was fifteen at the time.

Elspeth, the wife of another striking miner from County Durham and mother of two girls, Sarah and Clare.

Flis, who was also active in Sheffield Women Against Pit Closures, had a partner on strike and a young son at the time.

Gayle, who was four at the time and Jayne who was sixteen and whose Dad was a miner in South Yorkshire and Mum was active in Women Against Pit Closures.

Karen, a miner's wife from South Yorkshire and mother of one son, Andrew.

Jean, whose husband also worked at a mine in South Yorkshire, and whose son Sean was born during the strike.

As well as collecting stories relating to the Christmas of the strike and the politicisation of children and young people, the testimonies focus on the day-to-day recollections and experiences of families and communities both during and after the strike. The voices of the contributors have been placed together to create sections that relate to specific themes. Where relevant, parent and child testimonies have been placed together, to provide a coherent insight into their experiences.

Christmas 1984 – solidarity, presents and generosity

The Christmas of the strike was probably the most difficult time for the families of striking miners, particularly for those with children. After ten months on strike, it is probable that all financial resources available to miners' families would have been exhausted, and yet a similar pattern can be seen in the testimonies from all the interviews.

Dave: Christmas was hard for everybody, and the NCB were putting pressure on people to go back to work, offering to give them accrued holiday pay if they went back before Christmas. People were drifting back. Support did come, and sometimes from strange places. Where you would have expected support, you got none, in fact in some cases all you got was hostility, but overall we were inundated with donations. One of them was a postal order for five pounds, with a little unsigned note saying: 'Please accept this, it is my Christmas bonus. It is sent in solidarity and not charity.' It was obvious from the lack of a name or a return address that the person did not want thanks. I think that I cried when I read that, when you are in a situation such as we were and you read something like that, it gets to you. I greatly regret not having kept that little note.

Sam: Christmas that year was just such fun. That Christmas it had snowed and everyone went outside from the chapel where we went for some meals, and I can remember there being a big snowball fight with all the guys. There are just so many memories, happy memories. I loved it. I did not get very much, but actually I did not care even a tiny little bit. I can remember there was a party but I cannot remember where it was, probably it would have been at the village hall. All the kids got a present from Santa, and some of them had come from abroad. I can remember getting a little parcel. On Christmas morning I got a cheap plastic watch and a coat that my Auntie had made, but I did not care because I was just having so much fun. My Dad was an electrician and he was quite well off and, being an only child, I was quite spoiled. Normally at Christmas there was always a settee overflowing with presents for me. That year it would not have even filled the corner of the settee, but I really did not care. The coat that my Auntie had made, I can't remember the style of it, but it was kind of a 'herringbone-type' coat, and the watch I got was a plastic, bangle type that was so cheap and tacky, cream in colour, and I can still see it now. I wish I still had it actually, I should have kept it, but I can still picture the watch. It was a really nice coat actually, I did complain about it at the time, but it was a nice coat.

Elspeth: I think we were all worried and anxious about Christmas. We received donations from lots and lots of people, and we got some presents, toys that we wrapped up, and we managed to have a disco and hot dogs for the kids, and I believe Santa Claus came on the stage and we handed out selection boxes to all the children at the end of the day. My own children did not go without and we had a lovely family Christmas. I know I mentioned to my friend Cath that we would not be having a real Christmas tree that year because things were a little bit tight. One day, leading up to Christmas, we had gone shopping and when we came back there was a Christmas tree in the back yard. Cath had gone out and bought a tree for us. Our children did not ask for a great deal, but the fact that our families were together and we were so close, they still had presents to open. Perhaps not a computer that they had wanted, but they still had lots of presents. They got books I think, more than anything. Sarah got a cuddly hippo I think, which she kept for many years.

Karen: Christmas had never been a spending time for me anyway. Andrew was brought up in a similar way, and you could say to him 'this is why you've not got much'. I think there was a drive to make sure that every child had something at Christmas. I always liked to have a real Christmas tree and I was thinking that we were not going to have one that year. I said that as long as I can smell pine needles I'll be fine. We found this broken Christmas tree in a pile of Christmas trees, so we bought it quite cheaply, it might have been a pound or something like that, if even that. I just put some cellotape round it and covered it with tinsel, and I said 'that's it I'm fine now, I can smell pine needles'.

Jean: We got a lot of children's clothes for Christmas, and I think that they came from East Germany, and with them I got a lovely letter. I cried when I read it and I'll start crying again now, it was lovely. I cannot remember the exact words, but it said, 'We are thinking of you, and how very brave you are, and we hope you carry on fighting for what is good'. I thought, I would not get this from next door, but I can get it from East Germany. We did get things from this country of course, but we got a lot from abroad, and that was really, really nice. All the kids had little red duffle coats that had been knitted. They all looked like extras in *Little Red Riding Hood* but we all laughed. Oh, our Shaun looked beautiful in his.

Gayle: At Christmas, we always used to get up and pile into my Mum and Dad's bedroom, and we would sit and open our Christmas present on Mum and Dad's bed. That happened every year, I cannot ever remember waking up or thinking, 'this is horrible, I have no presents'. But like I say, I was only four or five years old at that time. I cannot remember thinking, I have gone without, there were probably things that I wanted, but my Dad has always said it was as if I knew I could not ask for too much, because I knew it would not be there. I really wanted this recorder, really, really badly and I had a bit of a face on for a while, and then that was that. I do remember getting a plastic jewellery set with hair-slides that were like plastic tube bracelets that fastened together with a plastic clip. I remember going out one night, with my Mum and Dad, with all these hair slides and jewellery. I think I literally put every piece that were in this box on. I felt amazing because I had all this jewellery on, and the plastic hair slides. I absolutely loved them.

I can remember certain toys that I got that year, and I still have them. I got a Care Bear that is still at my Mum's. I also got a cup, some badges, some books, and there is one that has a story, taking the micky out of Maggie Thatcher. I've still got that book as well. Those toys just remind me of my Mum and Dad working, and I am trying not to cry. Sorry, I did not think I was going to cry, it is just thinking about what my Mum and Dad did, what they went through, to keep us all together and to get through the strike.

Craig: The only memory I have of the Christmas during the strike is Mum and Dad mentioning that a neighbour called Brenda, who lived a couple of houses up the street, came to our house with a week's worth of shopping, just to give to my Mum so that she could make it easier, you know, for us to have food in the house at Christmas. Whatever her reasons were, I remember my Mum being really taken aback by that, and not really knowing how to react, just because she thought it was an amazing gesture.

Food

The main problem facing the miners and their families during the strike was making sure that no one would be forced back to work through starvation. Feeding the families was the priority, and in every mining community women came together to ensure that there would be some system in place to make sure that happened. In some communities, weekly food parcels were handed out to striking families, in others hot meals were provided. In many, both were provided. The organisation Women Against Pit Closures was formed out of these initiatives. The women in these groups, at community, regional and national level, created an organisation that kept their communities fed, and many miners believe that without these women, the strike would not have lasted three months.

Gayle: My Mum was part of Women Against Pit Closures, obviously when the strike began, my Mum was out and about, sorting out food parcels and raising money to pay for them. I remember her not being there as much as she had been before the strike.

Jayne: I was also involved in our local women's support group. It was just a meeting place were all the women used to meet up locally, to sort out the food parcels. On food parcel days I would be so involved, and sometimes I would realise that I had forgotten to pick our Gayle up from school. I would have to run down the street to the school, but the teachers realised what I had done and they used to keep her until I got there.

Jean: Because I was working, I had a bit of money put by at the beginning of strike, so we did not take our food parcels. We were not going to take from someone else who had a lot less than we had. We decided that we would not take a food parcel until our money had run out. It was our contribution to the community and the strike.

Karen: I think that going to our soup kitchen was a big benefit for us, because you saw all of the food and other forms of support coming in. We would all be there; all sat together, all eating together. And I think that this was quite an important thing. I think that when you are sharing food together, and everybody has been involved in cooking it, you are all with each other, finding out what was going on. If you were not involved you would just be sat in your own little house everyday thinking, 'oh this is really awful'.

Elspeth: In our hallway we had boxes of tins of soup, beans, spaghetti, meat, corned beef, fruit, which were collected each week, to be handed out in the food parcels.

Sam: I do not remember there not being food on the table, ever. I remember the food parcels and how crap they were. You always got a tin of *PEK*, which nobody ate, so in the cupboard there would be forty six tins of *PEK* that were probably multiplying on their own. Nobody I knew ever ate it, but every week we got a food parcel from the group who were organising things in our community, and Dad would come in with it. I remember there was one guy, down our street near the bottom, who would start at the top with his food parcel and he would just give it away to other families as he went down the street. That's the kind of people they were, and by the time he got inside his own home, he just had an empty box. He would get told off by his wife every time, but he always gave it away as he was going down the street.

Politicisation

The miners' strike was not a strike about wages and conditions; it was about the protection of jobs and communities. In other words, it was a political strike, and lasted three days short of a calendar year. The miners were not simply fighting an employer; they were fighting the state itself, and they suffered significant numbers of casualties. Many miners were sacked, and many more were arrested. Communities were under siege from what some commentators have described as a militarised police force. Many communities were torn apart by the growing number of miners who returned to work. Because of this families were politicised by their experiences of the strike.

Sam: I was fifteen during the strike and I would listen to what people were saying, the discussions about the strike and I started to become aware of what was going on. It was like osmosis, I guess. I remember that someone spray painted someone's house. It was a scab's house I would imagine, and I have a suspicion that I know who it was that did the spray painting. They still hate each other, those that stayed out on strike, and those who went back to work. It is still the same, people are still scabs if they went back to work, and they will be scabs until the day that they die. I had a friend whose Dad was also on strike. The YMCA in our community was fantastic and they took all us kids away on a holiday. We were quite close friends after that. Then as time went on, unfortunately, her Dad went back to work, and became a scab. After that she did not speak to me again. That was a little bit upsetting because we had become very close and then obviously her Dad went back to work and we were not friends anymore. I found that quite hard. At the end of that year the people who were involved were like your best friends, you knew everybody because you had spent so much time with them. When people started to go back there was conflict in our community.

It was hatred, absolute out and out hatred. If somebody went back to work, that was it. It split our village down the middle.

I also hated the fact that because my Dad was on strike, I got free school meals. It was awful, you had to queue up for a ticket to get your free school meal and I hated that. I really did not like the fact that we were singled out, and you had to go and stand in this queue to get a ticket so that you could get your dinner. We refused to do it. My Dad said that we had organised a little strike, I don't know if you would say it was that organised, but we refused to do it. We just said that we were not prepared to go and stand in a line to get a ticket and that they would have to do it some other way.

I have always been a Daddy's girl, if I'm honest. I would have had the same views that my Dad had because I was just so proud of him. He was like this hero you know, he was at the forefront of it, he was the boss, and everybody came to him. If he had said the police are horrible, I would have said – the police are horrible. I had Arthur Scargill posters on my wall, and 'Coal not Dole' stickers everywhere. My bedroom was just a complete shrine to the strike. Every wall was the same, I did not have any Duran Duran posters up, it was all just strike stuff. Arthur Scargill was my pop idol.

Dave: I went in from picketing one day, it was freezing cold, and as I walked through the door, I saw Sam and my wife getting their breakfasts. They both had overcoats on in the house, and I thought they will never beat us, they'll never beat us if our families are prepared to do that. I can't tell you how proud I was of Sam and my wife. They never ever complained, throughout the whole year of the strike, never ever. Not once. All of that must have had an impact on my daughter, a fifteen year old, still growing up. All of us who were involved were politicised by the strike, but I think the children of her age, the older children, I think a lot of them were also politicised, by being involved in that dispute. My daughter certainly was, she will not let anything she thinks is wrong pass unchallenged, and often at some cost to herself. She's just like any other Geordie lass, out for a good time, but there is a line that she will not cross.

Dave and Sam in conversation

Dave: If you are in the NUM, and they strike, you are on strike. You never cross a picket line. It is unquestionable. It was for us anyway.

Sam: I must admit I really don't think I could cross a picket line. You would write scab on my garage door.

Dave: Would I?

Sam: He's got form I think.

Dave: No. It wasn't me.

Sam: I think it might have been.

Dave: It wasn't me honest. It wasn't me.

Sam: Mmm my Mam thinks it was.

Dave: Your Mam always thinks the worst of me doesn't she?

Sam: It would have been the red paint underneath your fingernails.

Dave: No it was white paint.

Sam: How do you know what colour the paint was?

Dave: I was told, and I saw the garage door.

Sam: Mmm I'm not convinced. I still think it was you.

Gayle: At my age at the time I would not have heard the word 'politicised' and I would not have known who were and who were not. What I saw was everybody doing what my Mam and Dad were doing and standing up for what they believed in.

Elspeth: In the early days of the strike my husband Bill took our daughter Clare to Herrington Colliery and told her that he wanted her to watch what was going on. The police were there playing football and at one point, this must have been in the summer, because they made fans out of twenty pound notes and waved them about in front of the pickets, to show how much they were getting out of the strike. I should not really say this, but the police were not the flavour of the month in our family. Whether my girls were influenced by the outcome of the strike, Sarah just knew that her heart was where it should be. They both know that you have to work hard for what you get, and they have both done that. Sarah would have been politicised, because she definitely felt that the year of the strike brought people together, rather than pushed them apart.

Craig: Growing up I was just told that Thatcher was bad, and that the Tories were bad. That was just something that I probably did not understand at the time, and something I never questioned. I guess by default, that is where my head is wired politically. My Dad never really talked about politics that much with me, unless it was bad and then the slipper was thrown at the television, that kind of thing. My grandma used to escort us out of the room because there was also a lot of effing and jeffing. I was pretty shocked at first and a had a kind of disbelief when she told me that he had been arrested at Orgreave. It is still pretty painful for him to talk about, and it was my Mum that sort of disclosed what I guess was a family secret. She still finds it quite difficult to talk about it. I think her experience of my Dad being arrested was: 'shit I'm on my own now, I've got a kid on the way and I've got two that I've got to get up tomorrow, feed them, get them to school. How do I do that when their Dad is facing three years to life?' I think the biggest thing for me is that my Dad was younger than I am now, when this happened to him. He was there at Orgreave, and he was beaten up, and arrested, and I still find it quite hard to believe that my Dad was left bleeding in a field just because he wanted to work.

Jean: I think the strike had a positive effect on my son Sean really. After the strike, I went to university and then his Dad went to university. Sean was about eight or nine when I went back to school, and knew that his Dad had worked at the pit, and saw that his Dad had made a better life for himself. Yes, I think the strike did impact on him quite a bit.

Family and community: day-to-day life during the strike

In talking to people involved in the strike, people are always willing to talk about the big issues, but little is ever said about the everyday experiences that had to be endured during that year. The financial hardships; the constant and negative images of the strike in the media; families, friendships and communities split when some drifted back to work. The worries about future employment and about the impact mine closures would have on communities. All of these issues will have been in the minds of those involved, but when you ask about the day-to-day life during the strike, people smile and remember only the good things that they experienced.

Jean: You do not get what we had in other communities outside of mining; you don't get that sense that everybody might know your business, but that everybody helps everybody else. They might talk about you, but when you are in trouble, they are there for you.

Craig: I remember growing up with such love and, there was a genuine collective feeling that you could go into someone's house on your street and they would know you. If your Mum or Dad had a problem they could just go to a neighbour and ask, 'would you watch our Craig for five minutes while I just nip to the shops?' The answer would always be yes, and they would just dump you. You cannot do that, anymore, and I kind of miss that.

Elspeth: My Dad was a miner, and all his brothers were miners, so we were not the only ones out on strike in our family. I remember taking Bill's mam to see Arthur Scargill speak, what a night we had; so as an extended family we were 100 per cent behind the strike. You know we were really well looked after, and well supported by family. An ordinary day would be to get the kids up for school, get them breakfast, and, if Bill was going on picket duty, he probably would have already gone. Once they got to school I went to work, I would come home, make the tea, and then go to some fundraising event. Went to working men's clubs and asked for donations, and we went to London, and I spoke at a rally with Tony Benn, and I was absolutely terrified. The impact of the strike was that we had reversed roles. I got a little job in a shop, and I got £37 a week, which was not a lot, but it kept the wolf from the door. It just sort of happened, I had presumed that I would not go back to work until the girls were older, but it happened and Bill just got on with it. He could make a dinner better than I could, but he could never grasp how to iron his shirts, but he got on with it. When he was not out picketing, he was just brilliant. I think the most difficult thing was that we always had to have someone with the girls in the house when I was at work and Bill was off picketing. Either that, or they went to Bill's Mam and Dad's house, but it was always busy.

Jayne: We had quite a lot of happy times during the strike. Spirits were quite high, considering that they were on strike, and people were skint.

Gayle: I remember a there were lot of parties, mainly at our house because we had a massive living room, and everyone on the street used to come to our house, and would all fetch a bit of whatever they had. Someone might fetch some rice, and they would make pot of stew, or whatever they could. They used to brew their own wine, and beer, I can remember that because the women did not actually like the wine so they used to just chuck it into a plant in my Mum's room.

Jayne: Yes, she used to have a big giant rubber plant, but the wine used to go into it, and this guy would come round and fill all glasses up again, and he could not understand why we were all stone cold sober. The plant thrived on the wine.

Stories and songs

Whenever people involved in the strike get together – whether adults or children – stories emerge: funny stories, sad stories, tragic stories; stories of grand events and stories of the mundane. Whatever the stories told, it is apparent that these recollections of the strike still have a huge emotional resonance for our contributors. The recalling and retelling of memories provoked heartfelt responses and at times, tears. Memories of kindness and generosity from others generated powerful emotions in all of our respondents. Positive stories of communities and families supporting and helping each other were much more prevalent than stories of bitterness and hardship. Often these stories recalled music from the strike. This acted as a portal to memory for many contributors. Even those who were young children at the time remembered the words of songs, poems and chants with great clarity.

Craig: In the aftermath of the strike there were the stories, not only from my family, but of other people that we knew; our extended family and cousins and uncles, people like that. I take great pride in my parents really, for going through the hardest of hardships and yet they can still laugh about it. They can still tell stories like the one when they were on the coal tipping site, pinching coal and throwing it into the back of my grandma's car. I can remember my Dad saying to her if the police come we just need you to drive the car away. The police did come and she just drove off and left them both stranded, and they had to run away. They tell stories like that, and they can laugh about them now, and I always think that being able to laugh about their troubles is of great credit to people involved in such struggles.

Flis: There was a lot of fun in the strike as well; we used to go picketing and we would sing on the picket line. We met so many new people and there were so many really positive aspects of the strike, the solidarity with other people, and just knowing there were people out there who really supported the strike. We always would sing the women's song written by Mal Finch:

We are women we are strong,
We are fighting for our lives
Side by side with our men
Who work the nation's mines,
United by the struggle,
United by the past,
And it's – Here we go! Here we go!
For the women of the working class.

And some funny ones:

If I had the wings of a sparrow,
If I had the arse of a crow,
I'd fly over Kiverton tomorrow
And shit on the scabs below.

Sam: Talking about songs in the strike, there was obviously the *Coal not Dole* album and I am sure there will have been some choice picket songs that I will have heard that I probably was not meant to. I can still remember the words to one of Jock Purdon's poems.

He was a folk singer, and also wrote and performed poetry. The one I liked the most was called *Pitracide*:

Who am I to ask them why?
This pit must live, that pit must die,
They say but Sir its economics
That's juggling by financial comics.
What maxim had the NCB?
The miner's lot or LSD
And further Sir, it can be said
A pit must die if in the red
Be this so I must resent
This anti-social precedent
So until the happy day
When every pit can pay its way
You cannot Sir rebuke the tide
Or get away with Pitracide.

Aftermath

The strike ended on 3 March 1985, when the miners returned to work without an agreement with the NCB. Within a short period of time, the mine closure programme began in earnest, and the first collieries closed in December of that year. As the closures progressed, the consequences of those closures started to emerge. Communities devastated by unemployment experienced levels of economic and social decay never before seen in mining areas. Other chapters in this book offer greater insights into the consequences of mine closures than we can here, but what we offer are views from those who directly experienced the aftermath of the strike. However, not all of our interviewees felt the same when the strike was over.

Craig: My Dad's job was phased out when he returned to work after the strike, and he was moved around a lot because all the pits were shutting. I think, because of this, their relationship became stressed, and they ended up getting divorced five years after the strike. So when I look back at it now, many of the things that have happened to our family you definitely link back to the strike. The effects the strike had on the wider community were also pretty devastating. Fundamentally, it resulted in the general erosion of workers rights, and now we have things like zero hours contracts. It is not at all what it could have been, had the strike been successful. The unions do not exist any more really, so workers are not protected any more.

Jean: Who really cares now? The communities that we live in have been decimated, and you can clearly see the decay in our village. The office my Dad used to work in at the pit is a gym now, and I walk past it twice a day, every day. There are times when I cry as I walk past because I think that this is all that's left. The whole pit is gone, with that one office left, and it is like it is taunting me. The strike impacted on all of us, and it definitely affected our marriage. When they eventually went back to work, my husband worked every hour god sent, simply because he thought this is not going to last very long, and we will need the money. When the strike ended, like all the other miners' families, we were left with nothing. As a couple we had lost touch, we really had, and we were both annoyed and angry about what had happened.

Elspeth: We had such a great time during the strike, and I cannot think that I ever said to Bill I wish you would go back to work. There were families with little kids, really small kids, who found it really, really difficult. The need just to get nappies and soap powder and things that babies need, brought a lot of hardship to these families in particular. For us, personally, it was just a wonderful year.

Gayle: Everyone was in the same situation, kids, adults, wives, husbands, they were all going through exactly the same thing. The kids, like myself and the other parents, well, we all got through it together, after the strike the kids just carried on playing, and the adults carried on helping each other.

NOTES

1 https://www.ncm.org.uk/news/a-share-of-a-pensioners-christmas-bonus-a-special-christmas-exhibition-and-toy-appeal-at-the-national-coal-mining-musum-for-england
2 http://echoes-of-protest.weebly.com
3 Whilst researching the 1984–85 miner's strike in the archive, we came across the Hilary Wainwright papers, a collection that included hand-written letters and cards from pensioners donating their Christmas heating bonus, to ensure striking miners' children could celebrate Christmas 1984. The personal nature of this material resonated with us and we began to develop our research in order to bear witness to these stories. We contacted individuals and their families who had been recipients of acts of generosity that Christmas, recorded interviews with them and wove these into an audio documentary. We also created a photographic series to accompany this that focused on their personal memorabilia from the strike. This original audio–visual research was then exhibited alongside a selection of the hand-written letters and cards from the Hilary Wainwright papers. The oral testimony interview transcriptions gathered for this project highlight a perspective of the strike that has seldom been explored.

Part 2

The Controversies

Chapter 6

'We shall not be constitutionalised out of a defence of our jobs'

David Wray and David Allsop

Introduction

Mick McGahey, Vice-President of the National Union of Mineworkers (NUM), spoke the words in the title of this chapter during the growing controversy over whether or not the NUM should hold a national ballot in the early weeks of the strike.[1] Of all of the controversies that emerged during that year-long dispute, the decision of the National Executive Committee (NEC) of the NUM not to hold a national ballot was by far the most contentious, and subsequently had the most damaging and lasting consequences for the NUM itself. The failure to hold a national ballot provided a haven for those in the NUM who opposed the strike and were looking for a credible way to continue to work in defiance of the calls to join the strike. The absence of a ballot also provided legitimacy to those in the wider trade union and labour movement who stood either in opposition to the NUM in its attempt to defend the jobs of its members, or did not support the NUM in order to protect their own organisations and or positions.

To properly address the question of the ballot, this chapter will provide a detailed examination of the historical background of the democratic processes within the NUM, and the impact those processes had on the legitimacy and prosecution of the strike. It will go on to identify those who wanted the ballot, and why, and will conclude with an assessment of the post-strike period that suggests the strike may have been successfully prosecuted, had a ballot for strike action been held, and won.

Background to the dispute

Prior to the Conservative Party coming to office in 1979 Nicholas Ridley, in his now infamous report to the Conservative Party Policy Group on nationalised industries, identified the coal industry as a key battleground for the implementation of government policy. His report predicted that, as a result of proposed Conservative policy, a major conflict with a public-sector trade union would be inevitable, with the coal industry seen as the most likely arena for that conflict. The report went on to identify the measures that should be taken in the event of industrial action by the NUM including: building up coal stocks at power stations; utilising non-union lorry drivers to transport coal; drawing up contingency plans for the importation of coal; ensuring that dual coal/oil burn facilities were available at power stations; and preparing a well-equipped and mobile police force ready for mobilisation to the coalfields. It also suggested that the confrontation, when it occurred, should be at a time favourable to the government.[2]

Committed to controlling government expenditure and increasing competition in the energy sector, the oil and gas industries had been privatised by the government in the early 1980s. Plans to privatise the coal industry were only tacitly acknowledged within both the government and National Coal Board (NCB) at that time, and were not made public until 1988.[3] In 1980 the Coal Industry Bill, designed to make the coal industry subsidy free by 1983-4, was introduced identifying the main strategic objectives for the industry. The implementation of this Bill meant the abandonment of the promised expansion of the industry outlined in the *Plan for Coal*,* and called for a more cost-effective use of resources, requiring the NCB to maximise output from a reduced core of high capacity collieries making full use of new technology and to close high cost, low capacity collieries. The achievement of these objectives would require a significant increase in the rate of colliery closures made on financial grounds, rather than on those of natural exhaustion, as had been envisaged under that 'blithely optimistic document', the *Plan for Coal*.[4] An unspoken objective of the Bill, as outlined in the Ridley Plan, was to reduce the power of trade unions overall, with the NUM identified as the key battleground for the attainment of this particular objective. As expected, the NUM denounced the Coal Industry Bill, arguing that 'neither the unions in the industry nor the NCB itself believe that these targets can be met at a time of industrial recession without huge price increases, unprecedented productivity increases, or the closure of collieries that are presently making a loss.'[5]

In January 1981, in reaction to the Bill, the Executive Committees of the Yorkshire and Scottish Areas of the NUM voted to take strike action,

* The *Plan for Coal* was introduced by the National Coal Board in 1950, and was an attempt to increase coal production by 18 per cent by 1965. This was to be achieved by the opening of 20 new collieries across the national coalfield. (Allen. 198, p. 34.)

under Rule 41,* to oppose the closure of any colliery on grounds other than exhaustion or irreparable unsafe working conditions.[6]

Becoming increasingly aware that it would be unable to meet the targets set by the Bill, the NCB began to accelerate the closure programme, informing the NUM in February 1981 that they intended to embark on the closure of between twenty and fifty collieries. The response to these announced closures was immediate, with unofficial strike action erupting first over the decision to close Coegnant Colliery in Wales followed by spontaneous, uncoordinated strikes across the national coalfields.[7] In the face of this unofficial action that saw half the miners out on strike, the NCB withdrew the proposed closures.[8] Superficially, this swift reversal of policy by the NCB could be seen as re-run of the 1972 and 1974 disputes over wages when 'the miners had flexed their muscles and even this tough government had climbed down'.[9] With regards to the issue of the democratic process within the NUM, it is significant that 'over half the British coalfield was on strike, including Areas such as Nottinghamshire and the Midlands, traditionally known as moderate'. It is also significant that 'this strike action took place without a ballot or even a conference decision'.[10] While the announced closure list was withdrawn, almost all the collieries identified in it were closed within a year, following local agreements.

In terms of what was to follow in 1984, particularly the controversy over the lack of a national strike ballot, it is important to understand the historical evolvement of the NUM itself, and the constitutional complexities of its rule book, which are explained below.

The organisational framework of the NUM

Trade unionism developed organically and spasmodically across the widespread coal measures that made up the UK coalfield.[11] Organised against massive employer resistance, the emergence of these early trade unions were local- or district-based organisations that, once established, set out to create a national organisation representative of all miners.[12] After some significant setbacks, the Miners Federation of Great Britain (MFGB), was finally formed in 1888. Despite its name, the MFGB was neither unified nor centralised, acting mainly as an umbrella organisation within which the objectives of the thirty-six District† unions could be coordinated. Within the MFGB power

* These rules are set out in full in an appendix at the end of this book.

† Some of the early regional organisations were called 'Districts' and others were called 'Associations'. To avoid confusion between the MFGB and the NUM, all pre-NUM organisations will be called 'Districts'. All regional organisations within the NUM will be called 'Areas'.

lay with the Districts, with miners loyal to their own District organisations, a local loyalty that was generated by the culture and traditions historically formed in the geographically isolated mining communities across the UK coalfield.[13] The primary loyalty of the miner was to the union organisation at his pit and then to the District that represented his pit. These cultural and traditional ties to the District union organisations were much more than an industrial work-based relationship. That the localised relationship between 'trade union', 'occupation', and 'place' impacted on all aspects of life within mining communities has long been recognised as more than just a relationship between a trade union and its members, being in fact an all-encompassing social institution. Given these unique circumstances, solidarity, both social and industrial, was a localised solidarity. While the cohesion of this type of solidarity was a great source of strength in times of need, at certain times it has also proven extremely problematic.[14]

As a result, the pattern of trade unionism within the MFGB was much more decentralised than would be expected of a national trade union. Having the ability to formulate policy, the MFGB did not possess the power to impose that policy on the District organisations. This was for two separate, though not dissimilar, reasons. First, as stated above, the District organisations had specific social as well as industrial identities, closely associated with their own mines and communities. Second, the coal industry before 1945 was privately owned, and each District would be negotiating with local employers willing only to negotiate with the District, and not the MFGB.[15]

This sectionalism remained a major issue for the MFGB throughout its history as the differences between high wage and low wage coalfields, owned by different individuals and companies, militated against a coherent national organisation. The extent of this sectionalism can be seen in the aftermath of a series of failed national strikes over wages between 1912 and 1926. The power of the employers were such that District level agreements were imposed rather than bargained, with the Districts becoming increasingly separated, and even competitive. The 1926 dispute was, in reality, a lockout as miners rejected an imposed reduction in wages (21 per cent) and an increase in the working day of one and a half hours. Lasting six months, the dispute ended in defeat for the miners, and brought into existence the Nottingham and District Miners' Industrial Union, a company union set up by the coal owners, with the connivance of the then Nottinghamshire miners' leader, George Spencer.[16] Once established, this union spread to other Districts in the national coalfield and such was the influence of Spencer in the creation and running of this union, that the term 'Spencerism' became a catchall phrase to describe company unionism in the UK. The existence of the 'Industrial Union', and its debilitating effect on the MFGB, allowed the employers to continue to impose District agreements, leaving the MFGB reduced to leading on legislative issues only. Spencer's union lasted until 1937 when, under the threat of a national strike, it was reabsorbed into the Nottinghamshire District of the MFGB. However, the impact of 'Spencerism' lasted for many years and, as we shall see, it's spectre returned to haunt the NUM in 1985.[17]

The creation of the NUM in 1945* was an attempt to overcome these organisational difficulties by creating a new relationship between the older county-based unions and a truly national union. After months of negotiation and compromise, the Districts organisations of the MFGB became Area Associations of the NUM with a constitution that had been 'emasculated' by the Area Associations (hereafter Areas), and was a union having the pretensions of a national organisation but which, in practice, remained a loose federated system little changed from what had gone before. The organisational and democratic problems inherited from the MFGB remained unresolved, leaving the NUM organised around the still autonomous Areas, free to formulate their own policies, collect their own revenues and, most importantly, maintaining their own historical and cultural identity.[18]

The 'emasculated' constitution created what can only be described as a democratic deficit within the NUM that can be identified through an examination of the role and structure of the NEC. Under the constitution, the NEC consisted of three nationally elected officials, with one elected representative from each Area.† The single representative from each Area created the deficit by leaving the larger Areas underrepresented on the NEC. For example, in 1970, one NEC member represented 16,373 members whilst another, with the same voting rights, represented only 914.[19] Attempts to change the level of representation by the Yorkshire Area were thwarted because the constitution of the NUM required a two-thirds majority vote to instigate a rule change.[20] The determination of the smaller Areas to protect this favourable but undoubted democratic imbalance, and the fact that solidarity within the workforce was firstly to their colleagues at their mine, then to the Area Association, and only then to the NUM, were the main hurdles preventing the creation of a truly unified, centralised, and national union.

Organisationally, the NUM mirrored the federated nature of MFGB with

* The nationalisation of the industry made collective bargaining in the industry much easier, as there was only one employer to negotiate with, both at a national level and also at the Area level.

† President, Vice President and General Secretary.

the Areas maintaining all the independence and separateness of the Districts. This federalism dominated 'the industrial logic of the union, effecting its veracity as a powerful national union'.[21] In this way, solidarity of the mine workforces and the Areas can be seen as organic, but in relation to the NUM itself, can only be seen as instrumental. The following quote from a member of the Durham Miners' Association graphically articulates this structured loyalty,

> When I talk about the NUM, I am really talking about the Durham Miners' Association. It is the DMA that was, and still is my union, despite the fact that I have not worked since 1985.[22]

Creating a national union?

In an attempt to address the sectional problems outlined above, the NUM agitated for a universal wage structure that would not only unify miners across the national coalfield, but would also strengthen the union. During the Second World War the NUM was able to negotiate national flat-rate increases in wages, and an industry-wide minimum wage was established under the Green Award of 1942 and the Porter Award of 1943. However, neither of these initiatives were significant in contributing to national wage parity.[23]

The first significant stage in the creation of a national wage structure did not occur until 1955, when the Revision of the Wages Structure Agreement rationalised mining occupations into nine grades, determined nationally. This affected close to 60 per cent of the workforce, namely those ancillary workers away from the coal face, and those working on the surface, placing them within a national wage-grade system. It was not until the increased use of mechanised mining provided both the now nationalised National Coal Board (NCB) and NUM with the opportunity to introduce a national wage grade system for face workers, known as the National Power Loading Agreement (NPLA) consisting of measured day rates for mechanised power-loading face teams.[24] By introducing the NPLA the NCB would, at the same time, reduce the physical demands on the men working at the coal face, and reduce the possibility, if not probability, of conflict over locally negotiated 'piecework' rates. The thinking behind this new payment system was clearly outlined in its annual report 1966-67, which stated: 'Piecework was becoming increasingly inappropriate as a means of payment for men on mechanised faces where productivity depends less on physical effort than on the utilisation of machines.'[25]

For the NUM, the introduction of the NPLA brought a further 2 per cent of the workforce into an industry-wide wage agreement and ended the divisive piecework system for the majority of coalface workers.* The NPLA was accepted by the membership by the narrowest of margins (8.6 per cent) in a national ballot under Rule 43 (See Appendix). Face workers in the high producing areas felt let down by the NUM because they no longer had the ability to negotiate locally over the effort bargain, and because, for a five-year period, they would have to accept pay rises that were less than those of other Areas to allow those Areas to catch up. During this period, face workers in Nottinghamshire saw their wages decline by 15 per cent, compared to a drop of only 1.8 per cent for face workers in South Wales.[26] Despite these anomalies the NPLA was generally well received because it created a centralised pay bargaining system that focused on industry wide agreements. Once the NPLA system was established, miners began to re-focus their efforts on re-grading and overtime payments to increase their earnings, with activists in more militant Areas beginning to organise in opposition to declining relative earnings and pit closures.[27]

This new found solidarity, particularly around the issue of wages, continued and in 1970 the NUM submitted a demand for a 3 per cent increase across all grades. Working within the strictures of the government guidelines, the NCB offered less than half of this demand. Following a national ballot under Rule 43, 55 per cent of 26,000 members voted in favour of strike action. As the vote was less than the 66 per cent required for strike action under Rule 43, the NEC could not call for a strike. As a result of what was seen as a constitutionally enforced defeat, Rule 43 was changed at the annual conference in 1971, to require only a 55 per cent majority for strike action. Although a significant reduction in the majority required to call a strike, many conference delegates were still unhappy with this situation.[28] The NEC member from the Kent Area stated that,

> No democrat, and I consider myself a democrat, can justify standing on any platform and argue for 55 per cent and be satisfied. No one can do that. But of course, if this resolution is achieved it should lead towards reaching a more democratic basis.[29]

Despite the failure of 1970, wage militancy continued and, in 1972 following an overtime ban and a 58 per cent vote in favour of industrial action, a seven week national strike took place. A Court of Enquiry headed by

* The remainder of the coalface workers not covered by the NPLA were working at collieries that were not mechanised, and who remained on locally negotiated piecework rates.

Lord Wilberforce concluded the miners' claim should be given exceptional national treatment, and wage increases representing a 27.7 per cent increase for surface workers, 31.5 per cent for underground workers and 15 per cent for face workers. The inquiry also called for discussions on the re-introduction of piecework payments for face workers, the implications of which will be seen below.[30]

The bargaining power of the NUM was further increased in 1973 when the price of oil trebled, increasing the demand for coal, all of which placed inflationary pressures on the economy. The consequent dependence of the NCB on the workforce to increase production levels enhanced the power of the NUM, who responded with demands for significant wage rises across all grades of the workforce.[31] When these demands were rejected, the NUM implemented a national overtime ban in November 1973, and in January 1974 a ballot was held with an 89.9 per cent vote in favour of strike action. That strike brought the introduction of a state of emergency, a referral of the wage claim to the Pay Board, and a general election that saw the fall of the Tory government. The strike was resolved when the Pay Board recommended that the miners should be given what they described as exceptional increases.[32] During this strike the NUM was able to claim proudly that there had been no cause to picket the mines, as all miners had answered the call to strike. The miners had come to see that if they stood together change could be implemented and significant gains made.[33]

Constitutional controversy

This increase in nationally unified militancy came out of the successful wage disputes in the 1970s, and reflected the rising power of the political left within the NUM. Previously, the right wing had dominated both the NEC and the annual Conference, with the constitution remaining relatively unchallenged and unchanged. However, 1973 saw Arthur Scargill and Owen Briscoe elected as President and General Secretary of the Yorkshire Area of the NUM, representing a major shift to the left in the Yorkshire Area. This movement to the left in Yorkshire was reflected in elections in other Areas of the NUM, with the left coming within a handful of votes of ending right-wing dominance of the NEC, while gaining a majority at Conference, constitutionally the supreme governing body of the NUM. Traditionally, the NEC with its right-wing majority, had acted as the final arbiter in decision making primarily because right-wing delegates also dominated Conference. Once the left gained a majority at Conference, the NEC had to comply, bringing into the open the factionalism that continued to exist within the NUM.[34]

This factionalism was brought to the fore by the issue of an incentive payments scheme signalled in the Wilberforce Report into the Coal Industry in 1972. Incentive payments were integral to the *Plan for Coal*, and the subject of negotiations between the NEC and NCB. Such was the controversy over the proposed introduction of an incentive scheme that a Special Conference was called on 26 September 1974, to receive the report on the draft incentive scheme proposals. The NEC were unable to make any recommendation on the issue as they themselves were deeply split on the issue. The left believed that any incentive scheme based at colliery level would destroy the unity within the NUM that had been achieved by unifying wages under the NPLA.[35] This position was best articulated by a Welsh delegate at the conference,

> We do not want to go backwards. We do not want to allow anybody to shatter this unity that we have now. If we allow ourselves to regress back to our divided directions, then it will be a crime against all those old miners who fought over the years to get what we have now.[36]

To avoid the re-creation of wage differentials across and within Areas, the left in the NUM would only support an incentive scheme based on national production levels, thus guaranteeing national wage bargaining. The right saw the scheme as a way to improve productivity levels and wages, all within the guidelines of government incomes policy. This became a major issue for the NUM, with factions from both left and right arguing over the proposed scheme. At the heart of the problem was the NCB's need to increase productivity, whilst the left of the NUM would only accept such a scheme if it would not create wage differentials between miners at different collieries, and between different Areas. In other words, a national incentive scheme.[37]

The draft agreement, negotiated at the Special Conference, was put to a ballot of the membership under Rule 43 (which states that national actions can only follow national ballots) on 20 November 1974, without recommendation from either the NEC or the Special Conference. Rejecting the proposed scheme (61.53 per cent against) opponents of the proposed incentive scheme believed the issue to be dead. However, officials from nine Area Associations wrote to the NEC seeking permission to negotiate Area-based incentive schemes. Eventually, a revised scheme was accepted by the NEC, to be submitted to the membership for its approval by ballot. Believing that the constitution was being ignored, the Kent Area took the issue to the High Court on 19 October 1977 insisting that under Rule 23 of the NUM Constitution only a Special Conference could call a ballot, and that a ballot over a national incentive scheme was inadmissible because the Annual Conference had previously rejected the issue. Therefore, under Rule 8, (See Appendix) the NEC could not act contrary to, nor in defiance of, any resolution of Conference. Finding for the NEC, the judicial review stated that, 'what the NEC is proposing to do is hold a ballot of all its members. This is the very essence of the democratic process … every member is free to vote: every vote counts; no one is shut out or left unheard.'[38]

With the proposed ballot now legally endorsed, the NUM membership again rejected the proposed incentive scheme, with 55.7 per cent of the membership voting against the proposal. The right-wing majority on the NEC refused to accept this result, calling for the ballot to be declared null and void, and suggesting that disciplinary action be taken against those members of the NEC who had not supported the decision to endorse the scheme.[39] The NEC also called for those Areas supporting the introduction of an incentive scheme to be given the authority to negotiate Area based schemes. At an acrimonious meeting of the NEC, the President ruled that while the NEC must accept the results of the ballot, they did not have the democratic right to stop individual Areas from negotiating Area schemes.[40]

This decision opened the way for individual Areas to negotiate their own incentive schemes under Rule 41. In response Kent, South Wales and Yorkshire Areas took legal action to prevent the NEC delegating such negotiating powers to individual Areas. Arguing that the ruling the High Court had previously made on the primacy of a national ballot, the NEC was behaving undemocratically by going against a decision undertaken by a national ballot. However, in what seems a contradiction of its previous decision, the High Court upheld the NEC action declaring that 'the result of a ballot, nationally conducted, is not binding upon the NEC in using its powers between conferences. It may serve to persuade the Committee to take one action or another, or to refrain from action, but it has no great force or significance.'[41]

> Within weeks of this decision, and with the backing of the NEC, all Areas were negotiating Area Incentive Schemes (AIS), including Yorkshire, which had voted 3-1 against its introduction. Within months, AIS agreements were operating throughout the national coalfield.[42]

By what can only be described as a duplicitous manipulation of its own Constitution and Rule Book, the NEC had achieved its objective of establishing an Area-based incentive bonus scheme across the national coalfield.

The contentious introduction of the AIS resulted in a weakening of national solidarity, and the re-igniting of factional rivalries within the NUM, as well as an erosion of confidence in the Constitution. By ignoring the wishes of the membership at a national level, under rule 43, and then sanctioning action at Area level under Rule 41, the NEC had opened the way for the left to use Rule 41 in opposition to mine closures in 1984. Similarly, by seeking redress in the High Court, the left had itself set a precedent it would come to regret.[43] The introduction of the AIS increased the divisions between Areas to the extent that 'thoughtful union activists conceded that they were a national union in name only'.[44]

The fight against mine closures gained momentum in the early 1980s, when the NCB began to introduce the notion of pit closures into the wage bargaining process. It became apparent that the NCB was willing to significantly increase wages for miners in the highly productive mines, if the NUM would agree to close loss-making mines. As the NUM saw these issues as linked they combined both in a series of ballots from 1981 until 1983, ignoring the fact that for many of the membership this was both confusing and fundamentally wrong. A vote for a wage rise was also a vote to accept mine closures, and a vote against mine closures was a rejection of a wage rise.

> The way a lot of people looked at it, there were two issues on the ballot paper and they had only one vote. It gave 'the shits' a way out. The sort of people who are always looking for a way out of doing something, the sort of people who would be able to say 'I would have voted for the pits but I only had one vote and I wanted a wage increase'.[45]

In 1983, in response to the failure of the national ballot to oppose mine closures, the Scottish and Yorkshire Areas, under Rule 41, voted to take strike action against any mine closures in their specific Areas, on any grounds other than exhaustion of coal reserves, or safety. These Area ballots were supported by the NEC, now dominated by the left and endorsed by a Special Delegate Conference. Individual Areas were now able, under Rule 41, to support any industrial action taken by other Area Associations threatened by mine closures.[46]

The beginning of the strike

On 1 March 1984, the NCB announced the closure of Cortonwood Colliery in Yorkshire, and on 5 March 1984 both Yorkshire and Scotland Areas approached the NEC to request official support for strike action in their respective Areas under Rule 41. The fault lines within the NUM were made apparent on 8 March when three of the 24 members of the NEC voted against offering official support,* and requesting a national ballot. In calling for active support from all Areas under Rule 41, the NEC was looking for a strategy that would oppose the closure of all the mines targeted, without the need for a national ballot.[47] Michael McGahey, Vice-President of the NUM, stated that 'we are not dealing with niceties here. We shall not be constitutionalised out of our jobs. Areas will decide and in my opinion we will have a domino effect.'[48]

This proved to be inaccurate as eight Area Associations held ballots, none of which achieved the 55 per cent majority required. However, a domino effect was indeed achieved by pickets travelling across the coalfields, spreading the strike as they went. Within a few days seven out of ten miners were on strike. This unofficial action was the foundation upon which the strike was built, demonstrating the extent of national solidarity at that time. A Yorkshire activist offered an insight into the situation miners found themselves in:

> It is here. There is no place to hide; we have to face it. Cortonwood is the acid test of loyalty to this union, fail this test of loyalty, abandon Cortonwood, and this union might just as well close down, lock stock and barrel.[49]

Despite that clearly defined situation, on 16 March the Nottinghamshire Area voted 74 per cent against such support, and sought a legal opinion on the legitimacy of this action under Rule 41. Despite the Nottinghamshire Area ballot result, the Area Executive Committee voted 11 to 2 to make the strike official in Nottinghamshire. On the 19 April, with 80,000 miners on strike across the national coalfield, a Special Delegates Meeting was held at the NUM headquarters in Sheffield. At that meeting it was decided that there would not be a national ballot and that in any future ballot the requirement would be a simple majority, and not the current 55 per cent.[50]

The majority of Nottinghamshire miners, following the outcome of their own ballot, ignored this call. In choosing to work, the Nottinghamshire miners were joined by significant numbers of miners from the Leicestershire and South Derbyshire Areas who, collectively, had the least to fear as the majority of mines in those Areas were the highest producers in the industry, and had the largest reserves of coal.[51]

* Those Areas requesting a national ballot were the white collar section of the NUM, COSA; the Midlands Power Group; and the North Wales Area. (Adeney & Lloyd, p. 87.)

In September 1984, the Nottinghamshire Working Miners' Association (NWMA) was formed to encourage striking miners in Nottingham to return to work through what became known as the 'Back to Work' movement. The stated aims of this organisation were not to break up the NUM, nor to replace it, but to reaffirm democracy within the union. Taking the NUM to the High Court in September 1984, the NWMA argued that the strike, as called by the NUM, was unofficial and therefore unlawful. While the Court found that the strike was unconstitutional, it stopped short of ordering the NUM to hold a national ballot. Having previously ruled that a national ballot was not binding on the powers of the NEC, the Court ruled that neither the Annual Conference nor the NEC could act without the mandate of a national ballot of all members.[52] The refusal of the Nottinghamshire miners to support the strike, and the existence of the 'Back to Work' movement that successfully encouraged miners in other Areas to return to work, meant that defeat for the NUM was inevitable. One day short of a calendar year, the NUM organised an orderly return to work on 4 March 1985.

The schism between the NUM and the Nottinghamshire Area (now controlled by miners who had worked throughout the strike) became a parting of the ways following the decision of the NUM to create a National Disciplinary Committee, designed to make Area Associations accountable to the NEC. This move was anathema to the NWMC, and in response the Nottinghamshire Area voted in favour of having a new Constitution, giving the Area greater autonomy from the NUM. After an acrimonious NUM National Conference, in September 1985, the National Disciplinary Committee was endorsed, and the Nottinghamshire Area delegates walked out of the Conference, and shortly afterwards formed a new union: the Union of Democratic Mineworkers (UDM).[53]

Creating the myth of the ballot

Following the end of the strike many commentators, looking for reasons to explain such a categorical defeat of what was the strongest trade union in the UK, point to the lack of a national ballot as the catalyst for that failure. What many commentators fail to mention, or perhaps choose to ignore, is that the 1984-5 miners' strike *was* a legitimate strike, based upon the Constitution of the NUM, and classified as a national strike by the NEC, under Rule 41, at a Special Delegates Meeting on the 19 April 1984. Indeed, it was the use of Rule 41 that enabled the Nottinghamshire Area to force through the AIS at an Area level, despite having been rejected twice in a national ballot. This point is also indicative of the debate over the tactics used by individuals within the NEC. One argument holds that the lack of a ballot was due to an unscrupulous section of the leadership manipulating their members out on strike, another view is that the call for a national ballot was never a democratic demand, but was seen as an instrument to circumvent a strike by those working in more secure, and better paid mines.

Those Areas demanding a national ballot have been accused of 'instrumental collectivism', acting in concert against the will of the majority, for their own benefit.[54] In this, the Nottinghamshire Area had history.

As stated above, during the 1926 lockout Nottinghamshire had broken away from the MFGB creating the Nottingham and District Miners' Industrial Union, and again in 1984 Nottinghamshire miners provided the 'core of strike breaking, its inspiration and its moral justification'[55] becoming 'the most important bastion of working miners and the home of 'scab unionism'.[56] The important word here is 'moral', and it is incorrect to state that the Nottinghamshire miners were standing on the moral high ground.[57] As striking miners themselves, the authors of this chapter both believe that the strongest argument against holding a national ballot was indeed a moral one. How can it be that a miner, working in secure mine, in a secure coalfield, could vote on the issue of pit closures that would not affect them, that may even benefit them? A ballot, had one been held, would have created a situation where 180,000 miners were voting on the economic futures of 20,000 of their fellow miners. Such a situation cannot be described as moral. Similarly, how can older miners, offered large redundancy packages, be allowed to vote on the future career of younger miners? The concept of collectivism is about solidarity, about workers standing together, with the strong protecting the weak, based upon 'we' rather than 'me'.

To reiterate another point made earlier, the 'instrumental' collectivism of the working miners meant that they would only stand and fight when they were directly involved, particularly where wage militancy was concerned, when they presented as 'aggressive and uncompromising'.[58] There is no concept of solidarity in this type of collectivism. We are using Nottinghamshire here as indicative of the working miners, but it should be noted that significant numbers of miners worked throughout the strike in the Areas of Leicestershire, South Derbyshire, the Midlands, North Wales, and Lancashire. It must also be said at this point that not all miners in Nottinghamshire worked. As one Nottinghamshire picket stated: 'When it's a strike you should have a greater allegiance to the national union – to all miners together.'[59] It is also instructive to note that other Associations, holding their own Area ballots and which voted against a strike, came out once the strike began as they were willing to stand with their union, and with their fellow miners.

To properly address the issue of the ballot we need to establish who wanted the ballot, and, more importantly, why they wanted it? The 'instrumental collectivists', particularly those in the Nottinghamshire Area, wanted a ballot as they saw it as a way to circumvent a national strike.* The NCB wanted a national ballot because, based on those Area ballots that had previously been held, they believed that the result would have been a return to work – an outcome the Conservative government would have also welcomed. At best, the TUC, the trade union leadership, and the Labour Party wanted a ballot to give legitimacy to any support they would be prepared to offer the NUM, if the vote was for a strike. At worst, they wanted a no strike vote to save any embarrassment they might accrue by supporting the NUM in such a bitter dispute. Without a ballot, all the NUM received from these organisations was prevarication. In spite of the limited support from these organisations, it must be said that many thousands of their members gave the NUM massive support throughout the dispute, both materially and personally.

Those who did not want a ballot were the 73.7 per cent of miners who were already out on strike when the calls for a national ballot were being made.[60] It has been argued that 'when you have 140,000 men on strike, whether they have balloted with their feet, or with a cross, it is still a ballot'.[61] It is also worth noting that at the end of that bitter year-long strike 60 per cent of miners were still on strike. Also, if the Special Delegates Meeting on the 19 April 1984 had agreed to hold a vote it would not have been a ballot, it would have been a plebiscite asking for confirmation of what was a current and ongoing situation. Unlike many other commentators on the strike, we have tried to avoid counterfactual propositions, but we believe that it is likely, if not probable, that a national ballot at that time would have been in favour of a strike.

According to the critics of the strike, particularly those in the media, the striking miners were being duped by militants within the leadership of the NUM led by Arthur Scargill, who had deliberately orchestrated them into the strike, and were denying them their own democratic voices in that decision. This gives too much credit to that leadership who, from any considered view, were themselves being led by the rank-and-file membership. It also does a great disservice to the intelligence of miners.

The catalyst for the strike was the closure of Cortonwood colliery in Yorkshire, a pit that had previously been marked as a secure mine that would receive workers displaced by the closure of unprofitable mines elsewhere in Yorkshire. The announcement of that closure resulted in 'spontaneous, uncoordinated strikes'[62] across Yorkshire as well as other Areas. It should also

* In 2002 the Union of Democratic Mineworkers called for a strike to combat mine closures. It did not hold a ballot.

be understood that 'a strike is not a controllable process, but a huge wave of happenings in which emergency succeeds emergency, and instructions and directives are constantly being overtaken by events'.[63] From the day pickets from Yorkshire spread out across the coalfields, asking for support in defence of their jobs, the 1984-5 miners' strike was inevitable. If there is a need to apportion blame for causing the strike to a single individual 'the man who brought the miners out on strike … was not Mr Scargill, but Mr MacGregor.'[64]

NOTES

1 Jonathon Winterton & Ruth Winterton, *Strike in Yorkshire,* Manchester: Manchester University Press, 1989, p. 70.
2 This document was leaked to the *Economist* magazine on 27 May, 1978.
3 J. Moor, *Why Privatize?* London: Conservative Political Centre, 1983.
4 Huw Beynon, Allan Cox & Ray Hudson, *The Coalfield Research Programme, Discussion Paper No. 1: The Decline of Coal,* University of Durham, 1999.
5 National Union of Mineworkers, *The Miners and the Battle for Britain,* London, 1980.
6 Keith Gildart, *North Wales Miners: A fragile unity 1945-1996,* Cardiff: University of Wales Press, 2001.
7 See David Howell, *The Politics of the NUM: A Lancashire view*, Manchester: Manchester University Press, 1989, pp. 65-66; Jonathon Winterton & Ruth Winterton, *Coal, Crisis and Conflict: The 1984-85 miners' strike in Yorkshire,* Manchester: Manchester University Press, 1989, p. 55.
8 Francis Beckett & David Hencke, *Marching to the Fault Line: The Miners' strike and the battle for industrial Britain,* London: Constable, 2009.
9 Howell, op. cit., p. 67.
10 National Union of Mineworkers, *The attack on union organization in the deep mined coal industry. A report on management strategy and the expansion of sub-contracting within the UK Coal Industry*, Industrial Relations Department Mimeograph, 1989.
11 George B. Baldwin, 'Structural Reform in the British Miners' Union,' *The Quarterly Journal of Economics,* 1953, Vol. 67, No. 4, pp. 576-597.
12 Huw Beynon & Terry Austrin, *Masters and Servants: Class and Patronage in the Making of a Labour Organisation,* London: Rivers Oram Press, 1994.
13 Malcolm Pitt, *The World on our Backs,* London: Lawrence and Wishart, 1979.
14 See: Allen, V. L. (1981). The militancy of British miners. Shipley: Moor Press..; Paul Ackers, 'Life after Death: mining history without a coal industry', *Historical Studies in Industrial Relations,* Vol. 1, pp. 159-170; Carol Stephenson & David Wray, 'Emotional regeneration through community action in post-industrial mining communities: the case of the New Herington Miners' Banner Partnership', *Capital & Class,* Vol. 87, pp. 175-199; David Wray, 'The relevance of community unionism: the case of the Durham Miners Association', *Labour Studies Journal,* Vol. 34, 2009, pp. 507-518.
15 Baldwin, op. cit.
16 R. Page Arnot, *The Miners in Crisis and War: A history of the Miners' Federation of Great Britain from 1930 onwards,* London: George Allen & Unwin, 1961.
17 Page Arnot, ibid.; Alan R. Griffin, *The Miners in Nottinghamshire, 1914-1944: A History of the Nottinghamshire Miners' Unions,* London: George Allen & Unwin, 1962; Allen, op. cit.; Beckett and Hencke, op. cit.
18 Baldwin, op. cit.; Page Arnot, op. cit.; Beckett & Hencke, op. cit.

19 Allen, op. cit.
20 Michael Crick, *Scargill and the Miners,* Harmondsworth: Penguin Books, 1985.
21 Huw Beynon, 'Introduction' in Huw Beynon, (ed.) *Digging Deeper: Issues in the Miners' Strike,* London: Verso, 1985, p.12.
22 Interview with a DMA member in 2015.
23 See M. Heinemann, *Britain's Coal,* London: Victor Gollance, 1944.; W. W. Haynes, *Nationalisation in Practice: The British Coal Industry,* London: Bailey Bros.; Swinfend, 1953.
24 W. H. Sales, & J.L. Davis, 'Introducing a new wage structure into coal mining'. *Oxford Bulletin of Economics and Statistics,* 1957, Vol. 19, pp. 201-240.
25 National Coal Board, *Annual Report,* 1966-1967, p. 37.
26 Joel Krieger, *Undermining Capitalism,* London: Pluto Press, 1984; David Allsop, *Restructuring management strategies and trade union responses in the privatized UK coal industry: a case of UK Coal,* Unpublished Ph.D. Thesis, 2007.
27 Allen, op. cit.; William Ashworth & Mark Pegg, *The History of the British Coal Industry, Vol. 5. 1946-1982,* London: Clarendon, 1986.; Gildart op. cit.; Pitt op. cit.; Krieger op. cit.
28 Pitt, op. cit,; Krieger op. cit.
29 Pitt, ibid., p. 110.
30 Allen, op. cit.
31 Richard Pryke, *The Nationalized Industries: Policies and Performance since 1968,* Oxford: Martin Robinson, 1981.
32 Allen, op. cit.
33 Allen, Ibid.; Krieger, op. cit.; Crick, op. cit.
34 For a wider view of these issues see Allen, Ibid.; Joe Gormley, *Battered Cherub: The autobiography of Joe Gormley,* London: Hamish Hamilton, 1982.; Krieger, op. cit.; Crick, op. cit.; Ashworth, op. cit.
35 Andrew J. Richards, *Miners on Strike: class solidarity and division in Britain,* Oxford: Berg, 1996.
36 *NUM Annual Report and proceedings, 1997.* p. 418.
37 Howell, op. cit.
38 Allen, op. cit., p. 277.9
39 Gormley, op. cit.
40 National Union of Mineworkers, *Annual Report and Proceedings,* 1977.
41 National Union of Mineworkers, Ibid.
42 L. J. Handy, *Wages Policy in the British Coal Mining Industry,* Cambridge: Cambridge University Press,1981.
43 For a more detailed discussion of the introduction of the Area Incentive Bonus Scheme see Handy, op. cit.; David Allsop & David Wray, 'The Rise and Fall of Autonomous Group Working in the British Mining Industry', *Employee Responsibilities and Rights Journal,* 24, pp. 291-232.
44 Beynon, op. cit.
45 Beynon, op. cit. p. 10.
46 See Crick, op. cit.; Howell, op. cit.; Gildart, op. cit.
47 Richards, op. cit.; Gildart op. cit.; Beckett & Hencke op. cit.
48 Quoted in Howell, op. cit., p. 75.
49 Richards, op. cit., p.104.
50 Beckett & Hencke, op. cit.
51 Keith Stanley, *Nottinghamshire Miners Do Strike,* Nottingham: Nottinghamshire Miners Association, 2010.
52 Martin Adeney & John Lloyd, *The Miners' Strike 1984-1953: Loss without Limit.* London: Routledge and Keegan Paul, 1986. p. 22.

53 Winterton & Winterton, op. cit.; Stanley, op. cit.
54 Allen, op. cit. p. 279.; For a broader view of these issues see also S. Matgamna, (ed), *Class Against Class: The Miners Strike 1984-5,* London: Phoenix Press, 2014. Beynon, op. cit.; Richards, op. cit.
55 Adeney & Lloyd, op. cit., p 258.
56 Richards, op. cit., p. 44 & 108.
57 Adeney & Lloyd, op. cit., p 258.
58 Allen, op. cit., p. 186.
59 Penny Green, *The Enemy Without: Policing and class consciousness in the miners' strike,* Milton Keynes: Open University Press, 1990, p. 144.
60 Richards, op. cit., p. 109.
61 Green, op. cit., p. 145.
62 Richards, op. cit., p. 89.
63 Raphael Samuel, Barbara Bloomfiled, & Guy Boanas, (eds), *The Enemy Within: Pit Villages and the Miners' Strike of 1984-5,* London: Routledge and Keegan Paul, 1986, p. 17.
64 Samuel, Bloomfiled, & Boanas, op. cit., p. 20.

Chapter 7

An Open and Shut Case? Reappraising 'Conspiracy' and 'Cock-up' Theories of the Strike

David Waddington

Introduction

This chapter considers the intriguing possibility that the year-long miners' strike of 1984-5 was deliberately planned for and provoked by one or more of the two principal parties to the dispute, namely the Conservative government, aided and abetted by the National Coal Board (NCB), and the left-wing leadership of the National Union of Mineworkers (NUM). Opinion varies between those commentators who consider that the outbreak and course of the strike was a 'matter of accident' or the result of 'blundering' by one side or the other (the 'cock up theory'),[1] and those who regard it as the outcome of carefully conducted 'open conspiracy' or master strategy.[2]

The most frequent version of the latter option – the conspiracy theory – is that the government and the board jointly planned to 'pull the miners on to the punch'; that the closure of Cortonwood Colliery in South Yorkshire, coupled with the near-simultaneous announcement that twenty pits were to close in 1984-5 over and above the twenty which had closed in the preceding twelve months, was a well timed and well executed strategy, with the specific aim in mind of stimulating a strike which would then be smashed.[3]

The more comprehensive version of this theory posits that the Prime Minister, Margaret Thatcher, was acting on behalf of the Tory Party as a whole in seeking to gain revenge for a pair of strike defeats inflicted on Edward (Ted) Heath's Conservative government of the 1970s, in which she was Minister for Education, and for a humiliating climb down in the face of a threatened miners' strike in 1981, a mere two years after her administration was elected to office.[4] The related view had also developed that Mrs Thatcher and her ministers had engaged in extensive pre-planning for a confrontation with the miners, knowing that it was necessary for them to 'crush' the NUM as an essential first step towards pacifying the entire trade union movement and driving through their monetarist agenda.[5]

A second, and not necessarily mutually exclusive, conspiracy theory alleges that the miners' strike was carefully engineered by the NUM's left-wing leadership under the presidency of Arthur Scargill with the thinly veiled intention of using industrial confrontation to 'derail' or 'bring down' the avowedly anti-union government of the day.[6] Even during the actual dispute, considerable discussion focused on the fact that, since Scargill's election in 1982, the NUM membership had voted in three national ballots not to engage in strike action, contrary to the recommendations of their leadership. The NUM National Executive's decision to sanction the 1984-5 strike on an 'Area by Area' basis (i.e. granting permission for such action in Scotland and Yorkshire in the anticipation that this would have the 'domino effect' of drawing in miners from other coalfields), rather than by recourse to a national ballot, was seen as a 'treacherous' (but ill-advised) attempt by Scargill and his allies to achieve their 'insurrectionary' objectives,

> Scargill was not prepared to risk another rebuff from the members, so he sought to impose a strike on them. All that has happened since is an inevitable consequence of the decision not to have a ballot ... Scargill chose to spread the strike area by area, using flying pickets to coerce brother miners. Picketing became a means of coercion, a substitute for winning minds.[7]

This chapter seeks to examine the veracity of the above conspiracy theories. It begins by elaborating on the relevant series of developments that have lent credence to each of these two versions. Considerable attention is paid to the alleged role of the closure of Cortonwood Colliery in South Yorkshire, which is commonly characterised by conspiracy theorists of all persuasions as having been a 'deliberate provocation' for the confrontation that occurred. Two further sections present evidence to repudiate the claims, either that the miners' strike was the product of a carefully orchestrated government 'plot', or that it reflected the politically subversive motivation of Mr Scargill and his left-wing sympathisers within the NUM. These sections will be seen as lending weight to the idea that key developments in the strike's instigation and subsequent development were not so obviously premeditated as to suggest an underlying conspiracy. The final substantive section of the chapter maintains that the Thatcher administration's conduct during the strike represented a series of improvised or pragmatic responses to changing circumstances, rather than the outright application of a well-rehearsed plan or strategy.

The foundations of conspiracy theory

It would seem a reasonable assertion to make that the Conservative government 'had a humiliation to expunge' in relation to the successive defeats they experienced at the hands of the NUM 1972 and 1974.[8] The earlier of these two disputes is forever linked in the public's imagination with the enforced closure by miners and other sympathetic trade unionists of the strategically important Saltley coke works in Birmingham, which constituted at that time the nation's last major stockpile of fuel for use in power stations. The miners' success on this occasion was due in no small measure to the deployment of 'flying pickets' under the direction of the NUM's future president, Arthur Scargill.[9] It was doubtless with the specific intention of avoiding a similar debacle in a second national miners' strike, two years later, that the Conservative Prime Minister, Ted Heath, called an emergency general election, based on the slogan 'Who runs the country?' This proved to be a miscalculation of prevailing public opinion, for it was the Labour Party that was returned to power, where they would remain for the next five years.[10]

It was in the immediate aftermath of the 1972 miners' strike that the Conservative Party first embarked on serious contingency planning 'towards mitigating the consequences of industrial strength exercised in the direct, Saltley manner'.[11] This led to the establishment in quick succession of the Civil Contingencies Unit (CCU or 'Cuckoo'), a high-level committee of senior police, military advisers and government representatives charged with offsetting the potential effects of future major stoppages; and the National Reporting Centre (NRC), a specialist provision within Scotland Yard, whose remit involved the provision and co-ordination of police mutual aid in the event of threatened or actual public disorder.[12]

Immediately following his election defeat, in the spring of 1975 Ted Heath was replaced as Tory party leader by Margaret Thatcher, his erstwhile Education Secretary. She later conceded in her memoirs that she had regarded the Saltley showdown with the miners as 'a frightening demonstration of the impotence of the police in the face of such disorder', while the fall of the Conservative government in 1974 … 'lent substance to the myth that the NUM had the power to make or break British Government, or at least the power to veto any power threatening their interests by preventing coal getting to the power stations.'[13]

Not surprisingly, the attention of her party focused on the type of methodology they might use to manage a future confrontation with the miners. A specially commissioned document by Mrs Thatcher's Shadow Cabinet colleague, Nicolas Ridley (the so-called Ridley Report) advocated that a future Conservative government should brace itself for possible strike action by: stockpiling coal reserves at power stations; having a contingency plan for importing coal; introducing dual oil- and coal-fired burning in power stations; reducing social security benefits for strikers and their families; and finally, setting up mobile police squads to thwart flying pickets, and obtaining sufficient numbers of 'reliable' non-union drivers who would be prepared to breach the picket lines.[14]

Although it could scarcely have been predicted at the time, the Ridley Report was gradually to assume something of a 'demonological status' by the time of the miners' strike. Indeed, 'dog-eared photocopies of it were available on miners' picket lines; it was promoted by the union and the left as being the secret blueprint for the breaking of the labour movement.'[15]

That lay in the future. Fresh from returning to power in May 1979, the Tory government set about delivering its pre-election pledge to pacify trade unionism. In the first three months of 1980 it took on and defeated a national strike by the steel unions. Soon thereafter, the introduction of the Coal Industry Act 1980, which required the industry to break even by 1983-84 by such means as reducing 'uneconomic capacity',[16] appeared to set the government and miners on an inevitable collision course. Mrs Thatcher appeared to be acknowledging this inevitability, by asking her Agriculture, Fisheries and Food minister, Peter Walker, to go to Energy because 'We're going to have a miners' strike'.[17]

The predicted confrontation almost became manifest in February 1981, when NCB proposals for the 'accelerated closure' of 23 collieries were sternly met by an NUM threat to ballot its members on strike action. Meanwhile, a proliferation of strikes occurred throughout the UK coalfields.[18] This immediate accumulation of resistance induced the government to 'climb down' in humiliating manner. The Prime Minister subsequently justified this response by explaining how coal stocks at the power stations had been considered inadequate to withstand a protracted strike. Thus, 'it became very clear that all we could do was to cut our losses and live to fight another day, when – *with adequate preparation* – we might be in a position to win'.[19]

Later that year, however, there was a clear demonstration of the state's growing capacity to respond to large-scale public disorder when the NRC was able to deploy 30,000 officers up and down the country in the form of mutual aid to those cities most affected by the urban riots.[20] The subsequent refinement of the relevant methods, training and equipment involved in the handling of collective disorder meant that, by the turn of 1984, the NRC had no fewer than 416 well-drilled mobile police support units at its disposal, comprising some 13,500 officers.[21] At this stage, 'Saltley' continued to represent 'a demon still to be exorcised in the contingency planning community',[22] but this was soon about to change.

The decision by the Thatcher administration to transfer Ian MacGregor from his post as chairman of the nationalised steel industry into the equivalent position within the National Coal Board was viewed as a clear signal by the NUM that the government was gearing up for confrontation.[23] It was a well-known fact that the vastly experienced American had previously presided over a large-scale closure programme in the American coal industry and had pushed through similar, more recent 'rationalisations' in the British Steel Corporation.[24] Soon after his appointment, MacGregor began speaking of the need to eliminate 'uneconomic output'. In the midst of this, the NUM was presented with a final pay offer of 5 per cent, which the union responded to by starting a national overtime ban, also linked to the question of possible pit closures.[25]

By this time, Arthur Scargill had gone from being president of the Yorkshire Area NUM to being elected as national president of the union in December 1981. It was during the short period that Scargill was only president-elect that the NUM balloted its members on strike action during a dispute over pay. In this instance and in two subsequent ballots occurring in the first two years of his presidency the membership cast majority votes against undertaking industrial action.[26] Conspiracy theorists have therefore deduced that Scargill and other left-wingers within the NUM leadership had become reconciled to the need to galvanise strike action by alternative means to a national ballot.[27]

Even though the NUM did not have anything like the resources available to the government, and could not, therefore, 'match the rigour of thought' invested in the latter's advance preparation for the stoppage, the union nonetheless devoted considerable planning in anticipation of a strike.[28] Two prominent analysts of the dispute refer to three pieces of anecdotal evidence to suggest that the onset of strike action was the result of careful strategic 'premeditation' by Scargill and his most trusted colleagues on the NUM National Executive.[29]

The first such piece of 'evidence' concerns the fact that, in the last few days before the strike, Mr Scargill had argued in a BBC radio interview that it would not be necessary for his union to have a national ballot in order to mobilise the entire union membership. Full-time officials in any one of the NUM's federated 'Areas' (Nottinghamshire, Scotland, South Wales, Yorkshire, etc.) would simply need to invoke Rule 41 of the union's handbook in order to obtain their National Executive's permission for local strike action. A successful application of this nature would undoubtedly be the prelude to sympathetic action by miners in other Areas.

A second piece of evidence concerns a conversation occurring in December 1983, in which the NCB's deputy chairperson, James Cowan, was allegedly tipped off by the NUM's deputy leader, Michael McGahey, that the union 'was building up to a damaging strike', which was due to be led by its Yorkshire Area. Cowan subsequently maintained that his old adversary had given him this warning 'in order to allow him to retire before the coming storm, keep his reputation intact and preserve his health, which had been bad'.[30]

The final and perhaps strongest indication that the NUM had 'specifically prepared for a serious engagement' was revealed shortly after the termination of the strike by the man appointed as official receiver of the NUM's assets in the tenth month of the year-long stoppage. It was this particular informant who divulged that he had witnessed written evidence of a plan hatched by the NUM in February 1984 to transfer the bulk of its assets abroad in order to defy any High Court attempt to punitively seize them.[31]

The point at which these two principal conspiracy theories converge concerns the announcement on 1 March 1984 of the NCB's decision to close down the Cortonwood colliery in South Yorkshire. In the four-month period leading up to the dispute, 'leading left-wingers in the union examined each local dispute for its potential to be generalised into a wider strike against pit closures'.[32] A strike over the duration of meal times at the Manvers Main pit and adjoining coke works (also in South Yorkshire) had already generated a spate of sympathetic stoppages, thanks in no small part to the deployment of flying pickets. The Cortonwood issue was now opportunistically seized upon as the emotive final straw around which the entire membership hopefully would rally.

The notion that the Cortonwood announcement *actually did* form part of an 'open conspiracy' by the government and NCB, aimed at goading the miners into a strike they could not win, remains widely subscribed to by union members and academic commentators.[33] The fact that local miners had only recently been told that Cortonwood had five more years of coal reserves and that men were being transferred into it from surrounding mines lent credence to suspicions that the decision was too illogical to be devoid of an ulterior motive.[34]

Both the timing of the dispute (in the spring, when the demand for coal was obviously at its lowest point), and the location of the closure, in the union's militant heartland, lent further weight to arguments that Cortonwood represented a deliberate tactical provocation by the Board.

The Coal Board could have completely closed down both South Wales and Scotland – as indeed was broadly their intention in the future – without touching the heart of the miners' union in the central mining districts. Yorkshire has 60,000 miners, out of a national total of 180,000; it had a militant leadership; and it was Scargill's home base. Nottinghamshire was the powerful centre of the industry, and Yorkshire had to be broken. Scotland and South Wales could remain on strike for five years, and the NCB and Whitehall could and would have forgotten that there were miners still living in those parts, and the shortfall in output would have embarrassed no one. If the Government was to break the power of the NUM, Yorkshire had to be involved from the beginning.[35]

It is quite conceivable that the NCB and government would have calculated that the NUM had in Arthur Scargill a president who, unlike his more 'moderate' predecessor, Joe Gormley, 'could not be cajoled or bought off' and was, therefore, likely to prove 'inflexible' on the need to reduce capacity.[36] Given that ministers were unlikely to be interested in engaging in sincere negotiation, it would also have occurred to them that 'Scargill's obduracy' could easily be employed to their advantage.[37] Putting it crudely but succinctly, the strike was therefore popularly conceived of in the following terms:

> On both sides it's been seen as a political showdown. Conservative Party leaders are still smarting from what they see as the humiliating defeats imposed on a Tory government by the NUM in the early seventies. Mrs Thatcher wants vengeance, and the added satisfaction of proving she's a better man than Edward Heath. The appointment of Ian MacGregor as chairman of the National Coal Board was a clear signal that if Scargill wanted a fight, he could have it. Arthur, for his part, was only too happy to oblige.[38]

This enduring notion that the miners' strike was deliberately engineered by its main protagonists (the Thatcher government, and/or Mr Scargill and his left-wing union colleagues) in order to further their political objectives is now examined in close detail. Particular attention is paid to evidence which appears to suggest that key developments in the dispute occurred in an essentially unplanned or, even, accidental manner, and often fell outside of the immediate control of the principal actors involved.

A Conservative Party plot?

Some commentators are adamant that any conspiracy theory linking the outbreak of the strike to intense preparation followed by a deliberate act of provocation on the part of Mrs Thatcher and her cabinet is fundamentally implausible.[39] They reason that government ministers would not have considered it sensible to pick a fight with the NUM while another opportunity still existed to cut capacity without triggering industrial action.

This view is consistent with the personal memoir of Peter Walker, who maintains that he was invited to become Mrs Thatcher's Energy Minister, not because she was intent on confrontation with the miners, but because she was fully anticipating a challenge by Arthur Scargill and was 'nervous' about its implications for the British economy:

> She said she felt there was no one in the Cabinet who could conduct the battle with Arthur Scargill as well as I could. She thought I would have the political knowhow and the communications skill to explain the government case to the public. This was essential in a major conflict of this kind. Industrial unrest in the coal industry was probably the greatest threat to her government and I was the best person *to see it did not happen.*[40]

In keeping with this objective, Walker conceived of as many ways as possible of ensuring that Mr Scargill would find it difficult to achieve a vote in favour of a national stoppage. The minister was adamant, for example, that there would be no possibility of any compulsory redundancies in the mining industry, lest the issue might provide a rallying point for industrial action. Walker therefore regards it as 'a total nonsense' to suggest that he and his cabinet colleagues wanted confrontation, while nonetheless conceding that 'if it was forced upon us we intended to win'.[41]

Similar contention surrounds the notion that Ian MacGregor was appointed by the Prime Minister with the intention of sending a resoundingly provocative message to the miners' union. MacGregor's appointment was actually the brainchild of Nigel Lawson, who found it a 'far from easy' task to persuade Mrs Thatcher to move the American from steel to coal. Mrs Thatcher had initially objected, not only that MacGregor was doing such a good job in his present post, but also that, 'his appointment to coal *would be highly provocative*: Ian was widely seen as an overpaid, over-aged, ruthless American whose main achievement at British Steel had been to slash the workforce'.[42]

Lawson only managed to secure the premier's 'hesitant agreement' by eventually convincing her that MacGregor had all but completed the task of restructuring British Steel and now had a capable successor waiting in the wings; that the coal industry had become a bigger challenge than steel and therefore demanded the best man for the job; and that, 'while a coal strike sooner or later was highly likely, a strike simply as a result of the appointment of Ian MacGregor was not on the cards'.[43]

It has been pointed out that, contrary to the popular belief that MacGregor had been brought in to 'butcher' the coal industry 'over the heads' of the unions, the new chairperson was actually determined to achieve his objectives by a process of agreement. Prior to the dispute, he was reputed to have sympathised with the view of other senior NCB managers, 'that everything possible should be done to push Scargill back without giving him the chance of declaring a popular war'.[44]

This is certainly not to deny that the government had been engaged in intense planning and preparation for possible industrial action by the NUM. Such activity had been taking place ever since Mrs Thatcher's election as Prime Minister, and had intensified in the wake of the government's 'climbdown' of 1981. Discussions about beating a future miners' strike (which had involved politicians, civil servants and outside advisers from the very moment that Thatcher arrived in Downing Street) acquired a new urgency. David Howell, who as secretary of state for energy had presided over the settlement with the miners and who was described by [Joe] Gormley [Arthur Scargill's predecessor as NUM president] as 'wet behind the ears', was replaced by Nigel Lawson. Lawson built up stocks of coal at power stations and increased the use of oil in electricity generation. He also made special arrangements, so secret that they were hidden from his own cabinet colleagues, to transport vital chemicals into power stations by helicopter. Against protests from his own constituents, he insisted that a new 'super pit' was opened in the Vale of Belvoir, thus helping to make the Nottinghamshire coalfield more productive and Nottinghamshire miners more secure than their colleagues elsewhere.[45]

It has been argued that the chief significance of the 'Ridley plan' in this process lay principally in the extent to which it eventually became perceived by the NUM as an instrument of government strategy and marker of its intention to defeat the miners. Otherwise, the plan itself 'was not much discussed in the inner circles of the Conservative leadership during the years immediately before the miners' strike'.[46] Other analysts go one step further by emphasising that few government ministers actually knew of its existence.[47] Certainly, 'the famous plan was nowhere to be seen' during the infamous debacle of 1981; and when one Conservative MP had asked to borrow a copy of the plan from its author, one year prior to the strike, even

Nicolas Ridley himself experienced difficulty in laying his hands on it.[48]

These commentators are categorically of the view that far more attention and credence was given to the outcome of a similar 'contingency planning' exercise, undertaken in the early 1980s by a committee chaired by Robert Wade-Gery, the head of the CCU. Echoing the earlier Ridley report, the Wade-Geary commission also advocated the creation of larger stocks of coal, the switching from coal to oil burning at power stations, and the recruitment of private hauliers for use in the event of a sympathetic rail strike. More significantly, however, Wade-Gery appeared to specify the need for government circumspection in its handling of the NUM,

> The object was, first of all, to deter miners from striking. If that failed, it was thought that the hardship suffered might cause splits and encourage a drift back to work ... It never once assumed that the miners would attempt to mount strike action without a ballot, and was informed with the assumption that should a ballot come out for a strike, support from the rest of the union movement was more rather than less likely.'[49]

A mood of government circumspection is certainly suggested by one recent review of the miners' strike which insists that, far from representing a deliberate provocation in circumstances considered highly unfavourable for industrial action by the NUM, the decision by George Hayes, the South Yorkshire Coal Board director, to inform Yorkshire Area union officials of the planned closure of Cortonwood resulted from a misunderstanding of the instructions he had received from London.[50] Mr Hayes had clearly jumped the gun in making this announcement,

> And it was all a mistake. The NCB never intended to include Cortonwood in the list of pits to be closed at that time. An internal report says: 'In procedural terms the Area Director was wrong to announce closure at a General Review Meeting ... Closure has not yet been confirmed by the Board ...' No proper closure procedure had begun at the pit which started the strike; it had all been wrongly handled from the beginning.[51]

A further rebuttal of the idea that Cortonwood was a calculated provocation is provided by Ned Smith, the NCB's Director General of Industrial Relations, who insists that, just prior to the closure announcement, Peter Walker had issued firm instructions 'to avoid flashpoints at area level, to avoid conflict, whatever they now say about a great master plan to drive Arthur Scargill'.[52] Unfortunately, George Hayes and other Yorkshire Area Coal Board officials appear either not to have received, or not to have heeded, such advice. Hayes has since admitted that he was behaving unilaterally in announcing the closure of Cortonwood, based on the benign view that the closure of a single colliery would lift the burden on the whole area. Cortonwood had been the one singled out according to this rationale because it was reasoned that it would be possible to transfer the pit's employees to nearby mines without any need for major redundancies.[53] It would soon become clear, though, that the damage had been done,

> By 5 March half the pits in Yorkshire were already out. At Yorkshire Main, managers trying to do safety work were stoned by pickets. The board was trying to recoup the situation. Peter Walker, as much taken by surprise by the Cortonwood decision as anyone, made sure the board put out a letter to the 830 Cortonwood men stressing that the pit's future would go through the proper procedure – but too late.[54]

Some refute the suggestion that, had the closure of Cortonwood been handled differently, the year-long strike would have been averted.[55] They argue that this episode formed 'only part, though an inflammatory part, of a process which at some point would have led to a strike being declared, and declared, necessarily, in the same terms as it was'. There is certainly good reason to suppose that the NUM's left-wing leadership may have been spoiling for a confrontation. However, as we shall now see, it was the powerful momentum generated by *the union's rank and file*, rather than the promptings of Arthur Scargill and his allies on the National Executive, which provided the impetus for the year-long strike.

Scargill's insurrection?

Any suggestion that the strike may have been dictatorially imposed on miners 'by an ideologically rigid national union leadership' is stridently rebutted by one academic, who maintains that the dispute reflected a rapidly growing rank-and-file opposition to management attempts to reduce costs via pit closures while showing an increasing disregard for processes of joint industrial regulation.[56] A second academic describes this more succinctly as employee resistance to an enhanced assertion by management of their' right to manage the industry'.[57] It was precisely this transformation of management's attitudes and conduct, particularly in NCB Areas like Scotland and Yorkshire, which had raised feelings of rank-and-file rebellion to boiling point by the time of the Cortonwood announcement. This theme has been further developed as follows:

> The ballot issue was used by opponents of the strike to argue that it lacked legitimacy. But the truth is that, in many areas of which Scotland is a good example, miners were driven not only to support a strike, but actually to go on strike, regardless of what the National Executive decided. The confrontation in Scotland between militant rank-and-file miners and the provocative Scottish Coal Board management team resulted in many pits being forced out on strike at some point in February and March 1984, notwithstanding the caution of their leaderships. The calls for strike action originated from the rank-and-file in comparatively democratic forums, including mass meetings and area delegate conferences. These calls were never opposed by the two foremost national NUM leaders, Arthur Scargill and National Secretary, Peter Heathfield, but they brought those who made them into collision with bureaucratic structures in the NUM, in particular with the NUM Scottish Executive led by Mick McGahey and George Bolton.[58]

The authors in question point out that, when the call for industrial action eventually materialised, more than half of all the 14,000 Scottish miners were already on strike or, at least, in dispute with management.[59]

Even more evidence of this rank-and-file impetus is apparent in the way that strike action developed in South Yorkshire. Following the revelation on 1 March of the NCB's decision to close down the colliery, 500 Cortonwood miners met for a branch meeting three days later, where they were emotively informed by their normally 'moderate' Branch Secretary that 'the body of Cortonwood was on the operating table [and that] the area director had got hold of the scalpel and it would seem that the body was going to end up in the morgue'.[60] Cortonwood did not have an especially militant reputation, but the vast majority of its workforce found it deeply objectionable to learn of the imminent closure of their mine (particularly as many of them had just been transferred from another recently closed colliery), and also to be told that branch officials had been given only five weeks' notice of Cortonwood's closure, leaving insufficient time for the case to go through the customary review procedure.

In their resulting anger, the men voted unanimously to fight the closure by asking all other miners in the Yorkshire Area to strike sympathetically on their behalf. One day later, Yorkshire Area officials invoked a ballot result established three years previously to undertake strike action in opposition to pit closures on any grounds other than exhaustion. It is therefore evident that, 'on its own, the proposed closure of Cortonwood might not have led to a national strike. But Cortonwood was a good example of what was happening in the industry generally.'[61]

There is equally strong evidence to suggest that, far from streaming into Nottinghamshire in compliance with Arthur Scargill's direction, Yorkshire pickets entered the neighbouring coalfield out of a strong anxiety 'to show militancy in the face of the leadership's more measured approach'.[62] This view is endorsed by one Yorkshire NUM activist who maintained,

> I don't think it was the intention of the Yorkshire officials, or our co-ordinating committee to go into Nottingham with mass pickets that early. But we've got pits right on the border of Notts. The lads drink in the same pubs and clubs as one another. And when one pit's on strike, and there's a pit down the road, it might be in Notts, but to the lads it's not like that. And what happened was that an immediate mass picket took place, the lads went into Notts.[63]

Similar opposition to conducting a national ballot also originated from the union's rank and file, with many branches resisting attempts by area representatives to override decisions reached at branch level.[64] Such resistance to the idea reflected a determination not to allow miners whose jobs were not immediately threatened to vote those whose collieries were in jeopardy out of their right to strike.[65] It was also indicative of the mistrust felt towards right-wing areas like Nottinghamshire, who could not be relied upon to support a strike in the event of a national ballot.[66] Following the authorisation of strike action under Rule 41, the idea of staging such a vote quickly became taboo inside strikebound mining communities,

> Quite honestly, you mentioned the word ballot at your peril in the miners' clubs and so on. They used to turn round and say 'We've said we're not having one and we're not having one'. They looked at it that Margaret Thatcher wanted a ballot, MacGregor wanted a ballot, the media wanted a ballot, and they weren't going to have one.[67]

During the strike, three-foot-high painted graffiti appeared on a bridge leading into Cortonwood, proclaiming 'We told Arthur what to say',[68] thereby dispelling the accusation that the NUM leader was leading an unwilling membership 'by the nose' in reckless pursuit of his insurrectionary objectives,

> We did tell Arthur what to say and he said it. He represented us, not himself and for possibly the first time in my memory a trades union leader

didn't sell his members out with compromise for the sake of a settlement. How can you compromise over your own destruction?[69]

There were few indications during the dispute that the NUM's left-wing leadership was especially committed to a 'revolutionary' or subversive agenda. The NUM's strike tactics were more or less identical to those the union had previously employed in the industrial action of the 1970s, and were no more 'insurrectionary' in nature than those witnessed in (say) the 1977 Grunwick or 1980 steel strikes.[70] Generally speaking, whilst it was true that the NUM president 'did occasionally speak of "rolling back the tide of Thatcherism", this ambiguous-sounding formulation was not amplified or developed further'.[71]

Premeditated or extemporised?

Evidence emerging from the memoirs of key government and NCB figures involved in the miners' dispute[72] and Cabinet papers released by the National Archives in 2014[73] contradicts the supposition that, once the strike was underway, the Thatcher administration simply activated a carefully prepared strategy in its determination to 'crush' the NUM. Rather, as we shall now see, it was a case of the Prime Minister and her cabinet colleagues making best use of the significant advantages and opportunities that arose out of the chiefly spontaneous and unpremeditated way in which the strike was instigated.

Although the Thatcher government had been anticipating a miners' strike for several years, they could never have dreamed that it would actually be called under conditions that were so patently unfavourable for the NUM.[74] Both the Prime Minister and her Chancellor, Nigel Lawson, claim to have been pleasantly surprised by the timing of the strike. Mrs Thatcher maintains that she and her cabinet had not bargained on a strike occurring before the winter of 1984, when demand for coal would be at its peak. Further still, the government did not consider that strike action was necessarily inevitable. They had reckoned on the NUM leadership following its long tradition of balloting its members before a strike, in which case it was likely that the vote would follow the precedent set by three preceding ballots by registering a majority against strike action.[75]

Nigel Lawson professes to have been less taken aback by the NUM president's decision to authorise strike action without a ballot, given Mr Scargill's determination to generate a confrontation 'come what may'. He does concede to having been surprised, however, by what he refers to as Scargill's 'astonishingly inept decision to start one in the spring, with the summer months, when coal consumption was at its lowest, immediately ahead. This inevitably greatly eased the power station endurance problem, which we had identified from the start as the key to winning any strike.'[76] Given that government planning was based on the anticipation of a complete halt to coal production, it came as a tremendous bonus to Thatcher and Lawson alike that so many NUM members continued working in the strike.[77]

It is undisputable that key elements of the NUM's strategy and tactics had an extremely significant bearing on the conduct and outcome of the strike. Thus, for example, when flying pickets from Doncaster descended on the most northerly pits in the Nottinghamshire coalfield, in defiance of official NUM directives, they undoubtedly did so in full expectation of soliciting the solidarity and support of colleagues from across the border.[78] Even if, as some maintain, the majority of Nottinghamshire miners were ideologically opposed to strike action,[79] it is highly probable that the anger and indignation expressed by pickets from South Yorkshire provided the former with a strong moral justification (or convenient excuse) for continuing to work.[80] Certainly, it seems fair to suggest that 'the way [the Yorkshire miners] carried out that picketing was to colour and blight the dispute, ending hopes of support from a united miners' union and representing to many in the trade union movement, including its titular leaders in the TUC, the unacceptable face of trade unionism'.[81]

The similar argument has been proposed that a successful national ballot would have constituted 'a potent symbol of legitimacy, not only in presenting the union's case to the world outside, but also in its internal relations'.[82] As it turned out, however,

> The absence of a national ballot weakened the position of the NUM executive. It made it difficult for leaders of the Labour Party and other unions to defend the strike. It made it easier for Nottinghamshire miners and their allies to argue that the strike was illicit. Ministers were, in fact, far from sure that a national ballot would not favour a strike. However, the NUM executive was trapped by its own rhetoric. Once Scargill and his allies had talked of not letting miners 'be voted out of jobs', it was hard for them to hold a ballot without appearing to have given in; the fact that so much Conservative legislation revolved around encouraging ballots exacerbated this position.[83]

The NUM's commitment to its flying picketing strategy and refusal to contemplate a national ballot provided welcome ammunition to senior government ministers, most notably Peter Walker, whose daily briefings with newspaper editors were extremely pivotal in persuading the general public that the strike was a constitutionally illegitimate Marxist plot which depended for its continuation on the intimidation of those individuals who were brave enough to continue going into work.[84] Media representations along these lines carried obvious implications for the conduct and eventual outcome of the strike,

> For if the dispute could be defined legally as 'unofficial', if Scargill could be directly associated with the support of 'picket-line violence' and if the pickets could be identified as unofficial strikers committing criminal acts against those going about their lawful business, i.e. work, then the policing of the dispute would cease to be a controlling function and become an enabling function. In this situation the 'right to work' has overridden the 'right to picket' and the police have provided an escort-agency for strike-breakers.[85]

The recently released cabinet papers of 1984 corroborate the claim made by the NCB chairperson, Ian MacGregor, that it was largely as a result of his direct appeal to Mrs Thatcher and her Home Secretary, Leon Brittan, that the police became so centrally and decisively involved in the miners' strike.[86] MacGregor admits to having been tremendously alarmed on realising, right from the outset of the strike, that relevant police forces were too 'ill equipped and tactically disadvantaged' to stand up to the flying pickets. Indeed,

> The police at local level seemed incapable, often understandably, of handling the situation. In some cases they were frankly unwilling to get involved in a fight they did not see as being theirs. I was particularly concerned by reports I got that some local left-wing police committees were putting heavy pressure on their chief constables not to get involved, with the implication that the financial future of their forces could be made quite unpleasant if they were seen to be adopting the role of strike-breakers.[87]

MacGregor maintains that it was after he had gone, 'boiling with a righteous indignation', to Downing Street that the Prime Minister immediately began to demand that the NRC play a more prominent, strategic role in the dispute.[88]

The American's characterisation of this early police reticence is consistent with the findings of one academic study which revealed that several chief constables harboured strong feelings of ambivalence regarding their role in the strike, especially in those cases where their working-class background predisposed them to sympathise with the miners.[89] Ultimately, however, they had bought in to the increasingly well-established ideological perspective that a perfectly sensible, law-abiding section of society was being 'led astray by militant, politically motivated leaders'[90] and that the police had therefore been 'forced' into the position, not only of protecting the law, but also of ensuring that 'a government properly elected, was not brought down, or a country's base ruined because of a group of people who wanted to bring about their way by unlawful means'.[91]

The 1984 cabinet papers reveal how, with the egging on of close advisers like the head of her Downing Street policy unit, John Redwood, Mrs Thatcher built on the above advantages by engaging in a 'calculated campaign' of misinformation (e.g. by approving a letter to all miners which disingenuously confirmed that the NCB was seeking 'only' 20,000 voluntary redundancies and not the 70,000 being alleged by the NUM), and by publicly vilifying the striking miners, as on the famous occasion when she referred to them to an audience of her own party backbenchers as the 'enemy within'.[92] The papers also demonstrate the importance of Mrs Thatcher's interventions in disputes involving rail workers, dockers and pit deputies, where in each case she advocated favourable settlements for the employees involved so as not to detract from the government's attempts to defeat the miners, and thereby 'ensure that Scargill was isolated and ultimately defeated'.[93]

Conclusion

The conclusion of this chapter is consistent with the earlier one arrived at by two fellow academics, who regard the popular notion that the government wanted, and therefore engineered a confrontation with the miners as 'not substantiated [and] inherently improbable'.[94] This verdict chimes with that of two well-known industrial journalists, who strongly contend that,

> Every piece of contingency planning, every appointment made by the government in the period between early 1981 and early 1984 has been seen in retrospect as part of a wholly conscious plot leading to the miners' downfall. It clearly was not: rather it was a series of zig-zagging, often opportunist, sometimes accidental moves, though deserving the name of strategy because imbued with a common purpose: to render the government and the state as protected as it was possible to be from a miners' strike. But it was still an object of real and present dread.[95]

The memoirs of prominent actors in the dispute, such as Ian MacGregor, Peter Walker and Margaret Thatcher herself, betray an obvious anxiety about taking on the miners, combined with a clear reluctance to create any sort of flashpoint that might trigger a confrontation of this nature. In this context, the announcement of the NCB decision to close the Cortonwood colliery was an unsanctioned error which the Energy Minister immediately sought to remedy and was, moreover, eager to atone for.

Corresponding evidence suggests that, whilst the NUM's left-wing leadership was undoubtedly on the lookout for any opportunity to persuade their members to embark on industrial action, the actual impetus for the strike came from the union's rank and file. Subsequent media and political vilification of the NUM leadership, both for its 'refusal' to hold a ballot and for its 'tyrannical' use of the secondary picketing strategy, was therefore misdirected. However, this process of castigation played a key part in helping to legitimise the decision by large sections of the NUM's membership not to strike, in turning public and political sympathy away from the miners, and in justifying the repressive policing of the strike.

This is not to pretend that government preparations for such a dispute had not been extensive and did not eventually yield dividends. For as we have seen,

> The government prepared for a strike and expected a strike and when it came it began at the worst time of the year for the NUM. Thereafter the government was determined that it would end only with the crushing of the NUM. There was a conviction in the government that the defeat of the NUM – the union that symbolised union power, which had brought down a government and which for Thatcherites was the socialist threat incarnate – had to be defeated if the Thatcherite revolution was to take root in British politics and society.[96]

The government may well have succeeded in this mission, but as we have seen, their victory was achieved not as the result of some carefully hatched and skilfully executed master plan. Conspiracy theories of the year-long miners' strike may well have a plausible and satisfying ring about them, but there is too much contradictory evidence at our disposal to allow such convenient but overly-simplified levels of explanation to go perennially unchallenged.

NOTES

1 For example: Martin Adeney & John Lloyd, *The Miners' Strike 1984-5: Loss Without Limit,* London: Routledge and Kegan Paul, 1986.
2 For example: John Saville, 'An Open Conspiracy: Conservative politics and the miners' strike 1984-5', *Socialist Register*, 1985/86. pp. 295-329.
3 Adeney & Lloyd, op. cit., p. 70.
4 Saville, op. cit.
5 Bill Schwartz, 'Let Them Eat Coal: the Conservative Party and the strike', in Huw Beynon, (ed.) *Digging Deeper: Issues in the Miners' Strike*, London: Verso, 1984.
6 See Nicholas Ridley, *'My Style of Government': The Thatcher Years*, London: Hutchinson, 1991; Margaret Thatcher, *The Downing Street Years*, London: HarperCollins, 1993.
7 Jimmy Reid, 'What Scargill means', *New Society*, 17 January, 1985. pp. 90-93.
8 Adeney & Lloyd, op. cit., p. 70.
9 Andy Beckett, *When the Lights Went Out: What Really Happened to Britain in the Seventies*, London: Faber and Faber, 2009.
10 David Waddington, Chas Critcher, Bella Dicks, & David Parry, *Out of the Ashes? The Social Impact of Industrial Contraction and Regeneration on Britain's Mining Communities*, London: The Stationery Office, 2001.
11 Sarah McCabe & Peter Wallington, *The Police, Public Order, and Civil Liberties*, London: Routledge, 1988, p. 239.
12 Martin Kettle, 'The National reporting Centre and the 1984 miners', strike', in Bob Fine & Robert Millar, (eds.) *Policing the Miners' Strike*, London: Cobden, 1985.
13 Margaret Thatcher, *The Path to Power*, London: HarperCollins, 1995, pp. 340-41.
14 See 'Appomattox or civil war?', *The Economist*, 27 May, 1978.
15 Adeney & Lloyd, op. cit., p. 72.
16 Jonathan Winterton & Ruth Winterton, 'Coal', in Andrew Pendleton & Jonathan Winterton (eds.), *Public Enterprise in Transition: Industrial Relations in state and Privatized Corporations*, London: Routledge, 1993.
17 Saville, op, cit., p. 395.
18 Waddington et al., op. cit.
19 Thatcher, 1993, p. 139, emphasis added.
20 Kettle, op. cit.
21 Kettle, op. cit.
22 Keith Jefferey & Peter Hennessy, *states of Emergency: British Governments and Strikebreaking Since 1919*, London: Routledge and Kegan Paul, 1983, pp. 236-37.
23 Winterton & Winterton, op. cit.
24 Adeney & Lloyd, op. cit.
25 Saville, op. cit.
26 Saville, op. cit.
27 Adeney & Lloyd, op. cit., pp. 82-3.
28 Adeney & Lloyd, op. cit., p. 80.
29 Adeney & Lloyd, op. cit., p. 83.
30 Adeney & Lloyd, op. cit., p. 83.
31 Adeney & Lloyd, op. cit., pp. 83-4.
32 Winterton & Winterton, op, cit., p. 80.
33 Saville, op. cit.
34 Brian Towers, 'Posing larger questions: the British miners' strike of 1984-85', *Industrial Relations Journal*, 1985. Vol. 16, No.1, pp. 8-25.
35 Saville, op. cit., p. 306.
36 Saville, op. cit., p. 307.
37 Saville, op. cit., p. 307.

38 Reid, op. cit., p. 91.
39 Adeney & Lloyd, op. cit., p. 70.
40 Peter Walker, *Staying Power*, London: Bloomsbury, 1991, p. 166, emphasis added.
41 Walker, op. cit., p. 169.
42 Nigel Lawson, *The View from No. 11: Memoirs of a Tory Radical*, London: Corgi Books, 1993, p. 157, emphasis added.
43 Lawson, op. cit., p. 157.
44 Adeney & Lloyd, op. cit., p. 84.
45 Richard Vinen, *Thatcher's Britain: The Politics and Social Upheaval of the 1980s*, London: Pocket Books, 2010.
46 Vinen, op. cit., p. 156.
47 Adeney & Lloyd, op, cit., p. 73.
48 Adeney & Lloyd, op, cit., p. 73.
49 Adeney & Lloyd, op, cit., p. 79.
50 Francis Beckett & David Hencke, *Marching to the Fault Line: The 1984 Miners' Strike and the Death of Industrial Britain*, London: Constable, 2010, p. 47.
51 Beckett & Hencke, op. cit., pp. 47-48.
52 Quoted by Paul Routledge, *Scargill: The Unauthorised Biography*, London: Harper Collins, 1993, p. 139.
53 Routledge, op. cit., p. 139.
54 Adeney & Lloyd, op. cit., pp. 86-87.
55 Adeney & Lloyd, op. cit., p. 87.
56 Jim Phillips, 'Workplace conflict and the origins of the 1984-85 miners' strike in Scotland', *Twentieth Century British History*, 2009. Vol. 20, No. 2, pp. 152-172, p. 171
57 Peter Gibbon, 'Analysing the British miners' strike of 1984-5', *Economy and Society*, 1988. Vol. 17, No. 2, pp. 139-94.
58 Terry Brotherstone & Simon Pirani, 'Were there alternatives? Movements from below in the Scottish Coalfield, the Communist Party, and Thatcherism, 1981–1985', *Critique*, 2005. Vol. 33, No. 1, pp. 99-124, p. 106.
59 Brotherstone & Pirani, op. cit., p. 112.
60 Michael Crick, *Scargill and the Miners*, Harmondsworth: Penguin, 1985, p. 98.
61 Crick, op. cit., p. 99.
62 Adeney & Lloyd, op, cit., pp. 97-98.
63 Quoted in 'The miners', strike: a balance sheet - a roundtable discussion', *Marxism Today*, April 1985. pp. 21-27, p. 24.
64 Huw Beynon, 'Decisive power: the new Tory state against the miners', in Huw Beynon (ed.), *Digging Deeper: Issues in the Miners' Strike*, London: Verso, 1984.
65 Peter Gibbon & Simon Bromley, '"From an institution to a business"? Changes in the British coal industry 1985-9', *Economy and Society*, 1990. Vol. 19, No. 1, pp. 56-93.
66 Victor L. Allen, 'The year-long miners' strike, March 1984 – March 1985: a memoir', *Industrial Relations Journal*, 2009. Vol. 40, No. 4, pp. 278-291.
67 NUM activist, quoted in 'The miners', strike: a balance sheet - a roundtable discussion', *Marxism Today*, April 1985. pp. 21-27, p. 24.
68 Bernard Jackson with Tony Wardle, *The Battle for Orgreave*, Brighton: Vanson Wardle Productions Ltd, 1987, p. 11.
69 Jackson with Wardle, op. cit., p. 11.
70 Gibbon, op. cit.
71 Gibbon, op. cit., p. 149.
72 Lawson, op. cit.; Thatcher, 1993; Walker, 1991; Ian MacGregor, *The Enemies Within: The Story of the Miners' Strike, 1984-5*, London: Collins, 1986.
73 For useful synopses see: Nicholas Jones, 'The Cabinet Papers: Thatcher and the police', in Granville Williams (ed.), *Settling Scores: The Media, the Police and the Miners' Strike*,

London: Campaign for Press and Broadcasting Freedom, 2014a; Nicholas Jones, 'The Cabinet Papers: misinformation and cover-ups', in Granville Williams (ed.), *Settling Scores: The Media, the Police and the Miners' Strike*, London: Campaign for Press and Broadcasting Freedom, 2014b.

74 Vinen, op. cit., p. 164.
75 Thatcher, 1993, p. 344.
76 Lawson, op. cit., p. 158.
77 Vinen, op. cit., p. 164.
78 Beynon, op. cit.
79 Gibbon, op. cit.
80 Adeney, Lloyd, op. cit., p. 91.
81 Adeney, Lloyd, op. cit., p. 91.
82 Richard Hyman, 'Reflections on the mining strike', *Socialist Register*, 1985/86. pp. 330-354.
83 Vinen, op. cit., p. 164.
84 Walker, op. cit., p. 174.
85 Phil Scraton, 'From Saltley Gates to Orgreave: A history of the policing of recent industrial disputes', in Bob Fine & Robert Millar (eds), *Policing the Miners' Strike*, London: Lawrence and Wishart, 1985.
86 Jones, op. cit., 2014a.
87 MacGregor, op. cit., p. 191.
88 MacGregor, op. cit., p. 191.
89 Robert Reiner, *Chief Constables*, Oxford: Oxford University Press, 1991.
90 Reiner, op. cit., p. 183.
91 Reiner, op. cit., p. 185.
92 Jones, 2014b.
93 Jones, 2014b.
94 McCabe & Wallington, op. cit., p. 22.
95 Adeney & Lloyd, op. cit., p. 79.
96 Andrew Taylor, *The NUM and British Politics, Volume 2: 1969-1995,* Aldershot: Ashgate, 2005, pp. 173-4.

Chapter 8

'Iron Hand': Representations and Ramifications of the 'Battle of Orgreave'

David Waddington

The story on every street

The title of this chapter is partly derived from the song *Iron Hand* from the1991 Dire Straits album, *On Every Street*. The song's lyrics vividly describe a scene during the mass picketing of the Orgreave coking plant in May/June 1984 in which scores of police officers, both mounted and on foot, moved in with the intention of dispersing the hundreds of miners and their supporters who gathered with the aim of deterring the transportation of coke to a Scunthorpe steel works. The very existence of *Iron Hand* constitutes a powerful testimony of the degree to which the 'Battle of Orgreave' has become so firmly embedded in British popular culture. The song not only reminds us of how 'The wood and the leather the club and shield/Swept like a wave across a battlefield'[1] but also highlights both the scale of the ensuing police violence and the widespread infamy it has since attracted,

> Oh the iron will and the iron hand
> In England's green and pleasant land
> No music for the shameful scene
> That night they said it even shocked the Queen.

Received wisdom has it that the miners had come in search of a repetition of the symbolic and strategic victory they achieved (albeit with the sympathetic support of thousands of other trade unionists) in closing down the Saltley coke works during the earlier national dispute of 1972 (see previous chapter). The strikers could never have bargained, though, on the sheer numerical strength and resolve of the well-organised police operation confronting them. 'The consequence was a series of mediaeval engagements in which the miners were first physically trounced and then subjected to an ideological battering with the aid of selective newsreel footage.'[2]

This chapter is less concerned with exploring musical or other artistic representations of the 'battle'[3] than with the analysis of: (a) the highly controversial media accounts of the conflict, which arguably had a great bearing on the outcome of the strike; and (b) the contradictory legal testimonies of what happened during peak phases of the violence, which have since helped to shape the contemporary philosophical and practical approaches to policing public order, especially in South Yorkshire.

The chapter begins with a brief overview of the way in which the Orgreave episode unfolded from start to finish. This preliminary narrative largely derives from the participant observation study of the mass picket undertaken by the present author.[4] Successive sections then address the origins, nature and objectives of the large-scale police operation mounted in opposition to the miners, and of the highly partisan media coverage of the associated conflict. It will become evident, even from this brief focus on media representations, that print and television reports consistently placed the blame for the violence on the miners and their supporters, but systematically downplayed corresponding instances of police aggression and portrayed such conduct as justifiable under the circumstances. The fourth section of the chapter reports on the nature and implications of evidence produced during the Crown Court trials of 15 miners who were arrested for 'rioting' at Orgreave on 18 June 1984. The section will show how such evidence totally undermined the accuracy and credibility of media (and police) versions of what actually happened on the day. The crucial final section highlights the way in which such conflicting representations of the Orgreave episode (combined with similar controversy surrounding the police role in the subsequent Hillsborough disaster of 1989) have compelled South Yorkshire Police (SYP) into adopting a far more permissive approach to public order policing which now regards the upholding of the 'right to protest' as one of its uppermost priorities.

An overview of events

Whilst anyone could easily be forgiven for assuming that the violence occurring at Orgreave was confined to the final and easily most memorable encounter of 18 June 1984, the mass picketing of the coke works actually constituted a three-and-a-half-week saga of activity, commencing on 23 May 1984 when some 500 pickets from the Silverwood colliery in South Yorkshire assembled outside the entrance with the aim of persuading lorry drivers to stop making their twice-daily deliveries of coke to the British Steel Corporation plant in Scunthorpe. This action had been mounted in response to a sudden decision by the corporation to increase supplies of coke to Lincolnshire over and above those jointly agreed with the Iron and Steel Trades Confederation (ISTC) and National Union of Mineworkers (NUM).[5]

It quickly became apparent that this exercise would be no pushover for the miners, who soon found themselves penned up against a wall by equally determined police units and thereby prevented from even approaching lorry drivers.[6] Four days later, similar numbers of pickets were joined by the NUM president, Arthur Scargill, who was given permission to enter the plant with the aim of addressing its employees. However, not long afterwards, Mr Scargill returned to inform his colleagues that the coke workers were not prepared to support them. The NUM leader had scarcely done telling his immediate audience of this outcome when police officers were given the order to form a wedge and clear the roadway, an action which resulted in Mr Scargill and several other pickets being unceremoniously bundled to the floor. Subsequent television news bulletins inevitably focused on this incident, which the NUM president bitterly condemned as a blatant example of 'police brutality' and called on all members of his union to gather in large numbers at Orgreave with the intention of emulating the famous victory they had achieved twelve years earlier at Saltley.[7] The following day was Bank Holiday Monday and there were no deliveries of coke; but on the day after that, hundreds of pickets duly assembled outside the plant, to be greeted in decidedly resolute manner by vast contingents of police officers, drafted in from eleven separate forces. The day's events had scarcely even begun when,

> One crowd of pickets was prevented from getting within a mile of the gates by lines of police officers, while a second group, who had managed to assemble earlier opposite the gates, was charged by police horses and dog handlers. When the convoys of coke lorries arrived, any attempt at picketing was rendered ineffectual: whenever serious pushing was exerted against police lines, snatch squads were instantly deployed. Sensing the futility of their actions, some miners threw stones. This was answered by the production of full-length riot shields and, as the throwing intensified, mounted horses with baton-wielding riders were sent in.[8]

This was to be the first of three such 'cavalry charges'. Each time that this occurred, the mounted police were followed in by the short-shield 'infantry', whose apparently undifferentiating hostility provoked widespread anger and indignation.[9]

The following day's proceedings began with an early reiteration of police resolve when Arthur Scargill was arrested for 'obstructing the police and the highway' whilst leading a compliment of ninety pickets up the entry road towards the coke works. The total number of pickets present had so far been relatively small in comparison to the previous day. However, following Mr Scargill's arrest, miners began to assemble in much greater number and the ensuing hostilities were on a par with those of a day earlier.[10]

The level of such violence declined in the course of the next two weeks, no doubt in response to the NUM's decision to maintain no more than a 'token' picket outside Orgreave. All this suddenly changed on 18 June when some 10,000 pickets arriving at the plant were met by an estimated 4,000 police officers.[11] The day actually began with the police momentarily finding themselves caught off guard by a secretly organised operation in which scores of pickets entered the coking plant by climbing over an unguarded perimeter fence. Some commentators maintain that these pickets not only vandalised machinery, but were in the process of unloading and immobilising parked up coke wagons by the time police dog handlers finally arrived and were able to clear the premises.[12]

The appearance, shortly thereafter, of the first coke convoy of the day provided the signal for the now-familiar ritual of pushing and shoving on both sides. This was initially carried out in a relatively good-natured fashion, and continued in such vein until the point at which a mounted police unit was suddenly ordered in – possibly in response to a group of pickets who had seized a riot shield, which they were about to set alight.[13] This intervention provoked a brief flurry of retaliatory stone-throwing, but there was no further violence during the rest of the morning and for most of the following afternoon.

However, just when it appeared that the day's hostilities had concluded, a small group of young pickets made an inept attempt to roll a huge tractor tyre towards the onlooking ranks of policemen. Most of the police remained still but some officers rushed out, giving the impression of a false start in an athletics race. Stones were immediately thrown at them.[14]

According to one local newspaper report, it was at this point that police in full riot gear were hurriedly called back from a break, having only just ceased 'standing for hours in blazing sunshine being taunted by men basking in the weather'.[15] The order was then given by the senior police commander, Assistant Chief Constable Tony Clement, for mounted police and short-shield units to advance into the pickets. In a nutshell, 'The struggle that followed was violent but unequal',[16] insofar as the police chased pickets over a nearby railway bridge into neighbouring streets and gardens, often meting out 'summary justice' and/or arresting anyone proving too slow – or simply too defiant – to flee beyond their grasp.[17]

In the midst of all this mayhem, the NUM president was one of the many individuals on both sides to incur significant injury,

> But there is disagreement and contradictory testimony over the circumstances. He claims he was standing on a grass verge when he felt himself struck violently on the back of the neck by the edge of a riot shield. This is corroborated by two pickets standing with him at the time but is flatly contradicted by Clement, who has always insisted that he was the policeman closest to Scargill when he went down. His version is that the miners' leader tipped backwards over some fencing, hit his head and suffered mild concussion. He called for an ambulance, and Scargill, with another injured picket, was taken off to hospital.[18]

Afterwards, Mr Clement maintained that he had been faced with no alternative than to drive the pickets into the estate, a tactic he deemed necessary to protect his men from the 'hail of missiles' raining down on them. It has been counter-argued, however, that the vast majority of stone-throwing by pickets was entirely reactive: 'Only after they had been attacked in this way did the pickets retaliate. Then barricades were built and set alight and missiles hurled at the advancing police. In the end, however, the pickets were no match for them.'[19]

Interpreting police conduct

The widely-held conspiracy theory that Orgreave was a *set-piece confrontation*, 'theatrically managed to publicly teach the miners a lesson'[20] continues to resound within the UK's former coalfield areas. There is abundant anecdotal evidence to suggest that the police road block strategy *generally* operated, in late May and early June, in such a way as to prevent pickets from entering the Nottinghamshire coalfield in particular, while making it relatively easy and more tempting for them to 'fall back' on Orgreave.[21] Nevertheless, there is widespread academic agreement that the mass picket of 18 June was the product of careful planning by the NUM, who seemed intent on catching the police off guard. On this occasion at least, the police hurriedly built up their numbers in response to intelligence which gradually came to their attention.[22]

There is a similar academic consensus of opinion that South Yorkshire Police were wholeheartedly committed, not merely to upholding the individual's 'right to work', but also to the achievement of a broader political objective. Speaking on 18 June, Assistant Chief Constable Clement warned that, 'If the pickets here win by force, the whole structure of industrial relations, and policing, and law and order, and civil liberties is all gone,' adding that, 'we cannot afford for people who want to go to work to be prevented by force'. Reflecting the clear significance of recent industrial history, Mr Clement further maintained that 'there is no chance that this will be the Saltley of 1984. The plant will remain open until British Steel decides otherwise.'[23]

The Assistant Chief Constable had insisted at the time of the Orgreave confrontation that the crucial, transformative decision he made to send in the mounted police on the morning of 29 May had been an altogether improvised response to a crisis situation which had arisen just before the first of the two daily convoys of coke lorries was due to arrive. It was at this point that a snatch squad of police officers had suddenly found themselves detached from the remainder of their colleagues and menacingly surrounded by a group of forty pickets:

> 'There's half a dozen of our lads getting a good hiding here,' one constable called back to Clement, and he had a sudden inspiration. He ordered the wall to break momentarily so that a line of eight mounted officers could move in to rescue the stranded six. The miners, who had never seen anything like it, fled instantly up the hill. 'To see the effect those horses had on them, the way they backed off and ran scattered,' says Clement, 'it immediately suggested that if you were about to be overwhelmed, the horses would be invaluable. At no time before had I envisaged using them that way.'[24]

An on-the-spot BBC local radio reporter was clearly sceptical of this account, contending that the military precision with which the horses were introduced betrayed a strong element of premeditation. According to this journalist,

> Like a military manoeuvre, the police swept into action. They say it was a coincidence, but it was moments before the lorries came out. But I remember looking up and suddenly seeing two lots of horses sweeping in from the left and right simultaneously on the pickets. It was like a scene out of war, a battle. They swept in, the police went forward.[25]

Strike supporters complained in large number that the subsequent actions of mounted police and short-shield units on 29 and 30 May, and especially on 18 June, were almost universally vengeful and over-aggressive, and that officers were clearly none too concerned about differentiating between 'guilty' and 'innocent'.[26] These claims are consistent with evidence arising from interviews with rank-and-file police officers, who admitted to enjoying 'the genuine power' associated with public order policing: 'You are just part of a vast crowd,' one individual explained, 'and if the whole thing is wrong and illegal, it's not you who's going to be picked up for it.'[27] Another officer described how there was a tendency, in the heat of battle, to 'hit the first person in front of you. All right you are going to hit some innocent people, but in general you are going to stop a riot.'[28]

These interviews also provide major clues as to why police attempts to disperse the Orgreave pickets were so explicitly uncompromising: 'We'd had so much bloody aggravation,' admitted one such individual. 'Like the miners were just getting away with murder'.[29] Until such time as the horses were ordered in, officers had been forced to stand there in their growing frustration while pickets tore up fence palings and waved them defiantly in the direction of the police: 'We should have gone in, taken them out,' another officer insisted, 'but for some reason we just stood there watching them.'[30] Not surprisingly, the decision to deploy the mounted police was greeted with mass approval,

> And when they came back, we all applauded. I've never been in a situation like it. It was great to see them smashing into all them bastards who'd been giving us grief all day. A lot of bobbies were injured. It was as though somebody thought, 'Right. We're not standing for this crap anymore. We'll sort it out.' And that's what they did. It was the greatest thing I ever saw.[31]

As we shall now see, police sentiments and actions of this nature were by no means acknowledged in subsequent media coverage of these events.

Media representations of Orgreave

Analysis of the media coverage of the Orgreave mass picket has largely focused on televised accounts of the climatic violent events occurring on 18 June 1984. There can be no doubting on this basis that, 'in its choice of language, film-editing techniques and subtle juxtaposition of images and commentary, television news delivered an entirely misleading and politically biased representation' of what happened on that day.[32] This claim has been substantiated by an academic analysis of BBC Nine O'clock and ITN's Ten O'clock news reports of how the day's disorder was first instigated and then caused to escalate.[33]

The author of this study describes how each of these commentaries created a very clear general impression that the onset of serious violence was precipitated by a burst of particularly aggressive behaviour on the part of the miners, in response to which the police acted in a fundamentally *restrained and justifiable manner.* According to the BBC's reporter, the conflict,

> ... reached a peak as miners surged in against the riot shields. Policemen hit out with truncheons under a barrage of stones and missiles. Mass picketing had turned to rioting. The police didn't give any ground and on the front line they handed out as much physical punishment as they received. Eventually, the senior officer ordered in the mounted police.[34]

This commentary clearly places the blame for the early development of violence on the miners, in that it was they who allegedly caused it to peak by 'surging in' against police lines. The fact that officers 'hit out with truncheons' is obviously regarded as justifiable, in light of the fact that they were being subjected at the time to a bombardment of stones and missiles. Viewers are implicitly informed that, while the police admittedly reacted with due firmness and control (they 'didn't give any ground'), officers nonetheless exercised commendable restraint, responding only *in like manner* to any violence directed at them. The insertion of the word, 'Eventually' suggests that the horses were sent in only after all due consideration and restraint.

The study further reveals how the ITN commentary unfolds in similar fashion. Unlike the BBC report, it emphasises how the first signs of trouble coincided with the entry into the plant of the convoy of coke lorries. It was evidently at this point that,

> Pickets charged straight into the police riot shields. In seconds, a pack of police, twenty deep, was fighting a shower of stones to hold the pickets back. The first cavalry charge came a few minutes later and it clearly worried the pickets. [Film shows pickets scattering across field.][35]

Here too, the introduction of the police 'cavalry' (with all its Hollywood-style connotations of the 'good guys' coming to the rescue) is seen as a *necessary defensive tactic*, designed to relieve ranks of beleaguered colleagues who were 'fighting a shower of stones' in their bid to contain the pickets. The disclosure that the cavalry charge 'clearly worried the pickets' arguably understates the levels of fear and panic induced by this intervention.

The analysis then relates how, in its attempt to show how the conflict escalated from these origins, the BBC report explains that, on the order of the senior commander, the police ranks opened up and the horses 'galloped in'. The mounted police were immediately followed into action by riot squads with short shields, whose entry became the prelude to some of the 'most vicious hand-to-hand fighting' so far witnessed in the strike:

> The attacks on policemen were horrific but the riot squads gave no quarter, using their batons liberally ... At all times, the police were in control and there were over one hundred arrests as the fighting ebbed and flowed.[36]

The condemnatory description of the 'horrific' attacks on policemen stands in marked contrast to the considerably more restrained characterisation of police action (they 'gave no quarter' and were 'in control at all times'). The conflict on the whole is clearly depicted as an *equal contest* insofar as 'the fighting [allegedly] ebbed and flowed'.

The ITN narrative corresponds more closely to the overview presented earlier in this chapter, emphasising how, following this initial bout of hostilities, there was a lull in the proceedings. The reporter maintains that this period of respite was brought to a close by a resumption of stone-throwing by the pickets (although no explanation is volunteered as to what might have prompted this sudden barrage). Viewers are told how the miners had been warned by Mr Clement to stop their throwing and disperse, but had chosen to ignore this directive. Thus, 'after two hours, the police were tired of being pushed and pelted with house bricks. The pickets knew what to expect: they'd been warned it could turn nasty and it did.'[37]

Not for the first time, viewers are presented with the very clear impression that the police violence was not only reactive in nature but was also totally 'understandable', in light of the two hours of aggressive behaviour that officers had endured. Furthermore, the linguistic device of agent deletion – the pickets were warned that 'it [not the police, per se] could turn nasty, and it did' – is used to obscure and downplay the nature and severity of the corresponding police offensive. This apparent reluctance to refer *explicitly* to examples of police violence is further manifested in a tendency for the reporter to *refrain from commenting altogether* in relation to visual imagery of such acts. This practice exemplified by a particular instance in which a policeman is pictured repeatedly truncheoning a crouching miner about the head, but for which there is no spoken narrative.

Ironically, it was the ITN's inclusion of the same incident which highlighted the fact that the BBC had edited their footage of it in such a way as to remove all evidence of police culpability,

> Close comparison of BBC and ITN footage shows that the BBC film has in shot the man who was most severely beaten by the police, but that *the film has been cut at precisely the point when the policeman begins to set about him with his truncheon.* What we cut away to are miners' retaliatory attempts to help their colleagues. But because the BBC film has not shown any examples of police violence, these de-contextualised images can only signify *unprovoked* violence by pickets.[38]

An even more telling indictment of such distorting editorial practices was provided by the BBC's own *Brass Tacks* documentary of 30 November 1985, which compared the above BBC News narrative of events with the only definitive record of what had actually happened on the day – ironically, a police training video containing comprehensive details of every second of the conflict. In contrast to the version of events given by the 'official' news bulletin, the police video indicated that it was *police behaviour* that served to escalate the violence. Having been invited by the programme's production team to study the first hour of the police video, John Alderson, the former Chief Constable of Devon and Cornwall, commented that,

> I think it's fair to say that although there was pushing and shoving by the miners and one or two throwing of missiles of one kind or another, the general, first escalation it seems to me came from the cantering of the horses in the crowd which merely heightened the tension and increased the violence.[39]

The Crown court evidence

Many striking miners and their families already knew of the existence and contents of the police video prior to the screening of the *Brass Tacks* documentary. This was because its unexpurgated version of the day's events had already been pivotal, not only in undermining media and police accounts of what actually happened on 18 June 1984, but also in securing the acquittal after 16 weeks of legal proceedings of 15 miners facing charges of riot at Sheffield Crown Court in May 1985. One of the 15 defendants maintains in his personal memoir of the trial that, had the police been absolutely confident of their account, they would not have shirked from producing the video in evidence for the prosecution. Clearly, though, 'they had no intention of showing it at all and to this day it would probably have remained a secret if our defence had not dragged it out of them'.[40]

In addition to proving conclusively that it was the premature intervention of the mounted police which sparked off the first serious violence of the day, the training video fatally contradicted two key assertions made by the senior police commander. Assistant Chief Constable Clement had maintained earlier in the trial that it was the arrival on the picket line of Arthur Scargill at approximately 8 a.m. in the morning, followed by the NUM president's reckless insistence on 'inspecting' the police lines like a senior military or royal dignitary, that initially incited the day's violence. However, as the same defendant caustically explains,

> Mr Scargill obviously wasn't a very good timekeeper because the video reached 8.10 a.m. and there was still no sign of him and there was still only the occasional missile appearing over police lines. If you had extremely good eyesight it was just possible to detect a baseball cap, partially obscured by bushes, a good distance away from police lines. It was impossible to make a positive identification but if it was Arthur he came nowhere near police lines.[41]

Other excerpts from the video were used alongside still photographs taken by members of the press, to undermine the second of Mr Clement's assertions – that he had *personally witnessed* the incident in which Mr Scargill had been injured, and could therefore vouch for the fact that the miners' leader had lied about having been struck on the head by a riot shield:

> Again it seemed that Mr Clement's reliability as a witness was questionable. He had stated quite categorically that Mr Scargill could not have been hit by a shield-carrying officer because they didn't go anywhere near him and yet here was a photograph which actually showed two riot police standing over him. Arthur himself was in no doubt about what happened neither were the three people standing around him. A riot policeman had run up behind him and simply hit him over the back of his head with a riot shield. At that point Mr Clement was nowhere in sight and appeared over the bridge after it had happened.[42]

Elsewhere in the trial, defence solicitors drew the jury's attention to a secret ACPO (Association of Chief Police Officers) *Tactical Options Manual* which demonstrated that key tactics employed by the police at Orgreave (e.g. the use of police horses to scatter the crowd, the frightening and provocative beating of truncheons on riot shields, and the use of short-shield units to 'incapacitate' missile-throwers or ringleaders by striking them about the arms, legs and torso) had not simply 'evolved' in relation to this particular conflict episode, but were actually well-established components of *official police policy.*[43] Here, then, was a clear indication that, far from having been primarily *reactive,* as senior police and media reporters insisted at the time, numerous instances of police aggression witnessed at Orgreave were, in fact, *strategically preordained.*

Police and media representations of the violent conduct of the day were further discredited when rank-and-file officers appearing as witnesses for the prosecution admitted, under cross examination by defence counsel, that their written statements relating to the events of 18 June had actually been dictated to them by senior officers, or even copied directly from earlier accounts. Some such statements had been submitted up to ten months after the criminal act in question had allegedly occurred.[44] A subsequent television documentary commemorating the thirtieth anniversary of the 'Battle of Orgreave' demonstrated how the statements submitted by no fewer than 31 officers from four different police forces had all included the recurring phrase, 'as we stood there in the line a continuous stream of missiles came from the pickets into the police line … there were no shields being used at this point.'[45]

When placed alongside the police testimonies quoted earlier, the oral and written statements produced at Sheffield Crown Court lend considerable weight to Jackson's claim that, on 18 June at least, short-shield officers had 'run forward knocking down and truncheoning anyone who was in the way, then the casualties were passed back to following officers to arrest. Charges and statements were then made to fit the occasion.'[46]

Major ramifications

There is little doubt that the outcome of the Battle of Orgreave was a source of great satisfaction and 'historic significance' to the police, in the sense that, in their eyes at least, 'It redeemed the Saltley coke depot affair and wiped the slate clean'.[47] It also marked a clear turning point in the direction of the miners' strike, insofar as it provided activists with a chastening lesson of the futility of mass picketing and enforced a major shift in the NUM's strategy, aimed at preventing workers at their own pits from drifting back to work. Seemingly emboldened by their victory at Orgreave, and revelling in the fact that media coverage had portrayed them in such positive light, the police meanwhile showed no compunction in escorting individual or groups of strike breakers back into the mines, even though it would have been impossible for such employees to have engaged in anything truly useful or productive, due to the absence of the wider workforce.[48]

The longer term ramifications of the conflict, and more especially the way that it was represented by the media and in court, were equally significant. Although Orgreave had undoubtedly constituted a 'victory' for the police, it was nonetheless 'a dangerous one', in light of the televised images of their treatment of fleeing miners.[49] The Chief Constable of South Yorkshire publicly conceded afterwards how one incident in particular – the one in which the police officer was filmed repeatedly striking his cowering opponent – had left an indelible stain on the force's reputation 'That incident very nearly lost us Orgreave, in the eyes of the public,' he acknowledged, giving 'credibility to all the other statements of police misbehaviour which were rife.'[50]

The key strikebreaking role subsequently occupied by the police also somewhat predictably guaranteed that,

> Immense ill-will was generated, especially in those closely knit mining communities where feelings of solidarity were outraged by the return of individual miners often not themselves resident in the immediate community. The consequent influx of pickets and police was a high price, paid by the community, for the individual's exercise of his freedom to go to work. The ill-will against the police was undoubtedly compounded by inexcusable conduct by some police officers, but the very exercise of providing police protection was enough.[51]

Searing anti-police resentment in the mining communities of South Yorkshire was compounded by the Chief Constable's steadfast refusal to heed the democratic influence of his local Police Committee by softening his approach.[52] The force's local reputation was further sullied, first by its disingenuous attempt to deflect blame for its mishandling of the Hillsborough disaster (in which 94 Liverpool supporters were crushed to death as a result of crowd congestion) onto the actual victims;[53] and then by the collapse of the Crown Court Orgreave 'riot' trial and the force's subsequent out-of-court settlement in 1991 of half a million pounds in damages to 39 miners arrested on 18 June, who were suing them for 'assault, wrongful arrest, malicious prosecution and false imprisonment'.[54]

Faced with the necessity not only to win back public support and confidence but also to reverse the profound demoralisation now existing at all levels of SYP *as an organisation*, the force formally committed itself to the radical transformation of its everyday dealings with the wider community in general, and its handling of public protest in particular. Such efforts are painstakingly described in one study which shows how, in the early 1990s, SYP used a wide-ranging consultation exercise involving the general public and members of their own organisation to produce a new document (a

Statement of Force Purpose and Values) which set out fresh protocols for the way in which the constabulary would relate to the individuals and communities under its jurisdiction:

> It exhorts staff to strive to act with 'integrity', to be 'honest, courteous and tactful' and to 'use persuasion, common sense and good humour'. It emphasises also that staff should display honesty, humanity and compassion, be willing to listen, to try new ways of working and to admit failings. It is, in sum, a statement which both provides guidance to members of SYP and also gives people expectations concerning how they will be treated in their dealings with the force.[55]

There is substantial evidence to suggest that, following this change of philosophy, SYP has remained steadfastly committed to a far more inclusive and 'facilitating' style of public order policing, which places a much greater priority on the 'right to protest'.[56] The highly repressive and seemingly vengeful way in which the police operation at Orgreave was first prosecuted and then disingenuously portrayed by the media was undoubtedly detrimental to the miners' chances of succeeding in their strike action. However, contradictory legal representations of what happened on 18 June in particular have helped to ensure that the most enduring legacy of Orgreave has been to morally compel the police to adopt a more democratic and permissive approach in their handling of industrial and political dissent.

NOTES

1 Mark Knopfler, 'Iron Hand', on the Dire Straits album, *On Every Street* Wea/Warner Bros, 1991.

2 Richard Hyman, 'Reflections on the mining strike', *Socialist Register*, 1985/86. pp. 330-54, p. 336.

3 Such as Jeremy Deller's partial re-enactment of the Battle of Orgreave, and David Peace's literary account of the mass picket in his novel, GB84. These are discussed in: Michael Bailey, 'The Battle of Orgreave', in Granville Williams (ed.) *Shafted: The Media, the Miners' Strike and the Aftermath,* London: Campaign for Press and Broadcasting Freedom, 2009; and Joseph Brooker, 'Orgreave revisited: David Peace's GB84 and the return of the 1980s', *Radical Philosophy*, 2005.133 pp. 39-51.

4 David P. Waddington, *Contemporary Issues in Public Disorder: A Comparative and Historical Approach,* London: Routledge, 1992; David P. Waddington, Karen Jones & Chas Critcher, *Flashpoints: Studies in Public Disorder*, London: Routledge, 1989.

5 Sarah McCabe & Peter Wallington, *The Police, Public Order, and Civil Liberties*, London: Routledge, 1988.

6 Waddington et al., op. cit.

7 Waddington et al., op. cit.

8 Waddington, op. cit., p. 105.

9 Waddington et al., op. cit.

10 Waddington et al., op. cit.
11 Peter Wilsher, Donald Macintyre & Michael Jones, *Strike: Thatcher, Scargill and the Miners*, London: Coronet Books, 1985.
12 Wilsher et al. op. cit.
13 Waddington et al., op. cit.
14 Waddington et al., op. cit., p. 87.
15 *Sheffield Morning Telegraph*, 19 June 1984.
16 McCabe & Wallington, op. cit., p. 76.
17 Waddington et al., op. cit.
18 Wilsher et al., op. cit., p. 104.
19 McCabe & Wallington, op. cit., 76.
20 Jim Coulter, Susan Miller & Martin Walker, *State of Siege: Miners' Strike, 1984 - Politics and Policing in the Coal Fields*, London: Canary Press, 1984, p. 5.
21 Robert East, Helen Power & Philip A. Thomas, 'The death of mass picketing', *Journal of Law and Society*. Vol. 12 No. 3, pp. 305-319; Waddington et al., op. cit.
22 Victor L. Allen, 'The year-long miners' strike, March 1984 – March 1985: a memoir', *Industrial Relations Journal*, 2009. Vol. 40, No. 4, pp. 278-91, p. 283; McCabe & Wallington, 1988, p. 76; Waddington et al., 1989, p. 87; Wilsher et al., 1985, pp. 102-3.
23 Waddington et al., op. cit., p. 84 and pp. 89-90.
24 Wilsher et al., op. cit., 99.
25 BBC Radio Sheffield reporter, quoted by Waddington et al., op. cit., p. 91.
26 E.G. East et al., op. cit.
27 Quoted by Roger Graef, *Talking Blues: The Police in Their Own Words,* London: Collins Harvill, 1989, p. 62.
28 Quoted by Graef, op. cit., p. 67.
29 Quoted by Graef, op. cit., p. 73.
30 Quoted by Graef, op. cit., p. 73.
31 Quoted by Graef, op. cit., p. 73.
32 Waddington, op. cit., p. 168.
33 Waddington, op. cit.
34 Quoted by Waddington, op. cit., p. 168.
35 Quoted by Waddington, op. cit., p. 169.
36 Quoted by Waddington, op. cit., p. 169.
37 Quoted by Waddington, op. cit., p. 170.
38 Len Masterman, 'The Battle of Orgreave', in Len Masterman (ed.) *Television Mythologies: Stars, Shows and Signs*, London: Comedia, 1985, p. 103, emphasis in original.
39 Quoted in 'A Fair Degree of Force', *Brass Tacks*, BBC 2, 30 November 1985.
40 Bernard Jackson, with Tony Wardle, *The Battle for Orgreave*, Brighton: Vanson Wardle Productions Ltd, 1987, pp. 77-78.
41 Jackson, with Wardle, op. cit., p. 78.
42 Jackson, with Wardle, op. cit., p. 81.
43 McCabe & Wallington, op. cit., pp. 49-50.
44 Jackson, with Wardle, op. cit., pp. 100-101.
45 Quoted in Granville Williams, 'Setting the record straight: *Inside Out* and Orgreave', in Granville Williams (ed.), *Settling Scores: The Media, the Police and the Miners' Strike*, Nottingham: Russell Press, 2014, pp. 59-60.
46 Jackson, with Wardle, op. cit., p. 106.
47 McCabe & Wallington, op. cit., p. 77.
48 Martin Adeney & John Lloyd, *The Miners' Strike 1984-5: Loss Without Limit,* London: Routledge and Keegan Paul, 1986.

49 McCabe & Wallington, op. cit., p. 77.

50 Wilsher et al., op. cit., p. 104.

51 McCabe & Wallington, op. cit., p. 132.

52 Sarah Spencer, 'The eclipse of the police authority', in Bob Fine and Robert Millar (eds.), *Policing the Miners' Strike*, London: Lawrence and Wishart, 1985.

53 Phil Scraton, 'Policing with contempt: the degrading of truth and denial of justice in the aftermath of the Hillsborough disaster', *Journal of Law and Society*, 1999. Vol. 26, No. 3, pp. 273-97; Phil Scraton, 'Death on the terraces: the contexts and injustices of the 1989 Hillsborough disaster', *Soccer and Society*, 2004. Vol. 5, No. 2, pp. 183-200; David P. Waddington, 'Public order policing in South Yorkshire, 1984-2-11', *Contemporary Social Science: Journal of the Academy of Social Sciences*, 2012. Vol. 6, No. 3, pp. 309-24.

54 Seumas Milne, *The Enemy Within: The Secret War Against the Miners*, London: Pan, 1995, p. 24.

55 Robert C. Mawby, *Policing Images: Policing, Communication and Legitimacy*, Cullompten, Devon: Willan Publishing, 2002, p. 119.

56 Hugo Gorringe, Clifford Stott & Michael Rosie, 'Dialogue police, decision making, and the management of public order during protest crowd events', *Journal of Investigative Psychology and Offender Profiling*, 2012. Vol. 9, No. 2, pp. 111-25.; David P. Waddington, 'A "kinder blue": analysing the police management of the Sheffield anti-'Lib Dem' protest of March 2011', *Policing and Society*, 2013. 23(1) pp. 46-64.

Chapter 9

The Minority Report: Being on Strike in Nottinghamshire

David Allsop with Eric Eaton
and Keith Stanley

Introduction

In the period since the 1984/5 Miners' strike, much has been written about that dispute and its aftermath. Indeed, many of the contributors to this book have done so in the past. However, little has been written about the experiences of those miners in Nottinghamshire who remained on strike for the duration of the dispute. When, at the end of the dispute, striking miners in other areas were able to march back to work behind their banners, and led by colliery bands, in Nottinghamshire those who had shown loyalty to the National Union of Mineworkers (NUM) rather than their own Nottinghamshire Miners' Association were disallowed that privilege. Most returned under the heavy hand of colliery managers and spiteful former colleagues, all bent on making life as difficult as possible for those few who had remained loyal to their comrades across the national coalfield.

This chapter is not just an historical commentary on the 1984-85 strike in Nottinghamshire, it is also the story of some of the people who made that history. The first two sections are written in the third person, and are designed to provide the reader with an understanding of the strike as experienced in the Nottinghamshire coalfield. The final part tells the story of the strike and its aftermath by people who experienced it first hand. We refer mainly to three collieries in Nottinghamshire – Sherwood, Newstead and Thorseby – because those were the collieries we worked at, and where our stories unfolded. These stories are in no way unique; similar stories can be found across what was the Nottinghamshire coalfield.

The strike in Nottinghamshire

In the late 1970s the National Coal Board (NCB) began to create divisions between the high and low producing coalfields, primarily through the introduction of an incentive payments system that favoured the high producing mines in Nottinghamshire.[1] It was somewhat prophetic of what was to come in 1984 when in 1977, in two national ballots, the NUM rejected the introduction of a national incentive payment scheme. Rejecting the outcome of both ballots, the Nottinghamshire Area held its own independent ballot for an incentive payment scheme, and voted heavily to support one. Soon after, other NUM areas were negotiating their own incentive payment schemes. (see chapter 5 for further details)

In 1979, the NCB announced the closure of Teversal colliery in Nottinghamshire due to difficult working conditions The NUM's National Executive Committee (NEC) made the decision that if the NCB closed the colliery it would ballot its members nationally for industrial action. However, a decision was taken by the Nottinghamshire Area delegates to hold its own pre-emptive ballot on the closure of Teversal colliery. In the period leading up to the Notts ballot, miners from Teversal colliery travelled to every Nottinghamshire mine calling for support in their fight to save their colliery. Despite these calls for solidarity, 72 per cent of Nottinghamshire miners voted against taking industrial action in support of Terversal colliery and only at the colliery itself was there a majority vote for strike action. These are examples of what Allen[2] calls 'instrumental collectivism', where individuals will only act collectively if it benefits them directly. So, when the call for national strike action came in 1984, it is unsurprising that the majority of Nottinghamshire miners turned their backs on their national union, and continued to work throughout the strike. The primary justification given for this refusal of solidarity was the lack of a national ballot. The beginning of the strike in Nottinghamshire was marked by confusion and uncertainty, as the media were reporting that Scottish and Yorkshire miners were on strike, with other areas expected to follow. The Nottinghamshire Executive Committee was split, with general secretary Henry Richardson and President Ray Chadburn in favour of strike action, while finance officer Roy Lynk and the pensions officer David Prendergast were against. As a consequence of these divisions, no decisions were taken in response to the calls for a national strike in defence of the closure of five mines: Cortonwood and Bullcliffe Wood in Yorkshire; New Herrington in Durham; Snowdown in Kent; and Polmaise in Scotland. It was only when miners at Cortonwood, the first colliery earmarked for closure, walked out at midnight on the 5 March 1984, that the stalemate ended and pickets from Yorkshire began to arrive in Nottinghamshire. After listening to the calls for solidarity from these pickets, many Nottinghamshire miners refused to cross the picket lines. As a result, in the early weeks of the strike, production levels in Nottinghamshire dropped significantly.

Early in the dispute, the Nottinghamshire Area officials who were in favour of the strike tried to stem the flood of pickets arriving in Nottinghamshire, fearing it would be counterproductive and would harden the working miners' attitudes. Once the strike had started events moved quickly and on the 6 March 1984, the National Executive Committee (NEC) of the NUM declared the strikes in Yorkshire and Scotland official, along with any other Area taking similar action under Rule 41.* In attempts to keep Nottinghamshire united, and to prevent the strike collapsing there altogether, Chadburn and Richardson gained approval from the NEC to ballot the Nottinghamshire miners. This decision brought much opprobrium to Nottinghamshire, particularly from the leaders of other area associations, who objected to the idea of working miners being able to vote on the livelihoods of striking miners, whose pits were under the threat of closure.

The date for this ballot was set for the 15 and 16 March 1984. On the 14 March tragedy struck during a mass picket at Ollerton colliery in Nottinghamshire when David Jones, a striking miner from the Yorkshire Area, was killed on the picket line. Scenes of violence between police and pickets following this tragedy were shown in the press and other media, and opponents of the NUM were able to use this tragedy to condemn the miners for the violence and intimidation. As a result, and to ease the tensions that existed, the Nottinghamshire leadership called their members out on strike until the ballot had taken place.

The question on the ballot paper was clear: 'Do you support strike action to prevent pit closures and a massive rundown of jobs.' Out of 27,473 votes cast, 73.5 per cent voted to continue working, and with working miners now in the majority in the Nottinghamshire coalfield, the leadership decided there should be an immediate return to work, a decision that was devastating for those miners already on strike.[3] This left a situation where, with miners across the national coalfields on strike, the majority of Nottinghamshire miners had decided to carry on working. It was not long before the Nottinghamshire Executive Committee, led by Lynk and Prendergast, declared the strike to be both unofficial and unconstitutional. Nottinghamshire had become the key to the strike, and both the government and the NCB knew that if they could keep one of their most productive coalfields working, it would be much easier to defeat the NUM.

* These rules are set out in full in an appendix at the end of this book.

Following the ballot in Nottinghamshire, the NCB obtained an injunction preventing pickets from Yorkshire visiting mines outside their own coalfield. To enforce this injunction Nottinghamshire became a county under siege, with an enormous police presence in the county intent on thwarting the pickets and ensuring working miners had easy access into their mines. Roadblocks were used extensively, primarily to keep pickets from other coalfields out of the county, but equally importantly, to restrict the movement of pickets based there.

On 19 April 1984, at a special NUM Delegates Conference, it was made clear to every miner in Nottinghamshire that the strike was official, in accordance with the national Rule Book, and superseded all decisions taken at Area level. On 25 April 1984, the national president, Arthur Scargill and general secretary, Peter Heathfield, attended a meeting at the Nottinghamshire headquarters to underline the decision taken at that conference. The following day the Nottinghamshire Executive voted 11 votes to 2 (the Executive Committee members voting against were David Prendagast and Roy Lynk) to circulate a notice to all Nottinghamshire branches stating that the strike was now official, and that all branch committees and branch officials should abide by the decision, and should not canvass their membership against that decision.

The following week, the offices of Nottinghamshire were again the centre of attention, when working miners arrived to protest against that decision. Area officials appeared on the balcony of the building to give their own individual perspectives on the strike, and those who were in favour were faced with chants of 'resign or you're sacked'. When Lynk spoke, he told the protesters: 'you voted to work, so carry on working''[4] At an NUM Special Delegates Conference in August 1984, it was deemed necessary to clarify the NUM rulebook regarding strike action after various challenges from working miners. As a result of these deliberations Rule 51 was introduced, to enable the NUM to remove from office any official who had actively worked against the union.

The Nottinghamshire officials sought legal advice on how they could change their own Area rulebook in a way that would allow them to ignore Rule 51 and still retain membership in the NUM. The advice they received suggested that their Area rules could be changed to allow noncompliance with Rule 51, and in December 1984 the Nottinghamshire leadership met to amend the Area rules. The day before that meeting, NUM officials had sought to legally challenge the proposed changes to the Nottinghamshire rule book. In making the judgement, the judge refused to grant an injunction and concluded that if Nottinghamshire did introduce the rule change it would effectively be disaffiliated from the NUM. This warning made no difference and Nottinghamshire officials proceeded with ratifying the amendment.

The tactics for breaking the strike developed by the NCB, the police, and the government were based on the Mohawk Valley Formula, developed in the American steel industry in 1936, for whom Ian MacGregor, the chairman of the NCB, had previously worked.[5] The specific tactics that were implemented from this comprehensive strike-breaking formula included propaganda campaigns; identifying striking union leaders as 'agitators'; placing the 'right to work' at the heart of all communications with the public; describing the police tactics dealing with pickets as 'law and order issues'; using police from other regions; generating a back-to-work movement; and attacking and, whenever possible, raising the issue of trade union democracy.

David Hart, a rich property developer who had made a fortune during the property boom in the early 1970s, played a crucial role in helping to organise and finance a network of disaffected strike breakers around the national coalfields. In three months he travelled over 3,500 miles, holding clandestine meetings with miners in hotels and pubs. He adopted the alias David Lawrence, whilst John Liptrott, branch secretary at Sherwood colliery took the name John Joseph, and was one of the central organisers and litigants of the working miners.[6] Chris Butcher, a blacksmith at Bevercotes colliery in Nottinghamshire, using the nom de plume of 'Silver Birch' to hide his identity, was also financially supported by Hart.

Taken around the national coalfields by the *Mail on Sunday*, Butcher encouraged strike breaking and assisted in setting up other 'back to work' groups in mines wherever he could. With financial help form Hart, Butcher donated £10,000 to help finance legal activities aimed at crippling the NUM.[7] Colin Clark from Pye Hill No.1 colliery and Liptrott from Sherwood colliery held meetings with legal advisors, with the intention of seeing a legal declaration that would make the strike in Nottinghamshire unofficial.

In May 1984 Butcher, along with several other working miners, formed the 'Nottinghamshire Working Miners' Committee' (NWMC) and at that meeting were Liptrott and Clark. The NWMC instigated a legal offensive against the NUM, writing to constituency Labour parties requesting funds, responses to which were generally expressions of disgust. Liptrott then approached the local Conservative associations for financial help and, while the Conservative associations themselves provided no formal financial support, many individual members provided significant funding throughout the strike.[8] Butcher has since admitted that he discussed these strike-breaking initiatives with NCB chairman Ian MacGregor on several occasions. Eventually, Hart was able to fund a National Working Miners' Committee, with around 25 branches of working miners to rally to the call for a return to work. Hart would report regularly to Thatcher and MacGregor, who later wrote: As we chatted I began to realise he was the man I had been looking for. Someone like David could assist in launching campaigns to go after the NUM on legal grounds. [9]

Creating the Union of Democratic Mineworkers

It should be noted that the return to work in most coalfields was more or less a return to normal conditions. In Nottinghamshire, however, things were very different. The pro-strike Nottinghamshire secretary was sacked and complaints were made against the pro-strike Nottinghamshire president. At the same time John Liptrott, the Sherwood branch secretary who opposed the strike, was insisting that striking miners were to be deemed un-financial and therefore should be forced to repay the contributions missed during the strike if they wanted to maintain their membership.

On 22 April 1985 the National Executive Council of the NUM met to hear complaints about Lynk and Prendergast, who were called to answer for their actions during the strike. Lynk was found guilty of gross misconduct, and his contract of employment as a Nottinghamshire official was terminated. Prendergast received a severe reprimand for acts of gross misconduct, with a further threat of the termination of his employment should he continue in his misconduct. The Nottinghamshire Area immediately made provision to negate these findings, and organised a ballot to seek the support of the membership for the Nottinghamshire decision to oppose the rule changes, even if this opposition resulted in expulsion from the NUM. The ballot result was announced on 16 May 1985, with 73 per cent voting to oppose the rules changes made at the Special Delegates Conference in 1984, specifically Rule 51 that allowed the removal from office of any official who actively worked against the union.

In July 1985, following the NUM conference, the NEC accepted the recommendation to expel Lynk and overturned the decision to reprimand Prendergast, instead voting to terminate his contract. In response, Nottinghamshire called a meeting of all branch officials and committee members on the 6 July 1985 to hear reports from the NUM conference, eventually voting 228 votes to 20 in favour of breaking away from the NUM. In September 1985 Nottinghamshire changed its name to the Union of Democratic Mineworkers (UDM), known to loyal Nottinghamshire members as the 'DUM club'.

Shortly after this, and to the disbelief of loyal NUM members, the NCB arbitrarily deemed that every miner, previously a member of the Nottinghamshire Area of the NUM, would automatically become a member of the UDM. Union subscriptions to the NUM, taken directly from wages, were to be sent to what was seen by NUM loyalists as a 'scab' union. To address this problem those NUM loyalists in Nottinghamshire had to reconstitute themselves as a trade union as the law courts had previously ruled that all finances, colliery banners, and properties should be transferred to the UDM, leaving Nottinghamshire with nothing.

Once the Nottinghamshire Area Association had been reformed, Nottinghamshire miners were then offered the opportunity to re-join – a process that was often undertaken in the presence of a member of the management team at each colliery. At each mine the Nottinghamshire Area requested that the 'check off' system for union subscriptions from its members be redirected away from the UDM and paid to the Nottinghamshire Area. The NCB deemed that the administration of a dual system was too arduous and costly and as a result they would not countenance a 'check off' system for the Nottinghamshire Area. This refusal was a blatant tactic designed by NCB to bankrupt the Nottinghamshire Area. To counteract this attack, Nottinghamshire set up its own system for direct debit payments from the membership, a system that largely worked, with many union loyalists signing up immediately.

The situation of Nottinghamshire was further weakened when the NCB, in 1985, unilaterally abandoned the traditional arrangements that had been in place since 1946 and gave notice that, as from May 1986, it would only negotiate wages and conditions if the NUM agreed to accept the majority – minority principle. New conciliation procedures were also agreed with the UDM, again based on the majority – minority principle.[10] The basic structure of these new procedures meant that the majority union, at colliery or Area level, would negotiate for all miners regardless of their union affiliation. Of course, this situation had major implications for Nottinghamshire membership, where the majority union at all collieries was the UDM. It meant that the NUM was no longer recognised for negotiation and representation purposes at any of the Nottinghamshire mines, and that the UDM was representing thousands of NUM members by default. It is important to note here that the decision as to which union had the majority at any individual colliery was taken by the colliery manager. The same majority – minority principle was not offered at national level where the NUM represented 80 per cent of miners, and would have given them sole negotiating rights. The NUM refusal to accept these new conciliation procedures meant that they were formally excluded from national pay negotiations. As a result, all wage agreements were negotiated with the UDM, the minority union nationally, and unilaterally extended to the NUM, who only accepted them as 'interim settlements', but with no further negotiation ever taking place.[11] Soon after this agreement was in place, all four of the elected NUM officials at Sherwood colliery were suspended for posting a leaflet criticising both the leadership of the UDM and the British Coal chairman.* Following these suspensions, the four officials were called in to see the manager and told that, as it would not be in their best interest to continue working at Sherwood colliery, they would be offered severance deals. Given the situation, all four men decided to leave the industry, and Sherwood colliery lost four fine leaders.

The existence of two trade unions representing miners in the industry was fully supported and facilitated by British Coal, whose industrial relations strategy was now based on the institutionalisation of dual unionism, promoting the UDM over the NUM in all bargaining situations, and imposing the agreements reached on wages and working practices on the NUM.

Being on strike in Nottinghamshire

Very early in the strike, as in other coalfields, miners' wives started to get involved in the dispute. Tina Worboys,† wife of Frank Warboys,‡ met with the Sherwood colliery Branch Committee and told them, 'we are either all in this together, or we are not in it at all'. Tina, along with Pam Oldfield,§ and other women at Sherwood, set up their own support group. For the Nottinghamshire women, the situation was tougher than for those in other areas, mainly because the funds of the Nottinghamshire Area were controlled by working miners' leaders Lynk and Prendergast.

Despite these difficulties, each Nottinghamshire mine soon had its own Women's Support Group and these eventually amalgamated to become the Nottinghamshire Miners' Support Group, providing support and advice to the various mining communities throughout Nottinghamshire. Mention must also be made here of Ida Hackett,¶ a key figure within Nottinghamshire Miners' Support Group, who was 70 years old at the start of the strike, and became a local heroine for her tireless work in supporting striking miners.

* The National Coal Board became the British Coal Corporation in 1987.

† Tina Worboys was a member of the Sherwood Colliery Support Group.

‡ Frank Worboys was NUM Branch President of Sherwood Colliery.

§ Pam Oldfield was a member of the Sherwood Colliery Support Group (and the wife of a striking Sherwood miner).

¶ Ida Hackett was a lifelong member of the Communist Party and trade union activist.

At Newstead colliery, Evelyn Stanley* and others set up the 'Annesley and Newstead Support Group' with the intention of raising funds to provide food parcels for striking miners. With the support of the Miners' Welfare Committee at Newstead they were given free access to the miners' welfare hall to provide meals for those families on strike using their own homes to store the food used for the meals. Similar actions took place across Nottinghamshire, and the women involved attended meetings with other groups to discuss ideas for fundraising and the general organisation of food kitchens.

One major problem that faced the women in Nottinghamshire was the lack of support, even animosity, from some in the local Labour Party who would not come out in support due to concerns over alienating working miners, who were the majority group. One example of this reluctance can be seen in the response of local Labour Party councillors to miners' wives from Sherwood colliery. When the women asked for the use of the local Labour meeting hall to provide meals for striking families, the councillors would only agree to the Hall being used by the wives and children of miners, and then only to provide tea and coffee. The miners' wives believe that this compromise was due to the councillors' unwillingness to alienate working miners, thus endangering their possibility of re-election.

Unlike the mining communities outside of Nottinghamshire, there was always the underlying problem of working miners living in the same village. An example of this can be seen in the attempts by the miners' wives from Sherwood colliery to bulk-buy food supplies from local shops. On approaching these shops, they would always be asked to come back when the shop was closed. This was to ensure that their assistance for striking miners was kept secret from the families of working miners, as they believed that such help would be detrimental to their businesses.

As in other areas involved in the strike, both the men and women became involved in all kinds of fundraising activities. They held jumble sales, painted houses and mended cars, anything to raise funds. Newstead became closely involved with a miners' support group in St Albans, which raised funds and also provided holidays for children. The support and friendship from people outside of the mining industry was extremely important, both practically and in terms of morale. Many of these individuals still remain friends today, exchanging Christmas cards and attending various events together. There were also links with mines outside of Nottinghamshire, for example Sherwood colliery forged close links with the miners at Kiverton

* Evelyn Stanley was a key member of the Annesely & Newstead Miners' Support Group (and the wife of Newstead Colliery Branch Delegate Keith Stanley).

Park colliery in South Yorkshire who, while on strike themselves, would offer help and support when they could.

The miners' wives and other supporters of the strike in Nottinghamshire played an enormous part in the strike. Their organisational skills were such that they were able to make sure every family was provided with food, and any other type of support that was required. They took the lead in fundraising, writing to various groups and organisations around the country, outlining the miners cause and seeking financial or any other assistance they could. These local support groups would meet regularly across Nottinghamshire, exchanging ideas and offering support when needed, and would also organise picketing by women. It was at a picket line outside Sherwood Colliery that Anne Scargill, the then wife of Arthur Scargill, was arrested.

Like the striking miners, the wives travelled around Britain explaining the reasons behind the dispute, and seeking support for the families. Many of them made speeches to large audiences, something they would never have dreamed of doing before the strike. As Tina Worboys recalls: 'I asked my husband to write out what I should say, but that didn't last long and I soon got into it, saying what I wanted to say.' The support and dedication of these women will never be forgotten, and many miners believe that without their efforts the strike would have ended much sooner.

Neither should the hard times the children of striking miners had to endure during the dispute be forgotten. Many found themselves queuing up for free school dinners for the first time in their lives, and it soon became clear that many of these children were becoming politicised by the strike. In one school, children of striking miners in receipt of free school meals were segregated from the rest of the children at lunchtime, even from other children receiving free school meals. At this school, the 14-year-old daughter of a striking miner organised a 'walk out' of all miners' children, rather than be humiliated in this way. The following day, and after protests about this segregation from some members of the school staff, the miners' children were allowed back into the general population of the school for their meals.

A more humorous intervention was made at another school when two sons of a striking miner decided to place a picket line outside the school gates, saying to the children as they arrived at school: 'Our Dad is out on strike and we should be supporting him and the other miners. Don't cross the picket line.' Obviously, the other children loved the idea of not going to school, and refused to cross the picket line. The sympathetic head teacher of the school contacted the father of these two boys and asked him to tell them that this was not what the miners wanted; the father willingly complied and the picket line was removed.

Going back to work in Nottinghamshire

On 4 March 1985, the day the strike was called off, I can clearly recall watching the TV news reports of miners from the other coalfields marching proudly back to work behind their banners and their colliery bands. None of this happened for the 37 of us at Sherwood colliery who had remained on strike for the full year, the so-called 'dirty thirty'. In Nottinghamshire, striking miners had been in the minority, and the 'dirty thirty' of Sherwood were instructed to queue up in the street, to wait to see the colliery manager for an individual interview, before we could return to work. On entering his office, it was made clear to each of us that the strike was over and that the union had lost. We were warned about our future behaviour, and we quickly came to realise that there would be a different regime for us than for the rest of the workforce.

We were all split up and placed onto different shifts, and in different parts of the mine, to keep us apart. We were all told the jobs we would be given, and also instructions as to when we were to start back. This was a very anxious time for me; I was put on the night shift and found I would not be starting back with any of my comrades from the strike, nor would any of them be working alongside me. As I walked into the locker room on my first shift back, I was met by an overwhelming silence. As I made my way down to the shaft I was met by 'Sarge', another of the 'dirty thirty', whose shift had just finished. He stopped me and said: 'Just look them in the eye, Dave. We have done nothing wrong or anything to be ashamed about. Just look them in the eye, and they will look away.' I took Sarge's advice, with the result that my worst fears of what might happen to me, being isolated underground with men who had chosen to cross picket lines, remained unfounded. While memories and bitter resentments about the strike ran deep, once back in the environment of the mine, personal antagonisms were in many cases set aside for the duration of the shift, as safety underground is only achievable by co-operation.

On returning to work the eighty miners who had remained on strike at Newstead colliery were also told that they would be seen by the manager on an individual basis. However, as Keith* recalls, 'we sent a message back to the manager informing him that if he would not see us all together then we would not be returning to work. We would not be intimidated. Luckily, we had a somewhat sympathetic manager at Newstead and he readily agreed to our terms.'

* Keith Stanley, was to hold several NUM posts: Newstead Colliery Delegate, Thoresby Branch Secretary, Nottinghamshire Area President, National Vice-Chairman, and National Vice-President.

Many of those miners who had stayed out until the end, especially those who had been vociferous during the strike, were selected by management for the worst jobs, and many were sent to the far reaches of the mine, away from others who had stayed out until the end. Regular work teams before the strike were split up if there was more than one or two strikers in the team. Many such miners in Nottinghamshire returned under the heavy hand of vengeful colliery managers, determined to make life as difficult as possible for the minority of men who had dared remain loyal to the NUM. This macho management strategy towards the NUM was aimed at undermining its power and influence within the workforce.[12] It has been well documented elsewhere that some of the NUM Branch officials were targeted, and sacked almost immediately after the return to work, simply for continuing to follow their union's national policies and procedures.

Paul Whetton was sacked for pinning up a NUM branch meeting schedule at his mine. Mick McGinty was sacked for sitting at a table in the canteen with a few other miners who had stayed out until the end, with the manager claiming it was an illegal NUM meeting on the mine premises. Retrospective action was taken against Mark Hunter and Tony Geddis because, prior the strike, they had leafleted the workforce on the day of a visit to the mine by NCB Chairman, Ian MacGregor. Following a short meeting with the manager, they were sacked. It is interesting to note that each of these individuals was successful in winning an unfair dismissal case at an industrial tribunal hearing. None, however, were successful in regaining their jobs.

Before the strike at Sherwood colliery, David Cope, the Branch Treasurer, would pay out monies from the Branch Benevolent Fund to retired and injured miners every Friday morning. When the strike started, and despite being on strike himself, he continued this practice with the agreement of the (non-striking) Sherwood Branch, and with management seemingly turning a blind eye to his activities. A few weeks into the strike he arrived at the Branch office to find the locks had been changed, and he could not gain access. To maintain this service, David arranged to continue his benevolent activities at a place outside the environs of the mine. He said: 'it was a lovely summer if you recall and I got a great sun tan working from my little wall outside the pit gates every Friday.' It should also be noted that despite being one of the minority on strike at Sherwood, David had been re-elected to the position of Branch Treasurer. His re-election was in contrast to the situation at other mines, where most Branch officials had been voted out, losing their positions to working miners. Jimmy Hood, who had lost the post of Branch Secretary at Ollerton colliery, placed the blame for this on the NCB 'whose disgraceful interference produced a "propaganda machine" against pro-strike union officials.'[13] This was also the case with the Nottinghamshire Area elections, with 29 out of the 31 council seats won by non-striking miners. This resulted in the Nottinghamshire funds falling into the hands of miners who had worked throughout the strike, and any meagre help that may have been forthcoming from sympathetic Nottinghamshire officials was now cut off, with the balance of power in the Nottinghamshire coalfield now decisively in the hands of miners who had remained at work throughout the strike.

Soon after the strike ended, however, there was evidence of miners who had been on strike being elected to Branch positions. When Sherwood colliery Branch elections were held in 1985, following the return to work, all four of the main branch official posts – treasurer, secretary, president, and delegate – were won by previously striking miners. John Liptrott, the branch secretary who had worked throughout the strike and was one of the main voices of the back to work movement, lost his position in the branch in these elections. I think that we can conclude from these instances of striking miners being voted in as Branch officials in Nottinghamshire that the miners in Nottinghamshire, despite working during the strike, still wanted to be represented by the best possible people.

Fighting back

In 1987 British Coal closed Newstead colliery, allegedly on the grounds of it being uneconomic, though Keith Stanley firmly believes that it was more to do with the fact that it was seen as having militant workforce and, like Sherwood colliery, miners there were re-joining Nottinghamshire and coming close to attaining a majority of the workforce. He believes that a majority of Nottinghamshire members at any Nottinghamshire mine would have caused major problems for British Coal. Whatever the reason for the closure, it resulted in well-respected Nottinghamshire officials and other miners who had been on strike, transferring to Thoresby colliery in north Nottinghamshire. Two of these individuals were Keith Stanley and Eric Eaton,* both very experienced and well respected as both trade unionists, and miners. On their arrival at Thoresby colliery, both started to attend the local Nottinghamshire branch meetings, and very quickly were elected as Branch officials. On taking office, they both recognised the massive task facing them, not just in terms of representing Nottinghamshire membership at the mine, but also in trying to win back members from the UDM, all against a background of serious management hostility.

* Eric Eaton. Former Nottinghamshire Branch Secretary at Thoresby Colliery, and Nottinghamshire Miners' Association Chairman

Not being recognised by British Coal meant that the Nottinghamshire Branch at Thoresby colliery had no office, no telephone, no notice board, and no direct route to management when problems were raised by their members. At disciplinary hearings, NUM members were not allowed formal representation by their own union officials, so all representation had to be undertaken by either Eric or Keith in the role of a 'friend'. Due to the industrial relations situation at Thoresby colliery, both developed a lot of new 'friends' as they struggled to represent their membership.

In order to maintain a visible presence and to continue to organise on behalf of Nottinghamshire they developed various strategies to overcome the obstacles placed in their way by a hostile management. Keith, the branch secretary, began to organise the membership in different way: 'I organised what I called "shift-contact people", people who were NUM members. There was at least one of these individuals present on every coaling shift, who systematically referred any problems back to the NUM officials.'

The aim was to demonstrate that Nottinghamshire had a visible presence at the colliery, was actively involved on behalf of the membership, and was able to provide information and support at shift level. This was achieved despite the presence of UDM representatives and hostile management attitudes. Given that the Nottinghamshire representatives had no base from which to operate, they worked from their changing room lockers. As Eric reported 'we had to keep all our paperwork in our lockers. It was the only way we could maintain a presence at the mine.'

The situation was complicated. In the coalfields where the majority of miners had been involved in the strike, those who had abandoned the strike were ostracised. In Nottinghamshire, the miners who had been on strike were the ones ostracised. The open hostility evident in other coalfields towards the 'scabs' was, in many cases in Nottinghamshire replaced, by 'leg pulling' and 'banter'. The term scab was used for those who had not just worked, but had tried to damage the NUM. Eric argues that this dual approach served two purposes: firstly, in the working relationships underground 'you need to look after each other down there, whoever you are. You don't mess about, but there was banter, there was definitely banter and leg pulling'. Second, the Nottinghamshire officials and Nottinghamshire members were actively engaged in trying to win back members from the UDM, and the 'banter and leg pulling' enabled them to engage in light hearted discussions about which union best promoted their interest. As Keith suggests:

> You've got to remember that most of our members were ex-UDM who had re-joined the Nottinghamshire Area and that's what we wanted, to

> break the back of the UDM. We started recruiting miners back into Nottinghamshire simply by spreading the Nottinghamshire gospel and exposing the weakness of the officials of the UDM.

The difficulty in working under such constricted conditions can be seen in an example given by Keith who, on one occasion, was contacted underground by the personnel manager, who told him to come to the surface to attend a disciplinary hearing as the 'friend' of a Nottinghamshire member. On arrival at the manager's office, the personnel manager informed him that the individual who was to be represented had not turned up for the meeting. The personnel manager then told Keith that he was considering stopping his time for coming out of the mine early. On suggesting that he came out of the mine on the instructions of the Personnel Manager himself, he was informed that he was to be made an example of, to discourage miners for not attending disciplinary hearings. This ludicrous situation was only solved when Keith threatened to take the matter to an industrial tribunal. The ridiculous position taken by the personnel manager can be seen as laughable, but Keith believes his intent was not.

In order to gain access to management, Nottinghamshire officials at Thoresby colliery often used Health and Safety legislation. At a branch meeting it was decided that the Branch Secretary should to write to the colliery manager to highlight their concerns over a range of health and safety issues at the mine. Keith reports that 'I wrote on many occasions to the colliery manager on matters of safety at the mine and never once received a response, not even when seeing him underground'. In response to this refusal to acknowledge his concerns Keith informed the local press, who then challenged the manager to say why he would not deal with these safety concerns raised by the Nottinghamshire Area. The manager responded by saying 'we take advice on what the unions are sending us, and if we feel it warranted action, we would look to do so'. Unhappy with this response, the branch took the decision to write to the Mines Inspectorate expressing their concerns about managements' refusal to meet with Nottinghamshire over health and safety issues at the colliery.

The response from the Mines Inspectorate was that, 'we cannot get involved in industrial relations issues and the politics of the industry'. However, they did promise to treat any health and safety reports sent to them by the NUM seriously, and to investigate if necessary. Fearing that this would mean constant mine inspections, the NUM were offered an 'open door policy' at all the Nottinghamshire pits on health and safety issues. This victory for the Nottinghamshire Area meant that they had created an opportunity to represent their member's health and safety concerns and, as Keith said, 'we took every opportunity to raise other issues with management in those meetings'.

The tactics outlined above, in dealing with working miners and health and safety issues, helped facilitate a significant increase in NUM membership across the Nottinghamshire coalfield. The Tory government's policy also assisted with this, as the banning of 'closed shops' for unions allowed workers to choose which union, if any, they wanted to represent them. However, any member of the workforce at Thoresby colliery who chose to sign over to the Nottinghamshire Area was interviewed by the management at the pit enquiring if they had been bullied into a return. Indeed, on losing a member to the NUM, the UDM officials immediately requested that the colliery manager intervene. Keith was asked on several occasions by management if he was coercing men to re-join, or was enticing them with false promises.

Keith also recalls that after a further productive period of membership recruitment he was told that the team he worked with underground (all Nottinghamshire members by that time) was being taken off its normal job, to be sent to another section of the mine, isolating them from the rest of the workforce.

> We were put on a permanent 7 a.m. shift, which meant that we would no longer be in contact with other workers, working the three-shifts system at the pit. Quite simply, I was taken out of the equation with regard to recruitment. We did, however, have a news-sheet/bulletin called *The Miners' Next Step,* which was regularly dropped in and around the pit-top canteen and baths, allowing our message to continue to be heard by the workforce.

Following the strike, the members of the Nottinghamshire Area faced thirty years of draconian tactics designed by the management, either under the NCB, British Coal or, following the privatisation of the industry in 1995, RJB Mining and UK Coal, to marginalise the union. Right up until Thoresby, the last working Nottinghamshire colliery, closed in July 2015 the union was never formally recognised. Throughout those struggles, Eric and Keith were told on numerous occasions by the manager that they were no more than militant dinosaurs of the trade union movement, and that they would remain ineffective and ignored by the miners. When they asked the manager if his description of them was true, why was it that miners continued to re-join the NUM, the manager simply walked away. Eric and Keith never did.

Since the strike, Keith and Eric have worked together trying to rebuild the Nottinghamshire Area. Keith has also done so on a national basis, through his roles as a branch official, Nottinghamshire Area president, national vice-chairman, and finally national vice-president of the NUM. Eric has done so, initially as branch official, moving up to become Nottinghamshire Area president. On 15 November 2005 they launched the Nottinghamshire Ex and Retired Miners Association, with Eric becoming its Chairman. Along with 400 others I am proud to be part of the association. Even though the last colliery in Nottinghamshire closed in July 2015, and although both Eric and Keith have retired from the industry, they still remain active in maintaining an NUM presence in Nottinghamshire. They continue to provide advice and assistance to ex miners and their families, and are vociferous in fighting the injustices forced on their communities by successive governments.

Epilogue

After a falling out with Clark and Liptrott, Butcher was eventually expelled from the organisation he had created. After Bevercotes colliery closed in 1993, *The Guardian* newspaper asked him if he had any regrets in the role he had played during the strike. He replied: 'No. If I regret one thing, it is that at the time I was running around the country as Silver Birch, I didn't know what the story was worth',[14] which suggests that his main motive and concern was to gain monetary value from his actions. Called 'Dutch Elm' by Yorkshire miners (a tree that rots from within), his actions, and the actions of others in Nottinghamshire campaigning against the NUM, still resonate today, with Mansfield Town and Nottingham Forest football fans bombarded by 'scab' chants from the supporters of opposing teams, as well as the more serious problems of inter-family disputes. The most serious of these occurred in the ex-mining community of Annesley when a murder was committed in 2004, following an argument about crossing the picket lines during the strike.

NOTES

1 David Allsop, Unpublished PhD. *Restructuring, Management Strategies and Trade Union Responses in the Privatised UK Coal Industry: A case study of UK Coal*, 2007.

2 Victor Leonard Allen, *The Militancy of the Miners,* Shipley: The Moor Press, 1981.

3 Harry Patterson, *Look Back in Anger: The miners' strike in Nottinghamshire 30 years on,* Nottingham: Five Leaves Publications, 2014, p. 79.

4 Patterson, op. cit. p. 91.

5 For a full explanation of the 'Mohawk Valley Formula' see Benjamin Stolberg, ''Vigilantism', *The Nation*, 1937, Vol. 145, No. 7, pp. 166–168; https://www.youtube.com/watch?v=9pexQ7_tueg

6 Seumas Milne, *The Enemy Within: The Secret War against the Miners*, London: Verso, 2014, p. 324.

7 *The Guardian*, 1 March 2004.

8 Patterson, op. cit., p. 93.

9 Ian MacGregor, *The Enemies Within,* London: Collins Sons & Co Ltd., 1986. p. 220.

10 Jonathon Winterton & Ruth Winterton, 'Coal', in Andrew Pendleton, & Jonathon Winterton, (eds.), *Public Enterprise in Transition, Industrial Relations in State and Privatized Corporation,* London: Routledge, 1993, pp. 69-99.

11 Steve Leman, & Jonathon Winterton,'New Technology and the Restructuring of Pit Level Industrial Relations in the British Coal Industry', *New Technology Work and Employment*, Vol. 5, 1991, pp. 54-64.

12 Winterton & Winterton, op. cit.

13 Patterson op. cit. p. 128.

14 *The Guardian*, 1 March 2004.

Part 3

Ongoing Issues

Chapter 10

Orgreave: the Battle for Truth and Justice

Granville Williams

'The trade union movement does not forget. That is one of the things that keep it alive, but sometimes the past seems to matter too much.'

The journalist and historian Andy Beckett made the above statement following his visit to the exhibition hall at the 2015 Trades Union Congress in Brighton.[1] His comment was directed at the stall of the Orgreave Truth and Justice Campaign (OTJC). For many people born after the strike, what happened at Orgreave on 18 June 1984 is history. This, however, is not the case for those miners who were brutally assaulted, arrested and charged that day, nor for their supporters. Orgreave, near Rotherham in South Yorkshire, was the site of a coking plant supplying local steelworks, and stopping the coal reaching that site was a key goal of the National Union of Mineworkers (NUM). On that day, in what became known as the 'Battle of Orgreave' police from ten separate forces were mobilised against picketing miners.

18 June 1984

Prior to the 18 June, the police had always kept the pickets well back from the site of the Orgreave coke works, ensuring that there would be no disruption. On the 18th, and to the surprise of the miners, the police made no attempt to prevent them reaching their works. There were no roadblocks, no halting of miners' vehicles on the motorways and other road networks leading to Orgreave. Instead of keeping them at a distance, the miners were advised where to park their vehicles, and were then directed into a field near the works. An estimated 10,000 miners were eventually gathered in an open area that was surrounded on three sides by massed ranks of police.

That June day was hot, and the miners were lightly clad, with many in shorts, tee-shirts and plimsolls. The mood was good-natured, with the usual humorous banter from the pickets. Without warning, the massed police ranks opened, and mounted, baton-wielding police officers charged forward. At full gallop, they hurtled into the ranks of the miners, battering all within reach with their truncheons. This mounted charge was followed up by police officers on foot, again wielding batons. The miners, now in disarray, ran from the onslaught, and as they did police, battering their backs and heads, continued their attack. Beaten miners, some with their heads bloodied, were arrested as the assault continued.

That day 95 miners were arrested and many of them were charged with riot, an offence that carries a potential life sentence. At the eventual trial, held in Sheffield in May 1986, which lasted 48 days, the charges were dismissed as evidence of police collusion in the preparation of statements became known. Those falsely charged miners were eventually paid collective compensation amounting to £425,000.

More than three decades after those events at Orgreave, the miners who were involved continue to live with the physical and mental trauma caused by their experiences that day. As a group, they are aging and some have died; the need for an inquiry grows ever more urgent. The Orgreave Truth and Justice Campaign (OTJC) was specifically established to get to the truth about who was responsible for what became known as the 'Battle of Orgreave'. This chapter explores barriers to the emergence of an answer to that question and how the OTJC has, in a short space of time, mobilised significant support for such an inquiry.

Orgreave: obstacles to the truth

The OTJC was set up 28 years after the miners' strike, which begs the question why did it take so long to organise a campaign for a public inquiry into the policing at Orgreave? After all, anyone involved on 18 June 1984 knew what the police tactics were, and who was responsible for the resultant carnage. Police leaders openly recognised the political purpose of the assault on pickets at Orgreave at the time, as George Moores, Chair of South Yorkshire Police Committee commented:

> No one was stopped from going to Orgreave. They wanted to get them all together and have a real go at them. The government engineered that confrontation. The crime should be laid at their door. Their message to the police was, 'Go in and hit them hard'. The use of dogs and horses was terrifying. They wanted Orgreave to be a media spectacle and then blame the violence on pickets. [2]

The answer to the question about the lack of a public inquiry lies, to a large extent, in the way in which the media distorted the actions of the police and in the confidence of the public in the neutrality and effectiveness of the British police.

Two accounts of events at Orgreave on 18 June 1984 were on the evening news that day. One account was to shape the way the media reported the miners' strike over the following months and years; the other was to be marginalised. The lead story on BBC1's early evening news was the events at Orgreave. A single violent image was projected behind the newsreader: a man, presumably a miner, taking a running kick at a policeman. The film extract of miners attacking the police from which this image was taken was shown again and again on BBC programmes over the following week. The scene setting introduction for the story stated:

> Over 5,000 pickets at Orgreave fought a pitched battle with over 2,000 policemen. Mr. Scargill, who had been directing operations on a two-way radio, was found sitting on a kerb looking stunned after policemen with riot shields had run by under a hail of stones. He believes he was hit by a riot shield. A senior police officer says he saw him slip off a bank and hit his head on a sleeper, but does not know whether he had already been injured.

John Thorne's report for the BBC followed, presenting three themes: the military style planning of the operation by Arthur Scargill; doubt about whether the head injuries he sustained were actually inflicted by the police; and the essentially defensive and reactive nature of the police role in the conflict. The violence at Orgreave was presented unequivocally as picket violence with Thorne stating, 'The attacks on individual policemen were horrific. The police commanders said it was a miracle that no-one was killed.'

ITN's coverage of Orgreave was completely different. Their report, and the images that accompanied it, made it clear that some of the worst violence was administered by heavily armed riot police on anyone they could catch. These actions by the police were not spontaneous, but were part of a planned operation. The images which followed, in contrast to the BBC who omitted any reference to the extraordinary scenes of police violence, showed a policeman repeatedly clubbing a fallen man. An arrested man – seen being frog-marched behind police lines – yells to the ITN the camera crew: 'You want to get in there and see what they are doing.' The report concluded that miners who went to help their fellow workers were being truncheoned, and the direction in which they were running demonstrated that the 'horrific violence' attributed to them was carried out in defence of fellow miners who were under attack from the police.[3]

How could two journalists, both at the same event, file such conflicting reports? After all, unlike newspapers, broadcast news was, and is, required to be impartial. The charge against the BBC is that it suppressed police violence that day, by selective editing, and the minutes of the BBC News and Current Affairs dated 19 June 1984 reveal that Alan Protheroe, the BBC's Assistant Director General, recognised this, stating that he 'had the feeling that the BBC's early evening coverage might not have been wholly impartial'.[4]

Over the course of the strike, the narrative of 'picket line violence' framed the BBC's reporting of the strike generally. Indeed, with the exception of Channel 4 News, which stood out for balance in reporting the dispute, broadcasters generally followed the BBC in presenting striking miners as violently out of control. This was powerfully reinforced by national newspaper coverage of the dispute.

In 1984 the average circulation of national morning newspapers was 15,487,000 and Sunday newspapers 17,827,000.[5] A key feature of 75 per cent of these was that, editorially, they were strong supporters of the Conservative Party. Even leading Tories were willing to openly acknowledge the propaganda importance of the press. Former Conservative MP Ian Gilmour claimed that they, 'scarcely could have been more fawning if it had been state controlled, and indeed a liberal use of the honours system to knight editors and ennoble proprietors produced much the same effect.'[6]

The consequence of this press bias was a stream of front page headlines, news reports and photographs, which projected a totally inaccurate and distorted picture of the causes and conduct of the miners' strike. The front page of *The Sun*, the day after Orgreave, had the bold banner headline 'CHARGE' and the subheading 'Mounties rout miners'. Bullet points listed 'Scargill's Toll of Shame' (41 police injured, 82 pickets held, 28 pickets hurt) and the report by Jim Oldfield started 'mounted police made an amazing cavalry charge on picketing miners yesterday. The officers faced a hate barrage of bricks, bottles and spears as they broke up a bloody riot.'[7] One miner commented on media coverage: 'I object to the way they have personalised the strike as if it's between Arthur Scargill and MacGregor because it ignores all of us on strike and our views, along with the issues we are striking for.'[8]

Distortion and bias are created just as much by what is not published, as what is. Headlines about violence against the police by working miners dominated, whilst violence inflicted on striking miners by the police was notable by its absence. David Thacker, a television and theatre director, commented on the interviews he recorded with striking miners after the dispute:

> Running through all the accounts we heard were two central themes. Firstly, there was the appalling violence and brutality by the police during the strike. They were outraged no one knew about these things. This was the second recurring theme, they were astonished by the wall of silence in the media.[9]

The now famous photograph taken by John Harris of Lesley Boulton at Orgreave, of a mounted policeman swinging his baton at her as she is calling for an ambulance to help an injured miner, was studiously ignored by Britain's national newspapers. Where it was shown, attempts were made to discredit it, as such a shocking image clashed with the dominant narrative of violent pickets assaulting the police at Orgreave on 18 June 1984.[10]

Len Masterman made the point in 1984 that challenging media distortions and lies about the strike is an essential part of establishing the truth about policing at Orgeave.

> One does not have to enquire very deeply into the miners' dispute to discover that police violence and intimidation are very much live issues and are, indeed, topics of major concern in many mining communities. And one does not have to be inordinately suspicious to suggest that the persistent absence from media accounts of this aspect of the strike may constitute a sanitizing operation of considerable proportions.[11]

Unravelling the rhetoric

If the dominant media narrative during the strike was hostile to the miners, another obstacle, in terms of public opinion, was the erroneous belief that the police forces deployed against the miners were really citizens in uniform and that allegations of systematic, officially sanctioned police violence, or the use of fabricated evidence, were not credible. It took some years for this viewpoint to unravel and the public's perception of policing to change.

The miscarriages of justice associated with the Guildford Four, the Maguire Seven and the Birmingham Six, revealed during the late 1980s and early 1990s, exposed police fabrication of evidence and confessions extracted through beatings. The death of Ian Tomlinson on 1 April 2009 after an assault on him by a police officer with the Metropolitan Police's Territorial

Support Unit, provided another insight. Tomlinson was not involved in the G20 protests taking place that day, and was attacked as he simply walked by. The first statement offered by the Metropolitan Police later that day said that police had been alerted that a man had collapsed, and that they had been attacked by 'a number of missiles' as they tried to save his life. On the 4 April, the City of London police issued a statement that, 'A post mortem examination found he died of natural causes. [He] suffered a sudden heart attack while on his way home from work.' It was only when *The Guardian* published video footage on 7 April, supplied by a bystander, that the full picture of what happened emerged. When *The Guardian* posted this on their website a police officer and IPCC investigator visited the paper and asked that it be removed as it was 'jeopardizing' their inquiries.[12]

Following these events, and with subsequent cases of deaths in custody, the excessive force and 'kettling' tactics used to contain peaceful student demonstrators protesting against the trebling of tuition fees in December 2010, mistrust of the police significantly increased.[13] During another demonstration, a mounted policeman grabbed the hair of a student and he fell from his horse; when the student's brother came to his assistance the police attacked them both with truncheons. After a trial, at which they were found not guilty, the two brothers sued the police for malicious prosecution and assault and battery, and on 22 September 2015 each received £25,000 in compensation and a written apology from the Metropolitan Police. One of the brothers commented:

> I used to have a very positive view of the police, now it's a very negative view. Through all these things that have happened I certainly don't trust the police. We were told by our lawyers that the likelihood of us being found not guilty, due to the number of police witnesses, was extraordinarily low. It's only due to the fact that we were able, with our mum, to put together a lot of data, a lot of video footage for the trial, that we were able to be found not guilty. I frequently worried that I was going to go to prison, that I was going to be incarcerated for something that was not of our doing at all.[14]

September 2012: the truth begins to emerge

Against the background outlined above, two specific events spurred a group of concerned people to set up the OTJC. The first of these events was the report of the Hillsborough Independent Panel (HIP), released in September 2012.[15] The second was the broadcasting of the regional current affairs programme *Inside Out* in October 2012.[16]

In April 1989, 96 men, women and children had been crushed to death at the Hillsborough football stadium in Sheffield. There are many parallels between events at Orgreave and what happened that day, particularly the misinformation and distortion of facts by the media, South Yorkshire Police, and politicians. The Hillsborough report concluded that football fans were innocent of any wrongdoing on that day, contradicting the widely disseminated media accusation that drunken Liverpool fans had played a major causal role in the disaster:

> There was no evidence to support the proposition that alcohol played any part in the genesis of the disaster, and it is regrettable that those in positions of responsibility created and promoted a portrayal of drunkenness as contributing to the occurrence of the disaster and the ensuing loss of life without substantiating evidence.[17]

The initial official report into the disaster, carried out by Lord Taylor and published in 1990, made clear that the main reason for the disaster was 'the failure of police control' and concluded that the South Yorkshire Police (SYP) senior officers in command on the day presented as 'defensive and evasive witnesses' who had refused to accept any responsibility for error. He went on to point out that, 'in all, some 65 police officers gave oral evidence at the Inquiry. Sadly, I must report that for the most part the quality of their evidence was in inverse proportion to their rank.'

The report also detailed the changes made in police statements following the disaster. A team of SYP officers and a solicitor were involved in this process and the report concluded that in total 116 statements were amended to remove or alter comments unfavourable to South Yorkshire Police. The report also made it clear that:

> Examination of officers' statements show that officers were discouraged from making criticisms of senior officers' responses, their management and deficiencies in the SYP operational response: key words and descriptions such as 'chaotic' were counselled against and, if included, were deleted.[18]

The media were also heavily criticised for spreading 'unproven and unsubstantiated allegations' which had persisted for years in public perceptions of the disaster. As the severity of the disaster became apparent on the day, SYP Match Commander, Chief Superintendent David Duckenfield, told senior officials that 'Liverpool fans had broken into the stadium and caused an inrush into the central pens thus causing the fatal crush'. This was a lie to which Duckenfield finally admitted at the Hillsborough inquests in March 2015. The report notes that 'this unfounded allegation was broadcast internationally, and was the first explanation of the cause of the disaster to enter the public domain'. It is clear that SYP, in the days after the disaster disseminated a distorted, emotive, and sensational version of events that was repeated by local, regional and national newspapers and the broadcast media.

Documents disclosed to the inquiry show that the allegations had been filed by White's News Agency, a Sheffield based company. The documents emerged as a result of meetings that took place over a three-day period between agency staff and several police officers, as well as interviews with Irvine Patnick MP, and the SYP Federation Secretary, Paul Middup. A further document recorded a meeting in Sheffield of Police Federation members on the morning of the now notorious edition of *The Sun* newspaper. Under a banner headline 'THE TRUTH', the paper alleged that Liverpool fans had assaulted and urinated on police officers resuscitating the dying, stolen from the dead and verbally and sexually abused an unconscious young woman. Paul Middup confirmed that putting the police side of the story to the press and other media had been a priority. The Hillsborough Panel, however, reached different conclusions, finding that there was:

> No evidence among the vast number of disclosed documents and many hours of video material to verify the serious allegations of exceptional levels of drunkenness, ticketlessness or violence among Liverpool fans. There was no evidence that fans had conspired to arrive late at the stadium and force entry, and no evidence that they stole from the dead and dying. Documents show that fans became frustrated by the inadequate response to the unfolding tragedy. The vast majority of fans on the pitch assisted in rescuing and evacuating the injured and the dead.[19]

On 12 October 2012, the Independent Police Complaints Commission (IPCC) announced an investigation into events at Hillsborough, the biggest independent review of the police ever conducted. By December 2013, the investigation had identified a total of 240 officers whose statements may have been altered and had interviewed 143 of these officers. Thirteen police officers refused to be interviewed. The IPCC sifted through a vast amount of information in preparation for the new inquests into the 96 deaths at Hillsborough that began in March 2014, 25 years after the tragedy.

The second event leading to the creation of the OTJC was the revelations in a BBC Yorkshire and Lincolnshire regional current affairs programme *Inside Out*, broadcast on 22 October 2012. Dan Johnson, a BBC journalist with strong connections to the NUM in South Yorkshire, presented the programme. The introductory section made a direct link between the evidence uncovered by Johnson on the 'doctored' police statements after Orgreave, stating that they 'could have led to the culture which five years later would see the cover up at Hillsborough'. The programme revealed that SYP senior police officers had deliberately edited the statements of junior officers to allow them to prosecute miners for the serious charge of riot. While generally well received, the programme also provided a focus for the bitter and long-standing feelings amongst miners about the role of the police at Orgreave, and more broadly throughout the strike. This programme prompted Barbara Jackson,[20] a former member of the white-collar section of the NUM, COSA, to call an exploratory meeting, in Sheffield in November 2012, to discuss what could be done about the role of SYP at Orgreave, with the outcome of the creation of the Orgreave Truth and Justice Campaign.

November 2012: The fight for justice begins

Following information that the IPCC would be releasing their decision as to whether there would be an investigation into events at the Orgreave coking plant in 1984, the OTJC met to outline their response to the this decision. What happened over the next two and a half days was truly remarkable for a fledgling organisation that had no paid workers and relied totally on the dedication of its supporters to function. It also provides an insight into the distinctive qualities of a campaigning group that has since made such an impact nationally.

In anticipation of the announcement, the OTJC had prepared two news releases to deal with either outcome, and the NUM agreed that their planned media operation could be organised from their headquarters in Barnsley. The OTJC had speculated that the IPCC decision would be negative, a speculation that was confirmed the following day. The IPCC eventually produced two documents, the result of a tortuous two and a half year exercise, to which the OTJC had provided a substantial amount of material.[21]

The first document published made it clear that the wider political and symbolic goal of the police and state actions at Orgreave were beyond the remit of the IPCC, but that these could be brought into focus through a public enquiry or an exercise similar to the Hillsborough Independent Panel. It noted, 'Nothing in this report precludes such an exercise; indeed the lengthy work done in finding and reading documentation would provide a starting point for it.' The IPCC also made some damning comments about the SYP. The heavily redacted paragraph 55 in the IPCC decision document states:

> There is no direct evidence that senior officers involved in Orgreave conspired to encourage or instruct officers to commit perjury. It is however of particular concern that our review found evidence that the senior officers became aware, after the event, of instances of perjury by SYP officers but did not wish it to be disclosed. [redacted] The unwillingness to disclose evidence of wrongdoing by officers does raise doubts about the ethical standards of officers in the highest ranks of SYP at that time. [redacted]

Paragraph 57 of the document states: 'The evidence from hospital records was that more pickets than police officers required treatment. Some injuries to pickets were serious, including head injuries.' The second document published pointed to the absence of any 'operational order' and comments:

> It would seem obvious that there must have been more detailed planning for the event, given the number of officers whose presence was arranged through the National Reporting Centre. However, if more detailed planning was recorded in a document, it has not been found during the review and does not appear to have been included in any list of documents for the civil proceedings that followed the events at Orgreave (which it should have been if it did exist).

Paragraph 36 also notes that 'some of those documents disclose that SYP acknowledged privately to their solicitors that many officers did "over react" (sic) and there was evidence of perjury relating to at least two arrests.'

In the end, the IPCC took the line that it all happened too long ago for them to investigate, and that they did not have the resources to undertake such an investigation. Nevertheless, the IPCC publications did provide the OTJC with a clear focus for their dealings with the media over the next day and a half.

That afternoon, at the hastily arranged press conference organised by the OTJC, the press and media focused on Kevin Horne, a miner arrested at Orgreave, and NUM member Dave Douglass. Others from the OTJC also provided interviews. The following day at the NUM headquarters building, an OTJC press conference was held with a range of individuals from the NUM and the OTJC. There was a poignant moment when Arthur Critchlow, a miner who had been badly hurt at Orgreave, spoke about his injuries. He was joined by Paul Winter, another other former miner who was also at Orgreave, who gave a powerful testimony:

> It was the most harrowing and terrifying experience of my life, but what I remember most vividly was seeing a man in his 50s wet himself through fear. We had nowhere to run. They made sure we were all enclosed in that one field, the Orgreave plant on one side, railway line to another, a road to the other side and then trees and woods. When you ran to the trees, you were met with dogs. I could hear people screaming as they were bitten.

With the IPCC report receiving prominent coverage across all national and regional media, the OTJC was able to press for a full public inquiry into the policing of the pickets at Orgreave. This call for a public inquiry became the focus for all OTJC activity. Seizing an opportunity to keep the issue alive, the OTJC organised a demonstration on the anniversary of the Battle of Orgreave, at Old Bridge near to the site of the infamous police action 31 years before.

On the Parliamentary front an Early Day Motion (EDM) had 61 signatures by 24 June 2015, stating that:

> This House strongly condemns the decision of the Independent Police Complaints Commission not to launch a full and comprehensive investigation into the behaviour of South Yorkshire Police at the Orgreave Coking Plant on 18 June 1984; it believes there is no time limit to justice and furthermore that mining communities up and down the country deserve the truth; and calls for a wider public inquiry covering not only the policing of Orgreave but of the entire country during the 1984-85 Miners' Strike.

Sixty-two Labour MPs joined with the OTJC in signing a letter asking for an urgent meeting with then Home Secretary, Theresa May, to make the case for a full public inquiry into the policing at Orgreave. The letter argued that:

> … in light of the seriousness of the allegations against South Yorkshire Police, including perjury, perverting the course of justice, misconduct in a public office, and whether the actions of the police were influenced by the highest levels of government and finally given the scale of public concern, the case for a full public inquiry into the events of Orgreave is clear.

In July 2015 members of the OTJC, including miners arrested on 18 June 1984, OTJC's lawyers and a delegation of MPs that included Louise Hague, Labour MP for Sheffield Heeley, met with Theresa May, to present the case for a full public inquiry. Following that OTJC worked with a team of top legal experts to prepare the legal case for an independent inquiry into policing at Orgreave. This was presented to the Home Secretary on Tuesday 15 December 2015. At the same time, the OTJC launched a campaign on social media to publicise this case and build wider support for the campaign's work.

Several months elapsed but the OTJC did not put pressure on the Home Secretary for a decision, as the inquests into the Hillsborough disaster were proceeding. After the Hillsborough verdicts were announced on 26 April 2016,[22] another problem arose. The referendum decision to leave the European Union prompted the resignation of the Prime Minister, David Cameron, in July 2016. Theresa May was elected leader of the Conservative Party and therefore Prime Minister. A new Home Secretary, Amber Rudd, became the focus for the OTJC's attention. At a meeting with Rudd on 13 September, the OTJC were informed that a decision would be reached on an inquiry in October. On 31 October 2016, Amber Rudd announced that the government had decided not to hold an inquiry.

Truth and Justice

Amber Rudd's decision not to hold an inquiry led the OTJC to call a news conference in the NUM Hall in Barnsley the next day. All the national television news channels were there, as well as local, regional and national newspapers. They were presented with a clear message. Far from the OTJC shutting up shop, Amber Rudd's decision had galvanised it into an intensive new round of activity.

Effective and persistent campaigning can and does work. The Hillsborough families have proved that, and they have inspired the OTJC campaign to get to the truth about Orgreave. The events that day at Orgreave, particularly the actions of the police and the gross distortions of the truth presented by the media, matter to us all. Confidence in a just and democratic society is founded on a free and truthful press, and a police force that is both responsible and accountable. The events at Orgreave and Hillsborough, as well as elsewhere, have created a marked decline in the public's trust, both in the state, and in the media. If this trust is to be rebuilt, then there must be a process through which the truth is made clear to everyone.

The claims of the IPCC that 'too much time has passed' is a feeble response considering the lies, distortions and misdirections that have clouded events on that day at Orgreave and since. If the truth really matters, then it matters as much today as it did on the 18 June 1984. A huge body of evidence is now available for public scrutiny, and the opportunity to talk directly to witnesses is quickly fading, as many of those involved are aging and some have died. The time for the truth is now, and a full public enquiry is the only way in which that truth will be established. As a wise man once said, 'Injustice anywhere is a threat to justice everywhere'.[23]

NOTES

1 Andy Beckett, 'Vuvuzelas Unite', *London Review of Books*, Volume 37, Number 20, 22 October 2015, p. 26.
2 *Labour Weekly*, 22 June 1984.
3 The quotes from BBC and ITN News are taken from Len Masterman, (ed.), 'The Battle of Orgreave', in *Television Mythologies*, London: Comedia, 1984, pp. 100-103.
4 Tony Harcup, 'Reporting the Next Battle: Lessons from Orgreave', in *Settling Scores: The Media, the Police and the Miners' Strike*, Granville Williams, (ed.), London: CPBF, 2014, p. 96.
5 *The Press and the People: 32nd Annual Report,* London: Press Council, 1985.
6 Ian Gilmour, *Dancing with Dogma,* London: Simon & Schuster, 1992, p. 2.
7 *The Sun*, 19 June 1984.
8 Jim Coulter, Susan Miller & Martin Walker, *State of Siege*, London: Canary Press, 1984, p. 190.
9 Granville Williams, 'The Media and the Miners' in *Shafted: The Media, the Miners' Strike and the Aftermath,* Granville Williams (ed), London: CPBF, 2009. p. 40
10 Michael Bailey & Julian Petley, 'The Making of an Icon and how the British Press Tried to Destroy It,' in Granville Williams, (ed.), *Shafted: The Media*, op. cit., CPBF, 2009.
11 Len Masterman, op. cit., p. 99
12 *The Guardian*, 9 April 2009.
13 Charlotte Gerada and Hero Austin, 13 December 2010, http://blogs.lse.ac.uk/politicsandpolicy/the-policing-of-peaceful-student-demonstrators-in-london-was-heavy-handed-and-disproportional-from-the-outset-and-it-got-worse-as-the-day-proceeded/
14 *The Guardian*, 23 September 2015.
15 Hillsborough: The Report of the Hillsborough Independent Panel, September 2012 at: http://hillsborough.independent.gov.uk/repository/report/HIP_report.pdf
16 *Inside Out*, 22 October 2012.
17 Hillsborough: The Report, op cit.
18 Ibid. p. 339
19 Ibid. p. 367
20 See chapter 2.
21 *IPCC decisions on matters relating to the policing of events at Orgreave coking plant in 1984* and *Annex 1: IPCC review of matters relating to the policing of events at Orgreave coking plant in 1984*. The two documents are on the IPCC website: https://www.ipcc.gov.uk/investigations/orgreave-coking-plant-referrals-south-yorkshire-police
22 http://www.bbc.co.uk/news/uk-england-36141858
23 Martin Luther King, 'The Letter from Birmingham Jail', 16 April 1963.

Chapter 11

Solidarity Forever or the End of an Era? Unions and the strike

John Stirling

It is not possible to understand the industrial behaviour of miners without first recognising their commitment to their union.[1]

Introduction

Globally, mineworkers have always been at the forefront of the labour movement. The reasons for this are not too difficult to assess. Miners live in localities where family and working lives are intermingled and interdependent; invariably, their shared experience and reliance on each other builds a solidarity that is focused on themselves and in opposition to the mine owners. The owners brought harsh conditions of employment in the nineteenth century and global corporations divorced from local communities try do much the same today. Miners commonly organise in the early stages of the development of the trade union movement and they are prepared to lead in militancy and industrial action. Miners in the UK are no exception to this global tendency, being amongst the earliest workers organised into unions, often faced with hostile and exploitive employers and prepared to take them on, sometimes in long and bitter disputes which they regularly, but certainly not always, won. It was common for mining disputes to be engaged with local communities to help build practical support and solidarity. In the nineteenth and much of the twentieth century, because coal provided the energy that drove the economy, disputes occasionally impacted on the whole nation.

This has led to significant political issues being raised that are beyond traditional trade union commitments to collective bargaining, such as state involvement in mine ownership and intervention in industrial disputes. Each of the above conditions underpin three key issues that crystalised during the 1984/5 strike: an embedded solidarity between the workplace and the local community; an involvement with other unions beyond individual workplaces, both nationally and globally; and a necessary engagement with political parties and the state.

This brings us to an important point that can be lost amongst the figures and the trends discussed later: that mineworkers and their unions can and do become a leitmotif for a wider labour movement. Miners find themselves leading rather than following. Disputes engage others in enormous acts of solidarity, and demands may be raised and support may be inspired that challenge the authority of union officials. The 1926 General Strike had encapsulated many of these tendencies and they were to be raised just as profoundly again in 1984/5. The rest of the trade union movement was once more asked to provide support for a dispute challenging a hostile government. Union leaderships were again often out of kilter with the solidarity forthcoming from the wider membership.

In summary, miners and their unions globally have been and remain at the forefront of a broader labour movement from which they regularly gain support – both in terms of solidarity in disputes and through political action. Such support can, and often does, pose challenging questions for other trade unions – leaders and members – as well as for the leaders of political parties representing labour. The challenge was again posed sharply in the strike, as the NUM sought the solidarity they had won in the 1972 and 1974 disputes, but on this occasion taking on a government prepared to fight to the bitter end. Many of the issues embedded in this short introduction are addressed elsewhere in this book, but in this chapter I want to focus on one question and its implications: was the defeat of the miners the defining point for the declining power of the trade union movement itself? As many of those arguing for support and solidarity at the time would put it: 'if the miners lose then we will all lose'. I want to answer the question, and contextualise the strike, in two ways. Firstly, by exploring the trends and the position of the trade unions in general before the strike and then by presenting a picture of developments since. I will argue that while the strike is, in an important way, beyond 'measurement', we can also see that the trends of trade union decline were well established before 1984-5. However, I will also seek to argue that, despite contrary arguments, there is the potential for a new vibrancy and new possibilities for trade unions in the twenty-first century. Perhaps surprisingly, one of these possibilities can be seen in precisely that solidarity between unions and communities that was characteristic of the NUM and at the heart of the strike.

A striking record?

As globally, so locally: miners in the UK have been a well-organised, powerful and militant section of the trade union movement. That organisation has always had a strong local dimension in the UK, defined partly by local geological conditions, partly by the policies of local coal owners (before nationalisation) and partly by local communities and historical traditions. This local organisation was a longstanding strength but also had the potential for divisions with different areas characterised for their 'militancy' or 'moderation' and this became crucial during the strike (see chapters 5 and 7 for example).

Mining union membership has fluctuated with the fortunes of the coal industry as employment in the sector, particularly underground, was normally associated with union membership even if there was no formal 'closed shop' agreement.[2] Membership has also focused on locality, with the union initially established in individual coalfields, eventually consolidating into the Miners Federation of Great Britain in 1889 although even then the Northumberland and Durham unions did not join until 1907 and 1908 respectively. The 1926 General Strike underlined the national nature of the union but local traditions and bargaining remained embedded and 'until 1966 there was no common interest in wage negotiations'.[3] It was the National Power Loading Agreement in that year that provided a common interest. Even this did not commit to a uniform national rate of pay until 1971.[4] This was followed by national disputes in 1972 and 1974.

Overall, mine workers' union membership has fluctuated with the industry itself. At its peak at the beginning of the twentieth century the membership of the Miners' Federation of Great Britain approached a million at 945,000. By the time of the Wilberforce Inquiry,[5] in 1972 there were around 287,000 workers employed in the industry and similar numbers of NUM members but the slide since these highs and the strike has seen a figure of just 1078 in 2014 following round after round of pit closures.

The miners' strike record is difficult to calculate given the localised nature of bargaining, the area structure of the union and the inevitable inadequacies of national statistics.[6] However, by the 1960s and the surfacing of Britain's so-called 'strike problem' in the media, a Royal Commission led by Lord Donovan was drawn to separate out mining strikes given their disproportionate impact on their overall figures. From 1957 to 1961 for example, the number of strikes in the industry easily outdistanced those in the whole of the rest of the economy (Table One), although the balance then began to shift.[7] Of even more significance to the Commission was the 'unofficial' nature of the disputes and, again, coal mining is listed separately and shown as well outdistancing its 'rivals'.[8]

Table One: Annual Average Number of Strikes 1951-2005.[9]

Dates	Total Strikes	Coal Strikes	Coal as a percentage
1951-1959	2202	1600	73
1960-1963	2509	1329	53
1964-1967	2233	686	31
1968-1974	2846	202	7
1975-1979	2310	277	12
1980-1984	1351	288	21
1985-1990	851	199	23
1991-2001	228	6	3
2002-2005	131	1	0.8

By 1972, the 'unofficial' had turned 'official' not only in the NUM but in other unions as well. Leadership of the major unions shifted leftwards and local shop stewards were taking actions that were demanding official support.[10] The upward trend in strike action is indicated in Table One but, significantly, it was the miners who were at the forefront with widespread local stoppages in 1969 and major national disputes in 1972 and 1974, both of which they won.[11] This created a media panic that became personified by the 'Marxist' leaders of the NUM, Mick McGahey and Lawrence Daly who were seen as playing a prominent role.[12]

Miners and their union have played an important role in the development of post-war British trade unionism, which has developed alongside shifts in membership patterns and militancy more widely.

Miners in context

British trade unions have commonly been characterised as 'pragmatic'.[13] The movement was a deal-making one that lived in a 'real world' of industrial relations where agreements could always be negotiated and members could be relied on to take industrial action should it be necessary. However, the pragmatism was a caricature as well as a characteristic and it could only take shape with similarly 'pragmatic' employers and governments. The sort that might be said to have existed as part of the post-war settlement with labour and referred to politically as Butskellism, after Conservative MP, RAB Butler and Labour Party leader, Hugh Gaitskell.

Moreover, unions were never averse to doing deals with governments so that the much-vaunted description of the UK's 'voluntarism' in industrial relations which was characterised by a commitment to free collective bargaining without government intervention can be matched by an equal 'corporatism'. The latter is typified by the inclusion of trade unions in Government institutions and the Trade Union Congress's (TUC) regular engagement with government in the post-war period in discussions over economic policy in general and prices and incomes in particular. As early as 1948 it was co-operating with the Labour government on a 'wages policy' and there were to be repeated periods of incomes policies until the Thatcher era began a UK commitment to neo-liberalism and the free market.[14]

The picture of quiescent pragmatism was, however, never a complete one nor even an entirely accurate portrait. Whilst the media picture of 'strike-prone' Britain was a headline grabbing stick to beat the unions with, the strikes figures were at historically high levels. By the 1960s, industrial action was significant enough for popular culture to embrace Fred Kite, a caricature of the militant shop steward from the 1959 film *I'm Alright Jack*. Equally, militancy was linked to trade union politics both internal and external. Frank Chappell's action in taking on the communists in the Electrical Trades Union was only the most well publicised action against Communist Party organisers in other unions such as Arthur Deakin's Transport and General Workers' Union (TGWU) or as in the politically divided elections in the engineering union.[15] All of this led *The Times* industrial correspondent to ask 'what's wrong with the unions'; to suggest 26 'cures' and to note that 'the patient won't take any of them'.[16] The reaction to this attempted stamp down on local, workplace based militancy and political action was the emergence of an even stronger shop steward based organisation and the election of left wingers to union leadership positions. Most notably, Jack Jones in the TGWU and Hugh Scanlon in the Amalgamated Union of Engineering Workers (AUEW): the former preceded unexpectedly by Frank Cousins, who was also well prepared to back strikes and take on the Labour Party leadership, and the latter breaking with the right wing exemplified by Jim Conway's leadership from 1965-75.[17]

Strike activity continued to increase and generate high levels of publicity in a generally hostile media. Alongside this was the less publicised emergence of strong workplace organisation allied with new legislation on workplace rights such as unfair dismissal, sex and race discrimination and health and safety. A critical factor in the new legislation was the right to time off for trade union training which saw an unprecedented growth in the delivery of cross industry and cross workplace programmes. Trade union activists could network and build local solidarities as well as learning from each other. This came alongside calls for workers' control or at least democracy at work with the climax captured in 1972 as a 'glorious summer' of class based trade union militancy.[18]

These trends had emerged from a strongly organised trade union movement that had significant power both in the workplace and with governments. Immediately before the strike, 95 per cent of large workplace establishments were covered by agreements with union recognition.[19] Moreover, pay agreements that were the result of collective bargaining had even increased slightly in coverage from 1980 to 62 per cent of manual workers and 54 per cent of non-manual. Strike days lost peaked during the strike in 1984 at over 27 million but were averaging 11.7 million 'days lost' in the previous five years.[20] They did not begin their rapid decline until 1990 although union membership itself had peaked in 1979 with over 13.5 million members.

Problems, what problems?

1979 is often regarded as a turning point for labour and the trade unions and is closely associated with the rise of 'Thatcherism'; within two years of the election Eric Hobsbawm and others were debating, 'The Forward March of Labour Halted?'[21] Whilst hostile Conservative legislation became the focus for trade union agitation the halting of the 'forward march' had a series of far more wide-ranging causes in the workplace and beyond and we can identify these at a number of different levels.

At the societal level, sociologists were arguing for the loss of 'class' as a defining category of analysis and its replacement in a post-modern world by 'identity'. In effect, that people identify themselves in terms of race or gender and through the products they consume rather than their employment relationship or occupation. This led to broader questions for trade unions in relation to whether 'class' was still a unifying force and a basis for organising.[22]

At the level of the labour market, the shift in class identity was associated with two factors: the changes in employment between sectors and the remaking of the employment relationship. The sectoral movement was away from mining and manufacturing and towards the service sector, with retail increasing in importance alongside knowledge-based sectors exemplified by the rapid growth of call centres. The employment relationship itself was moving from long-term permanent contracts towards more 'precarious' employment through agencies or on temporary and zero-hours contracts.[23]

At the political level, there were the inevitable clashes with the Conservative government over their trade union legislation. The piecemeal removal of closed shop legislation from the outset inevitably undermined union membership levels and union income. The prohibitions placed on secondary or solidarity action and union funding of the Labour Party were both to have significant long-term implications. Furthermore, the gradual privatising of public enterprises provided a significant challenge to unions in retaining their organisation and membership. Equally importantly, the unions' relationship with the Labour Party was changing as it metamorphosed into New Labour and the Blair-led governments.[24]

At the level of the workplace two significant trends emerged: the marginalising of trade unions and the development of new management strategies. The outcome of this was a major shift away from collective bargaining and a decreased role for shop stewards and workplace union representatives. At the time of the strike in 1984, the Workplace Employee Relations Survey recorded an 86 per cent coverage of collective agreements but this had declined to 67 per cent in 1998 and that decline was ongoing.[25] Marginalisation could also be associated with de-recognition of trade unions altogether, with confrontational disputes in the printing industry such as that at Messenger Group Newspapers. However, such direct attacks were rare and trade unions were faced with the more insidious problem of changing managerial strategies.[26]

Finally, at the level of the trade unions themselves there was a need for both structural reforms and the development of new strategic directions. The rapidly declining income led to pressure on their resources whilst at the same time, a decline in workplace organisation led to increased demands for support from full-time officers. Mergers became one option along with the closure of offices and internal reorganisations. Alongside this were strategic debates about a 'new realism' suggesting partnership agreements with employers and even so-called no strike agreements.[27] To respond to the 'consumer-driven' society, new services came to be seen as a key strategy to encourage membership and to distance unions from a class based identity. These were to be challenged by different strategies, as we shall see below.

After the strike was over

The impact of the strike on the NUM itself and the coal mining communities it was embedded in, is dealt with in chapter 12. In terms of the trade union movement generally, the first impact was the gradual sidelining of the mine workers' union from the offices and conferences of the TUC and the Labour Party. The union's role as a rallying point and focus for anti-government action, or at least, rhetoric, disappeared and was not easily replaced by another industry-based trade union. Firefighters and railway workers were later to take on this role with left-led leaderships, but with less of the historical muscle of the miners.

Equally, there was an uneasy truce during the years of the Blair-led Labour governments, as appeals for the withdrawal of the main tenets of the Thatcher era laws were sidelined, and European Union Directives and individual rights became the focus of attention politically. In this respect 'consultation' became a significant collective issue for the unions with the introduction of the European Works Council Directive in 1994 (1997 in the UK) and the 'Informing and Consulting Employees Regulations' (2004). Employers were generally opposed to these, but consultation itself was a strategy adopted to lessen the role and impact of collective bargaining, whilst seeming to offer employees a voice and non-union alternatives for workers.

Moreover, the Blair years saw a growth of private sector involvement in the public sector, both in terms of investment through private finance initiatives, competitive tendering, and the shift to a consumerist and target-led delivery mode. Each of these posed critical challenges to public-sector unions that were clinging on to national collective bargaining. Privatisation invariably meant membership loss or weaker collective agreements, but the shift to the target-led 'new public management' was more invidious and less easily challenged. However, it was critical in shifting a managerial function from 'production' and the workforce to 'consumption' and the customer. The culture that the public sector was the epitome of 'good industrial relations' was disappearing.

The other key question for the trade unions was, inevitably, the continuing membership decline and the failure of servicing and partnership strategies to make any serious impact on this. There is a distinction between services and servicing, although they are inter-linked. Trade unions have always provided different services for individual members, most notably in legal advice and support and compensation claims. Some unions sought to add to these services and became the providers of consumer goods as well, thus reinforcing a customer/provider relationship with members focused on individualism rather than collectivism. Servicing was more associated with a way of delivering the collective benefits of trade unionism through a focus on activity through the expertise of both lay and employed union officials. Collective bargaining, for example, was something conducted on behalf of members rather than with their engagement, other than a possible vote on a proposed agreement.

As the miners called for solidarity in their dispute, leaders of other unions were faced by their declining membership and consequent income loss alongside the reduction in collective bargaining coverage and a diminution of workplace influence. However, union branches and individual members often became the focus of campaigning for support and defending communities.

Organising and communities

The initial union responses to the changing environment in which they found themselves was, as we suggested above, to offer new services to members, new partnerships to employers and to look to Europe for political support rather than UK governments. However, given the continuing decline in union membership there emerged a new focus on an 'organising strategy'. This had its origins in the USA and a focus on a dynamic workplace unionism and an engaged membership. This is not the place for an extended discussion of an extensive literature of a bundle of different strategies.[28] However, in spite of its potential radicalism in motivating and engaging a 'new trade unionism', the strategy could easily become little more than a new recruitment drive, with a target driven approach to outcomes that was more directed to staunching membership loss than reinvigorating a workplace branch.

The second strand of a revitalised union agenda became a focus on 'community unionism', and a direct connection with the miners and the strike is clear.[29] Community is a slippery concept and community unionism is no easier to define,[30] and neither is it new. Trade unionism has historical roots both in geographical communities and occupational communities and these, as in shipbuilding for example, might easily be combined. Communities are inclusive, but also excluding, as the early history of craft unionism based on occupational communities clearly demonstrated, particularly in relation to women. Local geographical communities can become part of 'union life', as in steel towns, docklands and pit-based communities where unions take on a social role and character alongside their workplace functions.

Recent approaches to community unionism have seen the establishment of 'community branches' in the UNITE union for example, which are open to those not directly engaged in long-term employment. The intention is to engage in solidarity action with other local trade unionists, but also to identify issues of injustice that effect local communities and engage with them in a campaigning way. Public sector unions in areas such as health and education have the potential for a relationship with the communities their members serve and campaigning can be seen to be overlapping in, for example, protecting jobs or protesting against a hospital closure.

Shifts in policy and engagement are hard to measure and require qualitative as well as quantitative analysis. Almost inevitably, membership levels become the key, and sometimes the only indicator of change for good or for bad. Trade union membership overall since the strike has stabilised somewhat after the initial years of major decline. The public sector has become the centre of membership and since 2006 women outnumber men, but the central problems of recruiting and engaging with young people and organising in sectors such as retail remain.

Conclusion

The intention of this chapter is to set the strike in a context that takes us into a broader analysis of the trade union movement in the UK. I have argued that whilst the strike was, and continues to be, an iconic moment for the trade union movement, it must be situated within the framework of a wider challenge to trade unionism generally. It was not just coal mines that were closing and leaving devastated communities in their wake, the same was also true of shipbuilding, steel, chemicals, car-making and all those communities that grew up around islands of manufacturing industry. The economic shift from manufacturing to services and finance capital is easily documented today, but it was a process that was lived through, on a daily basis by working-class communities across the UK. In this sense, the strike had a meaning beyond individual mining communities – it was not just about jobs and keeping particular pits open but precisely about communities and daily lives.

The economic shifts had profound implications for trade unions, but so did the social shifts that went with them. Changing patterns of employment for men and women and old and young workers, as 'safe' career and job options disappeared, to be replaced by precarious employment forcing families to reorganise lives around shift working and multiple job holding, culminating in zero-hours contracts and, for a few, the exploitation of internships. Class identities became challenged by labour market fragmentation and organisational employment strategies. This is not the new social identity of choice and opportunity exemplified by 'consumerism', but an older history of casualised labour re-emerging and leaving workers with no choice at all. Exploitation, at the point of production or the delivery of a service, becomes painfully isolated for the individual and the opportunity for trade union organizing is undermined at the outset.

For the trade unions themselves, the research evidence often brings depressing outcomes, particularly looking back and comparing to the period immediately preceding the strike. The most recent Workplace Employment Relations Survey,[31] for example, shows that workplaces with any recognised union presence stand at 22 per cent overall although the public sector shows a 92 per cent presence.[32] Collective bargaining has similarly diminished and continues to decline with the percentage of workplaces with it, being reduced from 70 per cent in 2004 to 57 per cent in 2011.[33] Strike action has been historically low although with a slight upturn in 2011 with 1.3 million days lost.

Capital is reforming, and workplace relationships become disempowering, as contracts are individualised. However, the exploitation of workers in the workplace remains embedded in a labour process that continues to require the extraction of surplus value from a compliant workforce. This is powerfully exemplified in the 'target culture' initiated by Thatcher's Conservative government and adopted by her Blair-led Labour successors.

Capital has always had a 'target' – profit or 'the bottom line'. The production line organisation of work in 'one best way' provided the route to profit in large scale manufacturing industry, and its ideology permeated management culture. What can be done for a motor car can be done for a burger but, critically, it came to be seen that it might be done for the delivery of a service or in knowledge-based occupations. It could be done by using the consumer as the target setter, and the process was in train for the health service, education and the whole of the public sector, a sector that came into being to provide support and services for individuals and communities often in a time of need; a sector that begat a public service ethos based on collective organisation committed to delivering a service, but also looking after its workers to enable them to do just that.

A long way from the miners' strike? Not so. It is precisely this engagement with communities and those living in them as if they were people, not simply as individual consumers and customers, that was at the heart of the dispute. This is an understanding of community rooted in shared values and collective interests expressed in acts of solidarity.

These are critical issues for today's trade unions and trade unionists. The defending and improving of their members' interests as producers, is symbiotic with the public's relationship with them as consumers of products or services. Such an argument can appear divorced from defending further attacks on union organisation by Conservative governments, or seeking to preserve the remnants of collective bargaining, but it is by seeing trade unionism in this broader light, as the miners did in their strike, that we can begin to develop a new and sustainable trade unionism that links with other social movements, not just in the UK but well beyond. The local strike to preserve a single mining community is embedded in a global struggle against a capital, whether industrial or financial, that has little interest in those it employs or the increasingly depleted world in which they work.

NOTES

1 V. L. Allen, *The Militancy of the Miner,* Shipley: The Moor Press, 1981, p. 1.

2 The 'closed shop' entailed 100 per cent union membership and was widespread in 'union membership agreements' in the 1970s. Conservative governments took periodic legislative steps to undermine and then abolish such agreements.

3 Allen, op. cit., p. 126.

4 The National Power Loading Agreement was to cover all pits and its introduction was precipitated by the introductions of new technologies. See: John Hughes, Roy Moore (Eds), *A Special Case? Social Justice and the Miners,* Harmondsworth: Penguin Books, 1972.

5 Lord Wilberforce led an inquiry into pay comparisons in the mining industry at the time of the 1972 dispute. See Hughes and Moore for the details.

6 Strike statistics can be recorded in two main ways: number of strikes and number of working days lost. Small scale strikes often go unrecorded in national statistics. For a classic discussion of industrial conflict in the UK that remains relevant see Richard Hyman, *Strikes,* London: Fontana/Collins, 1972. For the period leading up to the strike and for the 1972 and 1974 strikes see, for example, Eric Wigham, *Strikes and the Government: 1893-1974*, Basingstoke: Macmillan, 1976.

7 Lord Donovan *Royal Commission on Trade Unions and Employers' Associations 1965-1968.* London: HMSO, 1968. p. 96.

8 Ibid., p. 98.

9 Adapted from Dave Lyddon, 'From Strike Wave to Strike Drought: The United Kingdom', in: Sjaak Van der Velden, Heiner Dribbusch, Dave Lyddon, Kurt Vandaele. (Eds), *Strikes Around the World, 1968-2005*, Amsterdam: Askant. 2007. P. 350.

10 For one account of this period see, for example, Sheila Cohen, *Ramparts of Resistance* London: Pluto Press, 2006.

11 See Allen op. cit., for a full account.

12 Paul Ferris, *The New Militants: Crisis in the Trade Unions,* Harmondsworth: Penguin, 1972.

13 See Richard Hyman, *Understanding European Trade Unionism,* London: Sage, 2001, for a more theoretical account of this 'common sense' understanding.

14 See for example Colin Crouch, *The Politics of Industrial Relations,* Glasgow: Fontana, 1979; Leo Panitch, *Social Democracy and Industrial Militancy: The Labour Party, the Trade Unions and Incomes Policy, 1945-1974,* Cambridge: Cambridge University Press, 1976.

15 For an account of the engineering union in this period see: Joseph Melling and Alan Booth, 'Waiting for Thatcher? Trade Unionism, Labour Politics and Shop Floor Bargaining in Postwar Britain', in Joseph Melling, Alan Booth, *Managing the Modern Workplace,* Aldershot: Ashgate, 2008. For the electricians' disputes see, C.H. Rolph, *All Those in Favour? An Account of the High Court Action Against the Electrical Trades Union & its Officers for Ballot-Rigging in the Election of Union Officials,* London: Andre Deutsch, 1962.

16 Eric Wigham, *What's Wrong with the Unions?* Harmondsworth: Penguin, 1961, p. 196.

17 Geoffrey Goodman, *The Awkward Warrior, Frank Cousins: His Life and Times.* Nottingham: Spokesman, 1979.

18 Ralph Darlington, Dave Lyddon. *Glorious Summer: Class Struggle in Britain in 1972,* London: Bookmarks, 2001. For workers' control see, for example, Ken Coates and Tony Topham, *Industrial Democracy in Great Britain,* London: Macgibbon and Kee, 1968.

19 Neil Millward, Mark Stevens, *British Workplace Industrial Relations 1980-1984,* Aldershot: Gower, 1986.

20 Ibid., p. 226.

21 Martin Jaques, Francis Mulhern, (Eds), *The Forward March of Labour Halted?* London: Verso, 1981.

22 Guy Van Gyes, Hans De Witte, (Eds.), *Can Class Still Unite?* Aldershot: Ashgate, 2001.

23 The various workplace employee relations surveys (WERS) provides the major research data for these trends. Anil Verma, Thomas Kochan, (Eds), *Unions in the 21st Century,* Basingstoke: Palgrave, 2004, provides an interesting global perspective (including the UK) on trade union responses.

24 See the discussions in Gary Daniels, John McIlroy, (Eds.), *Trade Unions in a Neoliberal World,* Abingdon: Routledge, 2009.

25 Neil Millward, Alex Bryson, John Forth, *All Change at Work?* London: Routledge, 2000, p. 160. The data is based on workplaces with over 25 employees and union recognition so the overall coverage of collective bargaining is likely to be considerably smaller.

26 See, for example, Dave Beale, *Driven by Nissan: A critical Guide to New Management Techniques,* London: Lawrence and Wishart, 1994.

27 See Tony Huzzard, Denis Gregory, Regan Scott, *Strategic Unionism and Partnership. Boxing or Dancing?* Basingstoke: Palgrave, 2004.

28 See Gary Daniels 'In the Field: A Decade of Organizing' in Daniels and McIlroy op. cit., 2009 for an overview, and Gregor Gall, (Ed.), *Union Revitalisation in Advanced Economies: Assessing the Contribution of Union Organising.* Palgrave: Basingstoke, 2009, for a wide-ranging collection.

29 Jo McBride, Ian Greenwood, (Eds.), *Community Unionism: A Comparative Analysis of Concepts and Contexts,* Basingstoke: Palgrave, 2009.

30 John Stirling, *Organising Communities and the Renewal of Trade Unions: Challenges & Changes.* 20 Years on from the Miners' Strike Conference, Northumbria University, 2005.

31 Brigid Van Wanrooy, Helen Beverly, Alex Bryson, John Forth, Lucy Stoker, Stephen Wood, *The 2011 Workplace Employment Relations Study: First Findings,* London: Department of Business Innovation and Skills, 2011.

32 Ibid., p. 14.

33 Ibid., p. 22.

Chapter 12

The Gala that Would Not Die: Memory and heritage in the post-industrial mining communities of County Durham

Carol Stephenson and David Wray

We believe that it is important to stress the capacity for self-expression of working-class people and communities, and the ways in which they draw on the past, and senses of place and tradition, to re-interpret and re-work contemporary identity, especially in the face of economic, social and political changes that have eroded long standing bonds of class solidarity.[1]

The first Durham Miners Gala took place in Wharton Park, a hillside to the north of Durham City, on 17 August 1871. Organised by the Durham Miners' Association (DMA),[2] this annual Gala has been held in the city since 1872. It has been described as the greatest unorganised ceremony in the world[3] and traditionally takes place on the second Saturday of July. While the Gala, or 'Big Meeting' as it is affectionately known, has altered in form over the years, its core elements remain unchanged.

Lodge Banners,* following brass bands, first parade through mining villages in the county. Lodge Officials and invited dignitaries march in front of the Banner, with families and supporters following behind. The Banners are then transported to Durham City, where they follow a traditional route through the city to the Racecourse.†

Since the first Gala in 1871, only wars and major strikes have prevented

* 'Lodge' is the term used in Durham to describe the trade union organisation at each individual colliery. We have capitalised the word Banner throughout the chapter to demonstrate the importance of these iconic artefacts.

† The route a Banner takes through the city depends on the geographical location within the county of the mine it represents, and thus the direction from which it approaches the city. There are three routes: one starting from the north, one from the south, and one from the east.

it from taking place, and the Gala of 2016 was the 132nd. Unlike many trade union marches and demonstrations, it has no starting time, no finishing time, and no formal starting point. It has been variously described as part union rally, part political rally, part community get-together, and part family picnic. Each Banner is the iconic talisman of the community it represents. The Gala also provides an opportunity for the people of each community to celebrate their identity and cultural heritage. From its inception it has been instrumental in allowing miners and their families to come together to publicly celebrate themselves.[4] This annual event has been, and remains, nothing less than the visible representation of occupational and class politics, and symbolic of the long established and deep-rooted relationship that exists between DMA and the mining communities of Durham that the union was created to represent.[5]

As the mining industry, and the people who depended upon it, are at the heart of the Gala, it would have been reasonable to assume that the end of deep coal mining would bring it to an end. This has not been the case. While the decline, and eventual end in 1993, of the mining industry in County Durham had catastrophic consequences in terms of unemployment and social deprivation for those living in the now post-industrial mining communities, the Gala continues to survive, and indeed grow.

This chapter examines both the decline and subsequent resurgence of the Gala since the 1990s, and explores the motivations behind that resurgence. That resurgence cannot be understood without reference to the deep-rooted sense of identity associated with both 'industry' and 'class', an identity that continues to exist within mining communities.

The decline of the Gala

The decline of the Gala can also be seen as indicative of the decline in the mining communities in County Durham. Many of these communities were constructed only to serve the needs of the mines,[6] and redundant miners meant redundant communities. It has been argued that such constructed communities, or occupational enclaves as they have also been described, divide 'those within from those without', creating 'homogenous identities, common interests and kinship links'[7] and 'isolated socially and politically, and from those of the same class when the work is different.'[8] Writing against a background of continued job losses in the industry in County Durham in 1974, local author Sid Chaplin feared that the 'decline and fall of the banner' would impact negatively upon the 'complex pattern of Lodge and village life'.[9] Chaplin was prescient in his concerns, as the full consequences of these industrial and social redundancies left individuals and families without work, and in many cases without even the possibility of work. We would differentiate these consequences as the 'visual' and 'hidden' injuries of redundancy.

The 'visual injuries' are caused by the loss of the physical structures that defined them as mining communities. The rise of an industry can be seen as the 'constructive narrative' that eventually provides the image of that particular community.[10] In this sense, the visual landscape contains all the shared memories that hold significance for the populations of that community. Indeed the social and spatial organisations of work are essential to the production of 'place'.

'Place' is also a central aspect in the creation of concepts such as 'identity' and 'community', and depends to a great extent on the memories that are associated with the 'symbolic buildings' that inhabit that 'place'.[11] The symbolic buildings in a working mining community consisted of the physical infrastructure of mining visible above ground and located within the footprint of the colliery: the winding engine house, the lamp room, the shaft superstructure known in Durham as the 'heapstead', and the colliery baths, etc.

We could also include in this list of 'buildings' the waste heap, where the unwanted detritus of coalmining was dumped. What remains of the old colliery sites are neutralised post-industrial landscapes offering little indication of the heritage of the mining industry. In some communities, small iconic memorials to mining are the only remaining visible evidence that a colliery had ever existed. We can also add to the list of visual injuries the urban landscapes that are defined by neglect and decay.

The 'hidden injuries', exacerbated by the loss of the visual ones, are those that are associated with the consequences of unemployment, for the individual, the family, and the community. Here we are thinking about the loss of identity that, in mining communities, is indelibly linked with employment. Occupational identity and community identity, along with norms and values are produced, and continually reproduced, by the networks within the workplace and the community.[12] The loss of these networks is responsible for the 'destruction of the fixed relations between locality and work'.[13]

With the loss of occupation, people are simply left with the networks that exist within the community, and such networks have been seriously curtailed through the loss of many focal points of social contact such as shops, public houses, and other centres of public life.[14] The consequence of these negative processes has been categorised as a state of 'emotional degeneration', which initially impacted negatively on the Gala.[15]

Throughout its long history, the significance of the Gala can be seen in the number of Lodge Banners carried and the number of people attending. The same is true of its decline. In 1919, 350 Lodge Banners were carried into Durham, and in 1952 over 300,000 people attended to commemorate the Easington Colliery disaster of 1951, in which 83 men were killed in an explosion. At the Centenary Gala in 1972, attendance had reduced to 140,000 following only 36 Lodge Banners.[16] By 1993, following the closure of Easington Colliery, the last mine in Durham, the numbers had reduced to less than 10,000, with few Lodge Banners carried. It was also a period when the DMA found itself on the brink of bankruptcy, and it was feared that the Durham Miners Gala, like many others across what had been the national coalfield, would cease to exist.

The Gala that would not die

In 1994, with no working miners paying subscriptions to the union, the DMA found itself unable to provide the funding for that years Gala.* In an effort to raise the required funding, an appeal was sent out to trade unions and to the general public. This appeal was seen by a New Zealand born entrepreneur who contacted the DMA with an offer to provide the funding for three years, which was eventually extended to four. In response to this generous offer the Secretary of the DMA said,

He is a very generous man. To find sponsorship from a man from the Southern hemisphere, without any connection with the North East or mining, is marvelous - we owe him a debt of gratitude that is un-repayable.[17]

By the time this funding had ended, the DMA was once again able to fund the Gala itself, primarily by taking a small amount from each of the compensation payments for industrial injury claims it was securing for its membership.† With the Gala once again financially secure, there was an annual increase in both the numbers attending and and in the number of Banners carried into Durham. In an interview, the Gala organiser said that,

> Despite the demise of the coal industry in County Durham, we have continued to organise the Gala in the memory of all the miners who endured past hardships and in particular the many miners who perished mining coal, and people continue to respond to our efforts.[18]

* In 1994 the estimated overall cost of the Gala was £20,000

† The claims were primarily for Vibration White Finger, Obstructive Pulmonary Disease, and noise induced deafness.

This is the official view, but the leadership of the DMA simply organise the event and partially fund the people who bring the Banners to carry at the Gala. The rise in numbers of Banners carried and people attending is primarily because of an increase in numbers, not only from the communities, but also from the general public.

We believe this resurgence of interest can be traced back specifically to 2001, when the Banner from New Herrington Colliery was once again carried in to the Gala. In order to do so, the people from New Herrington raised the funding to purchase a replica Banner, as the existing one was not in a good enough condition to be carried. The purchase and eventual attendance at the Gala of the New Herrington Banner started a trend that has slowly and continuously grown; significant numbers of new Banners have been consecrated in Durham Cathedral as part of the formal programme of the Gala.

Such has been the recent resurgence of interest that communities with no living inhabitant with any direct connections to mining, have raised the not insubstantial funds required to purchase replica Banners that were once the physical representation of those communities.* Much of the funding to purchase replica Banners has come from the National Heritage Lottery Fund, and over the years a great deal of expertise has developed in the writing of funding applications.

One major step in this resurgence has been the creation of the Durham Mining Communities Banner Groups Association, a voluntary organisation that was established in 2008. Its aim is to conserve, celebrate, and promote educational interest in the mining heritage of the northern coalfields, and in doing so, support the continuation of the Miners' Gala. The Association meets monthly in the headquarters of the DMA, and its support takes three forms. Firstly, it assists the DMA with the organisation of the Gala itself, particularly in policing the progress of the Banners through the City of Durham on Gala day;† second, they organise and co-ordinate the many banner displays and photographic exhibitions that take place around the mining communities of Durham throughout the year; third, they offer help, advice, and expertise to any new community groups seeking assistance to secure their own replica Banner.

* The cost of a new Banner, and the accoutrements to carry it, will be in the region of £10,000.

† Such has been the increase in the numbers of Banners' carried into Durham, and the numbers of people attending, that in recent years the city centre has been gridlocked for many hours.

In all, the Association is made up of sixteen groups across what once was the Durham coalfield, and membership has increased annually as new community groups continue to come forward. The success of this organisation, based upon the activities of its constituent membership, can be seen in the numbers attending the 2016 Gala. The police estimated that over 200,000 people had attended, making it the largest one-day festival in Europe.

The people involved in these Community Banner Groups can be categorised into three distinct types of individuals. It should also be noted that each 'type' of individual can be found within the membership of most groups. The first category are those who have very close connections with the mining industry. They are primarily ex-miners or close family members of ex-miners. These individuals fully understand what the Gala, and the Banners, represent, and their efforts can be seen as attempts to maintain the positive aspects of their previous lives, in a mining community with a working mine. Through their work within their groups, they have displaced the inactivity and loss of self-worth that came with long-term unemployment. Many of the men in these groups were, and in some case remain, active in the DMA.

The second category are from communities that lost their mines generations ago. Suffering the same sense of loss, though for different reasons, they see the Gala and the Banners as a way to bring back to their community something that is representative of a better time in their community's history. Many in this category have no connections to the industry, nor previously to the Gala itself, but are aware of the significance of the Banners, and are using their participation in the Association and the Gala, as a way of promoting, or maintaining, a sense of community.

The third category is people with little or no attachment to mining, or even a mining community, who have simply been attracted to the Banners and the Gala as an interesting activity to be involved with. One ex-miner, and founding member of the Association, described this category of people as 'just people who want to have a band to march behind, but are nonetheless welcome for that'. These individuals have very little understanding of the 'heritage' they say they are determined to maintain. Indeed, some of them have argued vociferously that 'politics' must be kept out of their activities, and even the Gala. This suggests that they have very little understanding of the mining industry, the imagery on the Banners that they carry, or of the significance of the Gala.

Whatever the motivation behind the activities of any of these individuals, whichever category they are in, when questioned about the factors driving them, the response has almost always been 'this is our heritage'. When questioned further about what that heritage is, was, or represented, very few offer a coherent answer. This inability to define 'heritage' is primarily due to the fact that 'heritage' is not just the tangible artefacts such as buildings and monuments, but also the intangible traditions that exist alongside them. Events such as festivals, commemorations, as well as personal memories of the past, and the notion of 'place' are also integral to 'heritage'.[19]

In the mining communities of Durham, the concept of belonging to a 'place' has always been central to any notions of culture and heritage.[20] If the Banners are to be identified as representative of that heritage, we can conclude that the Banners have replaced the now demolished heapstead as the 'symbolic building' of their communities, and should be seen as a part of a process of alleviating the consequences of the 'visual injuries' caused by redundancy.[21]

Such representations of the past may be more than just celebratory of that past, and may indeed be political. It is as if the Banners have gone through some anthropomorphic process and become individuals who possess the collective memory of the community they were created to represent.[22] If this is true then 'history is for all, and heritage is for ourselves'.[23]

Beyond the Banner groups, there are the tens of thousands of people who attend the Gala on an annual basis. While the Gala continues to speak to, and be controlled by, mining communities and their trade union, many of the participants travel to the Gala from across the UK, and even farther afield. In 2015, a group of activists from South African townships who were in the UK for a study visit, attended the Gala at the invitation of the DMA. On seeing what she called the 'spectacle of the Gala' one said that,

> Back home, I represent seven Townships, and I am determined that within one year every one of those Townships will have its own Banner. Watching the way these people venerate their banners is moving, and it is clear that they generate solidarity within their communities, and solidarity is what we need.

Research focusing on these general participants, rather than Banner groups, has identified a number of motivations, most of which refer to class based politics, heritage, and trade unionism. The most popular response to the question of why they attended the Gala related to political motivations such as left-wing, trade union politics, and/or family connections to mining.

> It's working-class tradition, people like to remember, and we are handing it down to the next generation. It's also something to hang on to. The communities need it, it's the spirit of community that is so important, Durham people are a solid community, we stick together.

> It's about community; it is in your blood. The unions have kept it going … they are still strong.

Many respondents said that they have always attended the Gala, even as small children, and that they want to pass this version of their political and social heritage on to the next generation. For these individuals, we can say that the Gala represents a complex process of socialisation. For others, the Gala and the Banners are the important visible symbols that embody their pride in their way of life, and the dignity of the work they did.[24] Our research suggests that the majority attend because it is about the past, about community, about heritage, and about family in terms of community. One respondent suggested that 'the need to parade our banner at the Gala, is generated by our desire to be part of something, to have a sense of belonging, and for our village to once more be known as a mining community'.

Others see the Gala as evidence of something that was better than the present. Commenting on her annual visits to the Gala, one respondent suggested her attendance was 'like putting flowers on a grave'.

It has been recognised by the DMA that the population of miners who participate in, and more importantly organise, the Gala are a slowly diminishing group of people. Equally, the DMA is finding it increasingly difficult to fund the Gala. In 2012 a decision was made to create an organisation that could take the Gala forward into a future without ex-miners, and without the DMA. As a result, appeals were made for public subscriptions to an organisation the DMA created called 'The Friends of the Durham Miners Gala'. Individuals who have contracted to provide the 'Friends' with a monthly donation are described as 'Marras'.* In order to assist with the establishment of this organisation, the New Zealand entrepreneur who had funded the Gala for several years was contacted, and he agreed to provide the funding to allow the appointment of two workers to take the 'Friends' forward, funding that is still in place as this chapter is written.

The organisers of the Friends contacted several trade unions to request their involvement, a request that met with a positive response from all that were contacted. In order to formalise the 'Friends' as a legitimate organisation a Limited Company was formed before the 2015 Gala. The Board of the

* 'Marra' is the term used in the mines in County Durham given to a close workmate.

Company is constituted from members from the individual trade unions, including the DMA, along with a local MP representing an ex-mining constituency. The Friends was launched in the old County Hall in Durham and since its inception, it has increased its formal fee paying membership, as well as the income from individual one-off donors. It has also established a specific website, and has a presence on a range of social media sites.[25]

The Gala, the strike and the assault on the idea of the working class

In accounting for the regeneration of the Gala we must recognise the legacy of the 1984-85 strike. For all who were involved in that great struggle, the Gala offers a continuing opportunity to recall their participation in the fight to save jobs and communities. The miners and their families saw the strike as an assault: an assault on their industry, on their communities, and on a way of life that was in many ways unique.

To fully understand the legacy of the strike, it must be understood that the Thatcher government used a range of tactics, including violence, to ensure the defeat of the NUM and, in doing so provided a warning to the trade union movement as a whole. Certainly, physical violence was clearly evident during the strike, as several chapters in this book describe.

However, ideas have also played a role in legitimating the tactics of the state, to ensure the submission of any who may be minded to challenge state policy. In the case of the 1984/5 strike it was suggested that the miners were the 'enemy within', working against the best interest of the country. Once the strike was over, and the miners were defeated, history suggests that a process of demonisation was then turned against any within the general working class who might be willing to take industrial action.

From television comedies to newspaper editorials, working-class culture, consumption, work, and identity have all been parodied, demonised and misrepresented. In particular, the poor and vulnerable working class, those dependent on welfare or insecure employment, are portrayed as feckless, inadequate, disgusting, a drain on the respectable, and a social cancer without merit.[26] This malign state assault speaks for a ruling elite, and concludes that there is nothing left of the old 'respectable' working class.

For many, there was only one legitimate path to avoid such stigmatisation: to reject working-class identity and to aspire to align oneself with the middle classes. Both Tories and New Labour politicians lined up behind this assault, telling us: we are 'all middle class now'. This was a neat trick. As the poor were blamed, they were politically silenced and their plight was made to appear illegitimate. Simultaneously they were distanced from others within that class, persons who feared contamination and the condemnation that results. Miraculously the working class disappears, and in its place what we see are the undeserving and the greedy, who are a drain on the welfare state.[27]

Many examples of the impact of the demonisation of the working class exist, from sentencing in criminal cases, to the legitimation of austerity, and there is evidence that working-class people believe and respond to this process.[28] The process of demonisation has multiple effects, it divides social groups while legitimating their social position, thus nullifying the likelihood of a challenge to 'the natural order'. Socially created injustices appear invisible, the oppressed are persuaded either to be ashamed of their situation, or to reject their past identity, in order to align themselves safely with their betters.

We would argue that the 1984–5 miners' strike marked the beginning of this process of demonisation. During the year of the strike, the very idea of mining, mining communities, collectivism and organised labour faced an unprecedented onslaught from the state and from the media. It was claimed that the miners faced 'a judicial system systematically hostile to the strikers and their union; agencies of public 'welfare' thoroughly subordinated to the repressive purposes of the state; press and television largely dedicated to distortion and abuse'. [29]

The Tory depiction of striking miners has been described as an hysterical, mythologised moral panic:

> … the [striking] miners, as so often in the past, were a 'lawless and misguided set of men'; their leader was destructive – a Yorkshire Hitler, according to the one much-publicised photograph of him. To stand on a picket line was threatening behaviour, even if, like those at Orgreave, one was dressed in T-shirt and trainers: to charge it with batons and horses was the rule of law.[30]

The British press, both TV and print, took a similar view. Striking miners and their communities were problematised, criminalised, and blamed. Their actions were an affront to the security of wider society; they were indeed the 'enemy within'.[31]

While unemployment rates soared in County Durham in the years following the strike, the assault on the old industries, traditions, cultures and identities associated with industrial communities continued. Deindustrialisation and high levels of unemployment in the once mighty industrial county were attributed to the backward attitudes of its people, their inflexibility, and their stubborn commitment to trade unionism.

Working-class culture, developed over generations was parodied as 'flat cap and whippets', and identified as a barrier to new investment. The industries of the past were now dead, and so too was the way of life that was associated with them. This was a brave new world based on individualism and competition, not collectivism. Redundant miners were told to cast off the negativity associated with the past, and look forward rather than backwards.[32] However, the Gala is a manifestation of an unwillingness to do that. As one individual stated, in response to the question, 'why do you still attend the Gala?' replied,

> 'Part of what we do is about letting people know that we are still here. They closed the pits and took the jobs, but every time we take that Banner out to the Gala, we are saying to them, we're still here, and we are still fighting for our communities.' [33]

Conclusion

The Durham Miners' Gala remains a highly visible celebration of a commitment to collectivism. For many of those who were at the sharp end of the 1984/85 strike, the Gala represents an act of defiance against a political doctrine that sought to destroy their trade union, their communities, and a way of life that went back generations. For the ex-miners and their families who attend on an annual basis, the Gala represents a rejection of state-imposed social and economic impoverishment, and a determination to maintain an identity associated with a now redundant industry, that offers a more solid and dignified way of life.

The Gala is a visible rejection of attempts to besmirch and belittle collectivism, trade unionism, and working-class ways of living associated with mining. While the assault on the miners and their communities, and subsequently the working class in general, have been well documented, those who attend the Gala have rejected those messages. This is an important lesson in the politics of identity: identities are not simply ascribed by others, but rather result from a complex process of reflection on social interaction and agency. Given the importance of the Gala as a long-standing process of socialisation, it is reasonable to assume that the thousands who attend are unlikely to take guidance unquestioningly from the *Daily Mail*, when constructing a sense of self.

That is not to say that no damage has been done by these assaults on the working class, but it would be wrong to underestimate the backlash. In an age of austerity, there is a growing discussion about the search for a better way to live than the one we are currently facing. The return of political confidence can be seen in the election of the left-wing Jeremy Corbyn as Labour leader, and the in the resurgence in Labour Party activism and membership.

The regeneration of the Gala is a rejection of the attempts to besmirch and belittle collectivism, trade unionism, and the way of life associated with mining. While the assault against the miners and their communities, and the subsequent assault on the industrial working class in general, have been well documented and cannot be denied, these messages are rejected by those who attend the Gala annually. This is an important lesson in the politics of identity: identities are not simply ascribed by others but rather result from a complex process of reflection on social interaction and agency. Given the importance of the Gala as a long standing process of socialisation, it is reasonable to assume that the thousands who attend the Gala are unlikely to unquestioningly take guidance from those who belittle collectivism.

We would argue that the Durham Miners' Gala remains a highly visible celebration of a commitment to collectivism. For the ex-miners and their families generally, who attend the Gala on an annual basis, it represents a defiance of the assault on their communities, and a determination to maintain an identity associated with an industry that offered a more solid and dignified way of life, one that stands in marked contrast to the individualism and vulnerability offered by 'the brave new world' created by Thatcherism.

Despite the best efforts of the state and the media to besmirch working class values, hundreds of thousands of people, through their attendance at the Gala, restate their existence, their resilience and their refusal to let their communities and culture die. This is their aspiration, an aspiration that has been described as a process of 'cultural self-determination'.[34] The lesson of the Gala is that we are not, in fact, 'all middle class now', nor do we wish or pretend to be.

NOTES

1 Laurajane Smith, Paul A. Shackel & Gary Campbell, *Heritage, Labour and the Working Classes*, London: Routledge, 2001, p. 1.
2 First formed in 1869.
3 Huw Beynon & Terry Austrin, *Masters and Servants: Class patronage in the making of a labour organisation,* London: Rivers Oram Press, p. 206.
4 Beynon & Austrin, op. cit., p. 211.
5 Carol Stephenson & David Wray, 'Emotional Regeneration through Community Action in Post-industrial Mining Communities: The New Herrington Banner Partnership', *Capital & Class,* Vol. 87, 2005, pp. 175-200.
6 Bill Williamson, *Class, Culture and Community: A biographical Study of Social Change in Mining,* London: Routledge & Keegan Paul, 1982.
7 Tamsin Wedgewood, 'History in Two Dimensions or Three? Working Class Responses

to History', *International Journal of Heritage Studies,* Vol. 15, No. 4, 2009, p. 285.

8 David M. Emmons, *The Bute Irish: Class and Ethnicity in an American Mining Town 1875-1925,* Chicago: University of Illinois Press, 1990, p. 66.

9 William A. Moyes, *The Banner Book,* Newcastle: Frank Graham, 1974, p. 3.

10 Sherrie L. Linkon & John Russo, *Steeltown U.S.A.: Work and memory in Youngstown,* Laurence, Kansas: University Press of Kansas, 2002, p. 2.

11 Robert R. Archibald, 'Real Places in a Virtual World', *Museum International,* 2006, Vol. 58, No. 3., p. 12.

12 Tim Strangleman, 'Networks, Place and Identities in Post-industrial Mining Communities', *International Journal of Urban and Regional Research,* 2001, Vol. 25, No. 2, pp. 253-267.

13 David Gilbert, 'Imagined communities and mining communities', *Labour History Review,* 1995, Vol. 60, No. 2.

14 David Waddington, Chas Critcher, Bella Dicks, & David Parry, *Out of the Ashes? The Social Impact of Industrial Contraction and Regeneration on Britain's Mining Communities,* Norwich: The Stationary Office, 2001.

15 Stephenson & Wray, op. cit., p. 177.

16 Moyes, op. cit.

17 *The Independent,* 21 December 1996.

18 Interview with George Robson, organiser of the Durham Miners Gala, 13 July 2002.

19 Smith et al., 2001, p. 1.

20 Bill Williamson, *Class, Culture and Community: A Biographical Study of Social Change in Mining,* London: Routledge & Kegan Paul, 1982.

21 Tamara K Haraven & Randolf Langenbach, *Amsokeag: Life and Work in an American Factory-City,* New York: Pantheon Books, 1978.

22 David Wray, 'The Place of Imagery in the Transmission of Culture: The Banners of the Durham Coalfield', *International Labour & Working Class History,* Vol. 76, No. 1, 2009, pp. 147-63.

23 Wedgewood, op. cit., p. 286.

24 See: Mary Mellor & Carol Stephenson, 'The Durham Miners Gala and the spirit of community', *Community Development Journal,* Vol. 40, No. 3, 2005, pp. 343-551; Lyn Dodds, Mary Mellor, & Carol Stephenson, 'And the Bands Played On: an exploration of the resurgence of the Durham Miners' Gala', *Northern Economic Review,* No. 37, 2006, pp. 72-91.

25 http://www.durhamminers.org

26 Owen Jones, *Chavs: The Demonization of the Working Class,* London: Verso, 2011.

27 Ibid.

28 Ibid.

29 Richard Hyman 'Reflections on the Miners Strike', *Socialist Register,* No. 86, Vol. 22, 1985. pp. 330-54, p. 330.

30 Raphael Samuel, Barbara Bloomfield, & Guy Boanus, *The Enemy Within: Pit Villages and the miners' strike of 1984-5,* London: Routledge & Kegan Paul, 1986, pp 4-5.

31 Granville Williams, (Ed.) *Shafted: The Media, The Miners' Strike and the Aftermath,* Campaign for Press and Broadcasting Freedom, 2009.

32 Philip Garrahan & Paul Stewart, *The Nissan Enigma: flexibility at work in a local economy,* London: Mansell, 1992.

33 Stephenson & Wray, op. cit., p. 192.

34 Jane Parry, 'The Changing Meaning of Work: restructuring the former coalmining communities of the South Wales Valleys', *Work, Employment and Society,* Vol. 17, No. 2, 2003, pp. 227-246.

Appendix

NUM Rules

All rules are taken from the NUM union rule book as of 1 March 1984, except the last, Rule 51, which was introduced in August 1984.

Rule 41 – Strikes and Lockouts. In the event of a dispute arising in any Area or applying to the workers in any Branch likely or possible to lead to a stoppage of work or any other industrial action short of a strike, the questions involved must immediately be reported by the appropriate official of the Area in question to the National Executive Committee which shall deal with the matter forthwith, and in no case shall cessation of work or other form of industrial action short of strike take place by the workers without the previous sanction of the National Executive Committee, or of a Committee (whether consisting of members of the National Executive Committee or other persons) to whom the National Executive Committee may have delegated the power of giving such sanction, either generally or in a particular case and no funds of the Union shall be applied in strike pay or other trades dispute benefit for the benefit of the workers who shall have ceased work without the previous sanction of the National Executive Committee.

Rule 43 – National Action. In the event of national action being proposed by the union in pursuance of any of the objectives of the union, the following provision shall apply: That a national strike shall only be entered upon as the result of a ballot vote of the members taken in pursuance of a resolution of a Conference, and a strike shall not be declared unless 55 per cent of those voting in the ballot vote in favour of such a strike. If a ballot vote be taken during the time a strike is in progress, a vote of 55 per cent of those taking part in the ballot shall be necessary to continue the strike. If a ballot vote be taken during the time of a stoppage is in progress, such stoppage may not be continued unless 55 per cent of those voting in the ballot vote in favour of continuance. (The words 55 per cent were replaced by the words 'simple majority' at the Special Conference on 19th April 1984).

Rule 23 – The Conference of Delegates. The Conference of Delegates (Conference) in which the authority and government of the union shall be vested, shall function in Annual Conference or Special Conference. The Annual Conference shall be held between the 1st June and 31st July in each year, or such other times as Conference may resolve. The duties of the Annual Conference shall be to transact the business of the Union and to discuss matters affecting the welfare of the membership; to consider resolutions submitted to the Annual Conference by the National Executive Committee and Areas; to receive the National Executive Committee's report of its proceedings and the financial and Auditor's report for the previous year.

Rule 8 – The Government of the Union. The government of the Union shall be by Conference as provided for in these Rules. In the periods between Conference the NEC shall administer the business and affairs of the union and perform all duties laid down for it by resolution of Conference, and shall not at any time act contrary to, or in defiance of, any resolution of Conference.

Rule 51 – The National Disciplinary Committee shall have the power to consider a complaint that a member has done any act (which includes any omission) which may be detrimental to the interests of Union, and which is not specifically provided for in this rule.

Further Information

Campaign for Press and Broadcasting Freedom
www.cpbf.org.uk freepress@cpbf.org.uk

Durham Miners' Association
www.durhamminers.org admin@durhamminers co.uk

Friends of the Durham Miners' Gala
http://www.friendsofdurhamminersgala.org admin@friendsdmg.org

National Union of Mineworkers
www.num.org.uk chris.kitchen@num.org.uk

Orgreave Truth and Justice Campaign
otjc.org.uk orgreavejustice@hotmail.com

Index